THE DARK AND DINGY UNDERWORLD OF THE VICTORIAN SLUMS

For my grandparents

Also by Bethan Watts

Inside the Tudor Home: Daily Life in the Sixteenth Century

THE DARK AND DINGY UNDERWORLD OF THE VICTORIAN SLUMS

BETHAN WATTS

PEN & SWORD
HISTORY
AN IMPRINT OF PEN & SWORD BOOKS LTD.
YORKSHIRE – PHILADELPHIA

First published in Great Britain in 2024 by
PEN AND SWORD HISTORY
An imprint of
Pen & Sword Books Ltd
Yorkshire – Philadelphia

ISBN 978 1 39903 698 6

A CIP catalogue record for this book is available from the British Library.

Typeset in Times New Roman 10/12 by
SJmagic DESIGN SERVICES, India.
Printed and bound in the UK by CPI Group (UK) Ltd.

Pen & Sword Books Limited incorporates the imprints of Atlas, Archaeology, Aviation, Discovery, Family History, Fiction, History, Maritime, Military, Military Classics, Politics, Select, Transport, True Crime, Air World, Frontline Publishing, Leo Cooper, Remember When, Seaforth Publishing, The Praetorian Press, Wharncliffe Local History, Wharncliffe Transport, Wharncliffe True Crime and White Owl.

For a complete list of Pen & Sword titles please contact
PEN & SWORD BOOKS LIMITED
George House, Units 12 & 13, Beevor Street, Off Pontefract Road,
Barnsley, South Yorkshire, S71 1HN, England
E-mail: enquiries@pen-and-sword.co.uk
Website: www.pen-and-sword.co.uk

or

PEN AND SWORD BOOKS
1950 Lawrence Rd, Havertown, PA 19083, USA
E-mail: uspen-and-sword@casematepublishers.com
Website: www.penandswordbooks.com

FSC
www.fsc.org
MIX
Paper | Supporting responsible forestry
FSC® C013604

‘I long to go through the crowded streets of your mighty London, to be in the midst of the whirl and rush of humanity, to share its life, its change, its death, and all that makes it what it is.’

Bram Stoker, *Dracula* (1897)

'The debt that each generation owes to the past it must pay to the future.'

Abigail Scott Duniway, Suffragette (1834–1915)

Contents

List of Illustrations

1. Inhabited room with stove, tubs, beds (New York Tenement House Department, photograph, New York, *c.* 1902). Item held at the New York Public Library, New York, b16563378.
2. Old Vennel off High Street (Thomas Annan, photograph, Glasgow, 1868). Item held at the British Library, London, L.R.404.g.8.
3. The Crawlers (John Thomson, photograph, London, 1881). Item held at the British Library, London, Wq4/6069.
4. Terraced Cottage Slum (Thomas Annan, photograph, Glasgow, 1868). Item held at the British Library, London, BL 6057.i.7.
5. Over London by Rail (Gustave Doré, illustrative engraving, London, 1872). Item held at the British Library, London, Wf1/1856.
6. Homeless Men in Salvation Army Shelter (unknown photographer, photograph, London, *c.* 1900). Image courtesy of the Salvation Army Heritage Centre salvationarmy.org.uk (2023).
7. Slums in London (Gustave Doré, illustrative engraving, London, 1872). Item held at the British Library, London, Wf1/1856.
8. Marylebone Workhouse Dormitory (unknown photographer, photograph, London, 1900). Image courtesy of Peter Higginbotham, *The Workhouse*, workhouses.org.uk (2023).
9. Doffer Boys (Lewis W. Hine, photograph, Georgia, 1909). Item held at the J. Paul Getty Museum, Los Angeles, 84.XM.221.7.
10. Edwin Chadwick (John and Charles Watkins, photograph, London, *c.* 1860–1870). Item held at the Wellcome Collection, London, 12458i.
11. Mrs Winslow's Soothing Syrup (unknown artist, advertisement, Mumbles, *c.* 1880). Item held at the National Library of Medicine, Maryland, D02927.
12. Bedlam Incurable Ward (unknown photographer, photograph, London, *c.* 1880s). Image courtesy of Bethlem Museum of the Mind, London.
13. A Plain Cookery Book for the Working Classes (unknown illustrator, wood engraved print), in Francatelli, C.E., *A Plain Cookery Book for the Working Classes,* (London, 1852), p.1.
14. The Coster Girl (H.G. Hine, illustration from Daguerreotype), in Mayhew, H., *London Labour and London Poor* (London, 1861).
15. London Coffee Stall (H.G. Hine, illustration from Daguerreotype), in Mayhew, H., *London Labour and London Poor* (London, 1861).
16. WH Smith Victoria Station, Manchester (unknown photographer, photograph, (Manchester, *c.* 1932). Image courtesy of WH Smith PLC, *History and Heritage*, whsmithplc.co.uk (2023).

17. Decorative Scrap (unknown maker, lithographic scrap, England, *c.* 1885). Item held at the V&A Museum, London, E.176-1952.
18. A Christmas Transformation (unknown illustrator, magazine illustration, London, 1881). Item held at the V&A Museum, London.
19. Foundling Girls in the Chapel (Sophie Gengembre Anderson, oil on canvas, *c.* 1850). Item held at The Foundling Museum, London.
20. Detail of The Condition and Treatment of Children Employed in the Mines (unknown illustrator, illustrative engraving, London, 1842). Item held at the British Library, London, BL 1509/353, p.41.
21. Tiny Tim (M.F. Taylor, line drawing), in Dickens, M.A., *Dickens' Dream Children* (London, 1926), p.12. Image courtesy of Allingham, P.V., *Victorian Web*, victorianweb.org (2010).
22. Finding Polly, Durward Street (Ferdinand Fissi, illustration, London, *c.* 1902). Image courtesy of Bennett, J., and Clack, R., *Casebook: Jack the Ripper Photo Archive*, casebook.org (2008).
23. Mary Ann Cotton (unknown photographer, photograph, *c.* 1870). Image courtesy of Herdman, I.S., *Mary Ann Cotton*, maryanncotton.co.uk (2023).
24. Oliver's Eyes are Opened (Harry Furniss, lithograph), in Dickens, C., *The Adventures of Oliver Twist* (London, 1910), p.72.
25. Cemetery at Bunhill Fields (unknown illustrator, wood engraved print), in Thornbury, W., *Old and New London: Volume 2* (London, 1878), p.204.
26. Albert, Prince Consort after death, the Blue Room, Windsor Castle (William Bambridge, carbon print, Berkshire, 1861). Item held at the Royal Collection Trust, London, RCIN 2506826.
27. Resurrectionists at Work (Hablot Knight Browne, illustration, London, 1887). Image courtesy of the Internet Archive, *The chronicles of crime; or, The new Newgate calendar*, OL24418973M, archive.org (2010), p.274.
28. Punctual Attendance Medal (unknown maker, medal, London, 1896). Item held at the Museum of London Docklands, London, 2001.94/1.
29. Thomas Barnardo (unknown photographer, photograph, London, *c.* 1867). Image courtesy of Barnardo's, *Our History*, barnardos.org.uk (2023).
30. Annie Kenney and Christabel Pankhurst (unknown photographer, photograph, London, *c.* 1912). Item held at the British Library, London, J2YF65.

Acknowledgements

I wish to thank a number of people whose kind support was very much appreciated during my time writing this book.

Firstly, to the team at Pen & Sword Books, whose faith and confidence in my writing led to this second book. I wish to thank my editor, Sarah Beth Watkins, as well as the lovely Rosie Crofts, Lucy May and Laura Hirst especially.

I wrote this book alongside researching and writing my PhD thesis. Although I am still only at the very beginning of my PhD journey, I nevertheless wish to thank the people who have always believed in my capabilities as a historian, and whose enthusiasm and passion for sharing the stories of the past have been a great inspiration to me. To my PhD supervisors, lecturers, colleagues and friends, thank you.

To all of you who have ever read my writing or followed my historical blog, I am so indebted to you. I will forever be grateful for all of the support and kindness that you have shown me.

To those of you who have bought, read or reviewed my first book, *Inside the Tudor Home: Daily Life in the Sixteenth Century*, thank you so much – I am so very grateful.

And finally, to my friends and family, whose unrelenting support and encouragement is so treasured. You have always sat patiently through my stories of the past – the weird and the wonderful – and have always been my favourite companions to the many museums, palaces, art galleries and cemeteries that I do so love to visit. This book is for you.

Author's Note

The slums of Victorian Britain were so widespread and far-reaching across the landscape of the country that for this book I have chosen to focus my writing solely upon London and its immediate areas. Sources, records and documentation have survived particularly well from Victorian London, which served the country not only as its capital city, but also as its principal centre for trade, culture and crime. Although my research took me to every corner of the Victorian United Kingdom – from the decrepit urban labyrinths of Edinburgh to the criminal-infested city of Birmingham, and to the misty, murky mining villages of South Wales – ultimately I decided that including detailed anecdotes from these places would run the risk of lengthening my manuscript by double. Therefore, although brief sections of the book do focus on socially significant events that occurred outside of London and helped shaped Victorian Britain, this book is principally concerned with the capital city and its inhabitants.

Perhaps in future I will revisit the stinking slums of the other towns and cities of nineteenth-century Britain, for indeed there are so many colourful characters that I encountered throughout my research journey whose stories deserve to be told. Although they may not be included explicitly within this book, rest assured that these people linger in the background of every page you will turn. In the process of researching this book, I read and consulted much more material than I could comprehensively include; to that end, you will find in the Bibliography an abundance of resources that will point you toward further material about life in Victorian Britain. This list is by no means exhaustive, nor is it inclusive of every individual city or county of the United Kingdom, yet the sources within are what I relied upon to conduct my in-depth research, and as such I can testify to their value both to seasoned historians and casual readers alike.

Any quotations used in the book have been lifted directly from the source material. As such, any spelling errors, outdated language or potentially offensive terminology is entirely original and has been included for purposes of authenticity.

There are instances throughout the book where original recipes for medicines, cosmetics and foodstuffs have been included. Many of these recipes are highly dangerous and should not be attempted or replicated.

Money Conversion

The value of money changed numerous times throughout the Victorian period. For purposes of simple conversion, I have used the mid-point of the nineteenth century as the base year.

In 1850, there were no less than eight types of coinage currency in Victorian Britain. These were farthings, pennies, shillings, florins, crowns, half-sovereigns, guineas and pounds.[1] Pennies were typically written as *d*, shillings as *s* and pounds as either *£* or *l*.

1 farthing	=	¼ of a penny
12 pennies	=	1 shilling
1 florin	=	2 shillings
1 crown	=	5 shillings
1 half-sovereign	=	10 shillings
20 shillings	=	1 pound
1 guinea	=	1 pound + 1 shilling

One penny (*d*) in 1850 cost the equivalent of 33p in today's currency. One shilling (*s*) cost the equivalent of £4.01 in today's currency. One pound (*£* or *l*) cost the equivalent of £80.19 in today's currency.[2]

On average, five days' worth of wages for a male labourer in 1850 came to around £1.[3] On average, a labourer could expect to make around £48 per annum solely through his wages, the equivalent of around £4,000 in today's currency.

Significant Dates

1837 The death of William IV. Victoria becomes Queen.

1842 Edwin Chadwick publishes his *Sanitary Report.*

The Association for Promoting Cleanliness Amongst the Poor is founded.

The *Children's Employment Commission Report* is published.

The Mines Act raises the starting age of children in collieries to 10 years old.

1844 John Snow publishes *On the Mode of Communication of Cholera.*

Ragged schools are founded.

The Factories Act limits the working hours of women and children to twelve hours a day.

1847 The Factories Act further limits the working hours of women and children to 10 hours a day.

1848 The Public Health Act establishes dedicated Boards of Health across Britain.

1849 A cholera epidemic kills approximately 54,000 in Britain.

1850 The Metropolitan Internments Act allocates dedicated spaces for burials in cities.

1857 Mary Ann Cotton commits the first of her murders.

1858 The 'Great Stink' occurs in London.

1860 The Coal Mines Regulation Act bans children under 12 from working in collieries.

1866 Thomas Barnardo establishes his Home for Children.

The Sanitary Act makes it compulsory for health boards to improve urban hygiene conditions.

1867 The Second Reform Act extends the vote to the male working class.

1868 The Pharmacy Act regulates the sale of dangerous drugs like opium and laudanum.

1870 The Education Act makes secular schooling available to every child.

The Married Women's Property Act allows married women to keep any of their earnings as their own legal property.

1871 A smallpox epidemic kills approximately 42,000 in Britain.

1872 The Public Health Act makes it compulsory to provide public health services.

Amelia Dyer commits the first of her murders.

1874 The Factory Act bans children under 9 from working in mills.

1876 The Education Act makes schooling compulsory for every child aged between 5 and 13.

1880 The Metropolitan Public Gardens Association is founded.

1884 The Mayor of London's Relief Fund for the poor is established.

The Third Reform Act extends the vote to every male aged over 21.

1887 Queen Victoria's Golden Jubilee.

The Thames Torso murders.

1888 The Jack the Ripper murders.

1889 Charles Booth publishes his *Maps Descriptive of London Poverty*.

1893 The Royal Commission of Aged Poor is founded.

1894 The Local Government Act establishes local councils and gives property-owning women the right to vote in local elections.

1897 Queen Victoria's Diamond Jubilee.

1901 Death of Victoria. Edward VII becomes King.

Preface

It had been a fine, bright morning on 1 September 1888.[1] Journeying through shaded avenues of yellowing sycamore and bristled Scots pine, the Queen's carriage made its ascent across the flat, manicured acreage of the Balmoral Estate.

Victoria had always been enamoured with the castle at Balmoral. She and her beloved Albert had bought it almost forty years prior, and it had never lost its allure as a haven of comfort, domestic bliss and romance. Even now, the Queen had fond memories of hazy evenings spent waltzing around the ballroom in Highland garb, of hunting grouse and roe along the heathery moors, and of indulging in dinner parties that continued well into the small hours of the morning.

But those days were long gone. Queen Victoria, now into the fifty-first year of her reign, was no longer the lithe, petite young woman she had once been. Multiple pregnancies had aged her, as had the early death of her darling Prince, a devastation from which she would never quite recover. Now, the Queen preferred quieter evenings spent in the company of her grown children and grandchildren, wiling away hours engaged in more domestic pursuits and quiet contemplation. Indeed, tonight she would be hosting her daughter Princess Beatrice (affectionately known as 'Baby'), as well as a number of other members of the Royal Family, with Prince Arthur of Connaught and the Grand Duchess Princess Alice of Hesse at the head of the guest list.[2] It shaped to be an evening of opulence and grandeur, of abundance and extravagance. Rich food would be consumed, expensive wines would be sipped and featherdown beds would be plumped for the royal bodies to sink into after the night had come to its close.

But this is not their story.

Earlier that week, Victoria had signed a government grant offering the sum of £50 to the poor people of Poplar.[3] The sum (the equivalent of around £3,500 in today's money) had been intended to assist in the airing, disinfecting and re-flooring of 969 houses in the Poplar district of London, which had been flooded by the burst banks of the River Thames just days prior.[4] Miraculously, no one had been injured or drowned in the currents, though it left hundreds of already struggling working-class people without homes. Belongings and sentimental items were lost or destroyed, and many livelihoods – particularly those of the women – were no longer viable to be conducted from home. The tragedy led to mass sympathy in the London-centric press, which, in a manner somewhat tone-deaf, continued to advertise cheap houses for sale that came with a 'constant supply of water' and very 'good drainage'.[5]

Across the Thames and away from the now-destitute victims, poor pleasure-seekers headed toward the Crystal Palace, which had been dismantled and moved from its previous site in Hyde Park to its new location at Sydenham Hill in Bromley. The Crystal Palace, so-called for its breathtaking engineering feat of glistening glass doming supported by iron beams, housed the Great Exhibition, perhaps the most exciting of all tourist attractions in the world at the time. As well as showcasing local and domestic talent, the Great Exhibition also exhibited exotic marvels, historical relics and items of cultural, scientific and engineering interest. Most importantly, it also hosted free evenings of entertainment that even the poorest of the population could enjoy. Tonight's showbill would be a ballet performance of William Shakespeare's *A Midsummer Night's Dream*.[6] It was later reported in the *Pall Mall Gazette* that 'thousands [watched] without extra payment'; indeed, the ballet had attracted crushing crowds of London's poorest citizens, who gathered in the hope of catching a glimpse of the performance for no cost at all.[7]

The ballet at the Crystal Palace was not the only form of entertainment that the poor of London had enjoyed that night. At 8.15 pm, the doors of the Lyceum Theatre opened to ticket-holders for the night's performance of *The Strange Case of Dr Jekyll and Mr Hyde*, which drew a considerable crowd of patrons longing to be spooked by the unnerving tale.[8] The Victorians – both rich and poor – had shared an innate obsession for spine-tingling stories. Chilling retellings of fictional supernatural entities thrilled the wealthy just as it did the ragged, who drew their shawls closer around their thin shoulders as they huddled round glowing lanterns to better hear the tales. Yet, as the Victorians would come to discover, some stories were not always the work of fiction; sometimes, the true horror lay closer to home.

The night of 31 August 1888 was cold, damp and murky. As delighted concert-goers made their way back to their cheap tenement houses and rabbit-warren hovels, none could imagine the horror of what was occurring elsewhere in the city. Nerves were already strung when walking through the pitch-black streets of London; just weeks before, mysterious corpses had been found throughout the metropolis, sometimes whole and sometimes – horrifically – not. Dismembered limbs had been found upon slag heaps; even aborted foetuses had been found along the foreshore of the Thames.[9] Knife-crime and the presence of gangs was at an all-time high, and many people feared to walk the streets alone. Poisoning had seen an uptick in recent weeks, with seven deaths to carbolic poisoning occurring in London in one month alone.[10] People were still regularly dying of infectious diseases such as typhoid, diphtheria, tuberculosis and cholera, which had been hastened by inadequate healthcare and a lack of decent public sanitation. The capital city's cemeteries were quite literally overflowing, yet were still being continuously added to with new, still-infectious festering corpses piled high into communal burial plots. One more would be added to that list that night: in the dark alleyways of the Whitechapel district, slick hands moved tactfully amidst blood and viscera. The world's most famous murderer had just claimed his first victim.

Victorian Britain was not a place for the weak-hearted. Crime, poverty and prejudice all culminated in what would perhaps be the most socially destitute period of modern British history. As Queen Victoria nestled into her featherdown Balmoral bed, blissfully unaware of the perils of her people, the murky underground was only just beginning to awaken.

Welcome to the dark and dingy underworld of the Victorian slums.

Chapter 1

The Dark Underbelly of Victorian Britain

> 'The slums of a mighty capital like London can never be effectually flushed … accumulations of wickedness and misery continue to fester.'
>
> *The Evening Standard* (1 September 1888)

The Industrial Revolution of the nineteenth century had changed the lives of every man, woman and child in Victorian Britain regardless of their social standing and fiscal wealth. Urban areas already dense with bodies swelled to even greater proportions following the introduction of machinery and technology to local trade. These machines, still very much in their infancy, lacked the sophistication of later technologies and as such required human manpower to ensure that they ran smoothly and without hitch. As more and more people uprooted their lives from rural pockets of Britain to settle in cities, beckoned by the promise of steady labour and good pay, places like London irrefutably changed forever.

The population and human density of London prior to the Industrial Revolution of the nineteenth century was estimated to be around 650,000, a considerable, but not wholly irrational number.[1] By the mid-point of the century, however, this number had skyrocketed to two million.[2] As more and more people struggled to squeeze themselves into the city, resources – from food to housing, medicine and promised employment – began to wear extremely thin. Whole families caught up in the storm of relocation were forced to reside in sub-standard dwellings barely fit for human inhabitation, paid for with whatever meagre pittance they could hope to earn. London landlords had capitalized on the opportunity to swindle their new lodgers, offering dilapidated hovels in exchange for lofty rents. It was a transaction many newcomers to London were loath to pay, though they knew that their only other option – life on the street – would be a reality much worse. As the tenants began to settle in to their new homes, they could not help but escape the feeling that they had been roguishly tricked.

Elsewhere, the now-wealthy landlords rubbed shoulders with rich tycoons and industrial moguls who had earned their fortunes from the exploitation of the poor and needy. Their mills, factories and workhouses had served their purpose of generating revenue; what happened to its employees was not the concern of those who owned them. As wealthy men reclined in their well-built, insulated houses, their bellies full and their wine glasses drained, the very same people who had earned them their keep sat mournfully on cold kerbsides, bare-legged and ragged. These were the people who worked long hours but had nothing to show for it, people who could not afford to purchase food for their children or medicine for their sick loved ones. These were the people of the dark and dingy underworld of the Victorian slums.

The chasm between rich and poor was widening.

Overcrowded cities and large towns were particularly problematic in the nineteenth century for the people who were forced to live there. In London, slums of destitute people spilled over from dilapidated tenement blocks and rapidly began to fill each corner of the city. The slums at Clerkenwell, Lambeth and Whitechapel were the largest and by far the worst of all in London, where hundreds – if not thousands – of people lived among rats and scurrying vermin down cold, cramped alley streets.

'The evil is becoming worse and worse as a larger and larger population crowds into these subdivided dwellings,' complained one contemporary who had hailed from the middling class.[3] No jaunt into the city would be without contact in some form or another with a member of the poorest rung of the societal ladder. Slums were unavoidable; even if you had tried your best to ignore them with your eyes, you would never be able to escape them with your nose. With so many bodies packed into such close quarters, it would only be a matter of time before disease and illness rapidly took hold. Indeed, the slums of Victorian London were so dangerous to human health that permanent disability and even death could be expected within mere years, if not months, of living there. 'Unless there is a change there will be someday a tale of horror never equalled,' wrote social campaigner Nellie Bly in 1887. It was true. As contagious diseases borne in the slum conditions threatened to kill its inhabitants, the average life expectancy for a poor Victorian fell from 80 to just half that figure, with 40 being the mean for men and 50 for women.[5]

Given the description of the places working class people had been forced to live, it was little wonder that death ravaged so many in the slums of Victorian London. In his investigative work into life in the slums, contemporary Richard Rowe described swampy puddles, mangy dogs, ungroomed horses, and men, women and children in soiled clothes along just one street.[6] Enveloping himself further into this dingy underworld, Rowe wrote of the discarded piles of brick and dried mortar that crunched underfoot with every step he took, as well as 'cheap and nasty new houses' without windows and doors.[7] Worse still, Rowe was nauseated by the fact that these slums had been built in such close proximity to undesirable locations such as sewers, tanneries and slaughterhouses, and that 'rag and bone men' had scavenged unfazed through slurry and waste in search of treasure.

Not only were London slums disgusting, they were also truly dark and dingy places. Eminent journalist and social commentator Henry Mayhew wrote that in the poorer areas of the city, only singular gas lamps guided the way along a labyrinth of streets and alleys.[8] These lamps would scarcely emit enough light to illuminate the surrounding area, and instead tinged everything with a reddish-orange glow. It was no wonder that many Londoners, regardless of their social standing, had done their best to avoid these dim areas, which emerged as hotspots for crimes ranging from simple delinquency to cold-blooded murder. As he reflected on a childhood spent in the slums of Victorian London in the 1860s, Donald Shaw wrote that when 'torturous alleys and dingy, narrow streets had to be traversed [...] officers returning late [from work] carried knuckle-dusters and short blades in their right-hand overcoat pockets, ready to jab any footpad who attempted to seize them from behind'.[9] It came as little surprise that 'men seldom returned but in parties of twos or threes', for their own safety.[10]

Beneath the comforting rays of the sun, however, these dingy alleys and dangerous street pavements became meeting grounds for the inhabitants who resided there. Backstreet lanes and communal courtyards would fill with the chatter of housewives and the laughter of children once daylight had broken, scaring away the evils of the night before. Even if their hovels had resembled nightmarish scenes during the night, the homes of the poor working classes of Victorian London brightened as neighbours, friends and family came together to congregate. For many of these people, it mattered not where you lived, but who you lived alongside.

Building Conditions

In the nineteenth century, no matter where you lived in the country, shared housing was a commonplace and expected part of life. Houses full to the brim with numerous families flood local censuses and records, the list of whose inhabitants seem never to end. In Edinburgh, for example, the average number of people living under just one roof was sixteen, and they did not necessarily have to have been related or even to have known each other at all.[1] It was estimated that 13,209 families lived in Edinburgh at the mid-point of the nineteenth century, yet there were only around 2,000 rooms.[2] That so many people would be forced into such tiny spaces, often single-roomed hovels or cramped tenement buildings, is unimaginable to us in modern society today. Further, of these 2,000 rooms, 120 had no windows or doors, and 900 were classed simply as 'cellars'.[3] Indeed, it was estimated that one-third of the entire population of Edinburgh lived in desperate poverty during the reign of Queen Victoria; it was not a stretch to imagine the statistics of London to be round about the same.

Indeed, in London, renters were forced to pay extortionate fees to their landlords in exchange for 'waterless, drainless, floorless, and almost roofless tenements'.[4] So too did they have to relinquish their meagre pittances to afford houses 'full of broken windows, leaking roofs, precipitous staircases, and open doors', as well as broken tiles, peeling plaster, crumbling overhanging jetties, chipped paint, splintered wood and cracked glass panels.[5] The term 'jerry-building' was applicable to many of the houses of the working class and impoverished in Victorian Britain, meaning those that been built cheaply, hastily and therefore inadequately using subpar materials and methods. Occasionally, the walls of these hovels would be constructed from wood panelling or sturdy brick, though in most cases they had been made from plaster and 'hairy mortar', which was quick to crumble and easy to destroy.[6] These earthen-derived materials also succumbed easily to wet and damp, thus creating perfect breeding grounds for mould and spores, introducing harmful bacterium into the air. There was little a Victorian could do when signs of damp and rot appeared upon their walls, for central heating had not yet been invented to the standards that we know today, and any meagre coal-fire could make things worse rather than better with the emittance of smoke.

The hovels of London's poor truly were 'lairs into which a starving dog might creep to die, but nothing more', with contemporaries even writing that 'no cow or horse could thrive in such a hole'.[7] It was all one could do to hope that their walls would remain erect around them, that they would not betray weakness at the brush of a keen breeze or the battering of the rain. Damp, sodden floors could be alleviated by sitting atop scraps of carpet or rug, though fixing enormous cracks sustained by the weather would prove to be far more difficult. Isabella Bird, one contemporary journalist, wrote that the poor would attempt to stave off the cold and the wet by boarding up whatever remains of a window they had with paper or rags, or even with garbage if no other option was available to them.[8] Gaps beneath doors would be stuffed with makeshift draft-excluders, while leaky ceilings and walls would be patched up with greased paper made from the melting down of animal fats.[9] 'What the poor know they need is, houses to dwell in; not dens to rot and perish in, morally and physically,' Bird concluded.[10]

In winter time, when life became particularly difficult for the Victorian poor, freezing temperatures brought new threats of burst water pipes, icy glass and even hypothermia. The winter of 1886 had been a particularly harsh one for Londoners, who had taken advantage of the deep frost by ice-skating up and down the length of the frozen River Thames.[11] Back at home, slum dwellers had been forced to break apart staircases and bannisters for firewood, their fingers and toes slowly turning into ice blocks of their own. 'It's nipping in winter, especially when you've got no fire, to turn in with nothing to lie on, and nothing to cover you,' confessed one pauper in 1881.[12] As if the frost had not been torment enough, heavy rains which followed in the January and spring months of that year deprived 'those who depend for their bread upon the number of people frequenting the public thoroughfares', meaning those who begged, seduced or stole from innocent passers-by wandering on the streets of the city.[13] With towns and markets emptier than usual on account of the weather, money for vendors, for prostitutes or for pickpockets was particularly abysmal. So much so, that after enduring days on end of torrential rains and thundering storms, 'hundreds belonging to this class in the metropolis are reduced to starvation by three or four days of successive rain', such was the lack of earnings available to them.[14]

Money under Queen Victoria was still circulated with the faces of her predecessors, Kings William IV and Georges III and IV, upon them.[15] In the nineteenth century, money took the form either of solid metal coinage, paper notes or flimsy cheques, which could be taken to a bank and exchanged for hard cash. Typically, members of the working class had been paid 'hand to mouth', earning pennies each day which would be put toward food, rent or other necessities. One problem frequently encountered by Victorians was the issue of counterfeit money, which would regularly be given by swindlers to honest hardworking people in exchange for a long day of hard labour. These notes, however, would be confiscated upon trade at the bank, leaving the already poor worker without their due payment for the day.

Even just one missed or late wage payment in the nineteenth century could make the difference between life and death for a pauper. With no life savings and little (if any) liquid assets to their name, the poor had to come up with a solution fast. Thankfully, the passing of a string of laws by the government throughout the nineteenth century had somewhat alleviated the plight of the poor, awarding them provisions intended to improve their situation in life.

Established in 1601 during the reign of Queen Elizabeth I, the Poor Laws were grants given on behalf of the government to the poor. These grants aimed to alleviate the destitute living conditions of the poor by injecting cash into much-needed provisions such as clothing, food and education. Prior to the reign of Queen Victoria, Poor Law provisions came to just £1.25 million annually.[16] Under her government, however, this figure would rise substantially, rapidly growing from £4.25 million to £7 million per annum in just thirty years.[17] Despite this, contemporaries complained that the system simply was not effective, and that the money that had been promised to improve their poverty had barely touched it at all. According to one, the Poor Laws were 'not designed to abolish poverty but to prevent the poor from being a nuisance', keeping them satisfied so that they would not demand any more government assistance.[18] In 1884, for example, the Poor Laws funding in deprived areas of London needed to be supplemented by a further Relief Fund on behalf of the Mayor of London. This had come about due to the tireless efforts of social campaigner Charles Booth, who undertook the gargantuan task of surveying each and every one of London's slums in vivid detail. Booth had drawn up maps of the most severely deprived slum areas, concluding that at least a quarter of the entire population of London lived in destitute conditions, with another quarter faring just slightly better.[19] These *Maps Descriptive of London Poverty* assisted the government to some degree in targeting particularly poor areas of the city, and allowing them to pour much-needed relief funding into the pockets of the local authorities which governed them. This would only be furthered when Charles Booth published no less than seventeen volumes of his encounters with the London slums, entitled *Life and Labour of the People in London*, toward the end of the nineteenth century.

Charles Booth was not the only social reformer who sought to improve the conditions of the poor when the government had failed to do so. Working in conjunction with his friend Henry Hyndman, the pair published a joint inquiry into the extent of poverty in London, which led directly to the establishment in 1885 of the Social Democratic Foundation, an association which championed the rights of the working classes.[20] So too did the efforts of Joseph and his son Seebohm Rowntree (of the confectionery empire). Both men, despite their wealth, had recognized that one of the main issues faced by poor working-class Victorians was the lack of sufficient wages, which led directly to their hardship. The pair rejected social ideals of the time which stated that the poor were responsible for their own poverty, and pressed Parliament into providing working-class paupers with increased wages and even pension schemes. Like Booth and Hyndman, the Rowntrees had conducted their own survey into the lives of the working classes, estimating that a whopping one-third of the city's working population made barely enough money to sustain themselves, and that those in unemployment – or too sick or old to work – were living entirely on the breadline.[21]

Another rich heir who, despite her social standing, campaigned for the rights of workers in Victorian London was Louisa Twining, whose family had made their fortunes in the tea trade. Twining, an early feminist, particularly focused her efforts on bringing exposure to the unfair working conditions of women, campaigning for the employment of females when many turned them away on account of their sex. Louisa Twining especially championed the rights of young girls in service, touched by their struggles of working tough, menial jobs for very little pay. She had also been a significant player in establishing the Metropolitan and National Association for Nursing, which aimed not only to give women a chance of employment within the nursing sector, but also to improve the living conditions of the very young, the elderly, the sick and infirm in subpar and hazardous slum dwellings.[22]

Without the labours of these high-profile social reformists, little may have been done to improve the lives of the working class in Victorian Britain. Certainly, it is reasonable to say that their plights may not have been put at the forefront of the Victorian government, who were otherwise feigning ignorance of the predicaments of the poor. That paupers in Victorian Britain had to rely on the kindness and charity of others to improve their standards of living was a heartbreaking reality. Though it is an enduring belief that there was no kindness in the Victorian slums, evidence very much suggests otherwise.[23] In *The Army of London Poor, by the River-Side Visitor*, written by Thomas Wright in 1882, the author was struck upon a visit to a London slum by the genuine 'self-sacrificing kindness of the poor to the poor, which never fails even among those who are themselves suffering the direst pinch of poverty'.[24] These people, who had very little of their own, did not hesitate to share whatever meagre possessions and provisions they could with their neighbours, friends and family. There was a sense of community within the Victorian slums that perhaps even the wealthier echelons of society could not subscribe to. These communities were arguably tighter-knit and certainly more familial than the networks of the rich. Queen Victoria herself was surprised at how jovial the working classes were, despite the dreadful poverty in which they lived:

> 'We drove back through quite another, & the poorest part of the town, which took ½ an hour. There was not a house [only] wretched looking slums, where the people were all in tatters, & many very Irish looking, they were most loyal & demonstration, there was not one unkind look or dissatisfied expression, every one, without exception, being kind and friendly.'[25]

Indeed, it was believed by social campaigners of the time that 'visiting the houses of the poor is the only practical way really to understand the actual state of each family', and that 'great advantages may result from visits paid to the poor'.[26]To put yourself in their shoes, it was believed, would be the best way to understand the plight of the poor. Many of the most significant of Victorian social reformists did just that, following in the example of Charles Booth and Henry Hyndman. Radicals like journalist Nellie Bly, who lived as a poor woman feigning madness, helped change the way in which mental health care was provided for in the nineteenth century. Other journalists such as Henry Mayhew, Isabella Bird and Richard Rowe did not fear communicating with the poor, but instead forged friendships with members of the working classes, visited their homes and even shared food and meals with them. Bird would later write that her opinions of the poorest classes had changed, and that she had since learnt that 'misfortune, not drink or vice, had brought them so low'.[27] Mayhew had no qualms in voicing his disapproval of the government in their apparent lack of social care for the poor. Criticizing the fact that Parliament would pour money into what he considered to be less-important ventures such as rail travel, Mayhew wrote scathingly that,

> 'to improve the condition of a class of people whose misery, ignorance, and vice, amongst all the immense wealth and great knowledge of "*the first city in the world*", is, to say the very least, a national disgrace to us.'[28]

There was no excuse for a lack of duty to the poor, especially considering that hefty funds already lined the pockets of Victorian Parliamentarians of the day, which helped support their own lavish living. Equal rights were supposed to be equal, challenged the reformists, and 'civilisation supposed to penetrate even to the lowest stratum of humanity'.[29]

Not everyone in the nineteenth century was sympathetic to the cause of the impoverished, however. There existed a sense amongst the prejudiced of society that 'circumstances make people what they are', and that the poor only had themselves to blame for their destitution.[30] Many wealthier Victorians did not see the point in concerning themselves with the issues of the poor; after all, they never met or mingled with them, and seemed to exist almost on a completely different social level. These bigoted opinions reached such a head that some even ascribed to theories of natural selection, the belief that the weakest and poorest of society should 'die off' in order for the wealthy to thrive.[31] Indeed, one contemporary source written in the late nineteenth century states that, 'if we cannot help our pariahs, it would be a kindness, I think, to kill them off [...] death for these is better than life'.[32] Even the famous poet and painter William Blake wrote that the government should 'compell the poor to live upon a crust of bread', adding that should their 'children sicken, let them die; there are enough born, even too many, and our Earth will be overrun'.[33]

The chasm between rich and poor in Victorian Britain was wider than perhaps it had ever been at any point of British history. That these two societies could co-exist seemed inconceivable, such was the prejudice and conviction of thinkers at the time. Radical on both ends of the spectrum, rich and poor alike in the nineteenth century would continue to bump heads for decades to come; the poor wanted more, yet the rich would not grant it. This was a sentiment nowhere more keenly felt than in London, a city so divided by wealth and status. There was 'the High Street of the city, with a royal palace at one end', and the cavernous labyrinths of poverty and vice at the other.[34] Being poor in nineteenth-century London could be the knife-edge between life and death; one late rent payment, or one day's missed work, could have fatal results.

'It is only after one is in trouble that one realises how little sympathy and kindness there is in the world,' one contemporary wrote.[35]

Chapter 2

City Dwellers and Street Urchins: Living in the Slums

'Home has few attractions to a man whose life is street life.'

Henry Mayhew, *London Labour and the London Poor* (1851)

Life in Victorian Britain was much as it is today. People were born, people lived, people died. Our Victorian ancestors were not too dissimilar to us; they loved, they laboured, they lost. They had favourite foods, favourite pastimes, favourite people. Yet history has consigned them to a life in the shadows, removing all of the traits and quirks that had made them human; that had made them like us.

To accurately think about a life in Victorian Britain, we must first think of our own lives. What are our most prized possessions? What are our goals? What makes us human? We must learn to see in our ancestors the same beating hearts which drive us in our ambitions today. We must treat history not as an encyclopaedia of dates, but as a mirror to the past.

We would be surprised at what we might find staring back at us.

He wandered across the litter-choked gutters, observant and mindful in where he placed his boot. One wrong step could land him – quite literally – in rotting refuse or puddles of raw sewage. Jotting down in his journal what he had seen so far on his travels, Richard Rowe continued past a row of tenement houses, their fronts blackened with the soot and smoke of the city. Staring back at him through makeshift grease-paper curtains and cracked window panes were 'sly-faced, swarthy, black-eyed women and children [–] skim-milk-eyed bumpkins'.[1] Rowe was undeterred; he had already met many of these bumpkins along his journey throughout London, and he was sure to meet many more.

Further still he walked, ducking beneath sagging lines of laundry and stepping over naked urchin children playing hopscotch in the street. There, sitting upon the street corner huddled between a crumbling brick wall and a refuse pit was a man; or a shadow of a man, he could not quite tell. The man was bent double, his hair white from age and black from dirt. His skin betrayed signs of malnutrition, his eyes betrayed sadness. Richard took out his pen. 'He had given up all hope of rising above his wretched condition,' he wrote of the man, 'it was as much as he could do to keep his body and soul together.'[2]

Richard Rowe had not walked far, scarcely an inch of the city, yet he had truly seen in it a microcosm of the world which until recently had seemed so foreign and alien to him. This was a world in which smells and sights and sounds had at times bordered on the sickening; this was the dark and dingy underworld of the Victorian slums.

In his *Life in the London Streets*, published in 1881, Richard Rowe had painted a vivid description of the lives of the masses in Victorian London. Doing what others had scarcely done before, Rowe communicated with these masses; he ate with them, sat with them and listened to them when they confided in him their worries and fears. In doing so, Rowe had forged relationships with the most marginalized members of Victorian society, and had taken up their cause when no one else had. And truly, their cause had been a difficult one.

In an age where 'families pawned their belongings to pay the rent', any sign of compassion had been welcomed by the poorest of Victorian society.[3] These were the same people who did all that they could 'to keep life in them', who worked, scrimped and struggled to survive in return for nothing at all. In Victorian London, the going rate of rent for a single hovel room per year was between £5 and £8, or 10*s* a week if renters were willing to further sacrifice their comfort.[5] For this price, tenants would be faced with shoddily built single-roomed dwellings in communal tenement buildings (often just a typical, standard house which had been divided into 'apartments') complete with softening wood plank flooring or cold stone, as well as walls divided by insufficient 'dividers' (which did little in keeping out noise, smells or even the weather) that were riddled with woodlice and beetles.[6] For a cheaper rent, tenants could expect to go without such luxuries as doors or windows, but for just slightly extra payment they could hope to enjoy perhaps a chimney or a room which had a small, yet prized, degree of privacy.

Tenement houses in Victorian Britain were inhabited by the poorest of the poor, who were forced to reside in these hovels to avoid a life exposed upon the streets or one of gruelling labour in the workhouse. Tenement houses, also known as 'lodging houses' or 'dosshouses', were intended to be but temporary homes, a last resort for people to stay in as they saved money for dwellings of their own. On paper, perhaps it had appeared a realistic plan; in practice, however, many slum-dwellers in the nineteenth century rarely moved out of these tenement buildings unless they had fallen behind on rent or were forced to be removed due to some other means. Even then, the newly evicted would wander aimlessly until they had found another tenement accepting new renters, whereby their transitory period would end and the cycle would begin again. It was very rare for landlords of tenement buildings not to accept new lodgers, however, for with every desperate homeless person came the attraction of regular sums of money. Being a landlord in Victorian London was a lucrative job, one which could amass relatively substantial wealth.

With landlords refusing to turn tenants away, these dosshouses grew fuller and fuller with every soul who passed over its threshold. If lodgers were lucky, then they could hope to move into a room of their own, away from the prying eyes of strangers and wandering nomads who also called the building 'home'. In one immense lodging house in Spitalfields, for example, 300 men and women filed into its rooms and corridors, settling in to whatever corner they could find to rest their heads for the evening.[7] If a lodger was fortunate, he or she could move into tenement houses built solely for people of their own gender, though this meant breaking up families and separating loved ones from each other. Nevertheless, same-sex dosshouses were popular particularly amongst the female population of Victorian London, who found comfort in sharing with women whose struggles mirrored their own. Though it meant that men, women and children had to share beds with complete strangers in mixed-sex lodging houses (such as was the case at the White Horse Dosshouse in East London), given the lack of space and cramped conditions of same-sex houses, acquaintances still found themselves sharing close quarters with people they had literally just met.[8] Life in a shared dosshouse was an unfair and unjust reality to which hardworking Londoners were unfortunately accustomed. 'Here was a home for deserving women and yet what a mockery the name was,' wrote one contemporary about the state of dosshouses; 'the most deserving of women, are asked to call this spot of bareness – home […] I could not endure that sort of business long.'[9]

Life inside a tenement building was cold, cramped and chaotic. As Karl Marx wrote in his *Economic and Philosophical Manuscripts*, published in 1844, 'the cellar-dwelling of the poor man is a hostile element'.[10] Devoid of character and warmth, these dosshouses were dirty and unfurnished due to the nature of their use as a transient place to stay. Even functional items like tables, stoves, wash basins and beds could be entirely lacking in these places. When journalist Isabella Bird visited a dosshouse in 1869, she found that one stonemason, his wife and their three children lived in one singular room decorated with items retrieved from refuse heaps.[11] The whole family had slept on sodden straw strewn upon the floor and had used a broken wooden box as a makeshift table. With no door and numerous holes in the walls, Bird declared this particular room unsafe for inhabitation.

In another room along the same street, Bird came across a family consisting of elderly parents, their two adult sons and their two unmarried adult daughters, who all had to share a single bed that was wriggling with vermin.[12] Such had been their discomfort that, despite both parents suffering from rheumatoid arthritis and one son suffering from fever, the family had decided instead to sleep upon the cold, hard earthen floor.

To have a comfortable bed in the Victorian slums was to have a luxury many could not afford. If the poor could afford a bed, it most likely took the form of a so called 'box bed', which had high sides and prevented sleepers from rolling out at night. One family in the slums of Edinburgh during the nineteenth century had owned a box bed, which had been shared by a mother, father and their three children.[13] Lacking in bedclothes, the family had recycled a scrap of worn carpet as their blanket, which was the only item of 'comfort' within the entirety of their hovel. Others had 'beds' that consisted of sole blankets upon the floor, or pillows made from sacking stuffed with straw. Mattresses and duvets (known as 'bolsters') certainly did exist in the nineteenth century, as did counterpanes (a top sheet which would be pulled taut atop the duvet), though these were luxuries that much of the poorest population simply could not afford. Indeed, even in institutions like workhouses, prisons and hospitals, beds tended to be hard, lumpy, 'cold and uncomfortable', with some contemporaries feeling as though they had awoken 'bruised' after their arduous sleep.[14]

In 1800, an attempt had been made to combat the dire sleeping arrangements of the poorest members of society. Aware that the wandering poor would 'sleep in barns, tents and casual wards', such was the lack of comfortable beds available to them, social campaigner William Booth (who later went on to establish the Salvation Army) introduced schemes aimed at alleviating homelessness.[15] One of these schemes was the establishment of sleeping halls, which were filled with 'one penny sit ups', 'two penny hang overs' and 'four penny coffins', all which allowed paupers a relatively comfortable night's sleep. As the names suggest, a 'one penny sit up' could be purchased for a penny per night, and would reserve a seat on a long, communal bench for the poor to sleep sitting upright. Likewise, a 'two penny hang over' cost two pennies, and allowed sleepers to perch upon a seat while they rested their upper body across a suspended rope. Finally, a 'four penny coffin' could be hired out by individuals or even shared by families each night, and resembled deep box beds with high sides that earned them the nickname of 'coffins'. Despite their name, these coffin beds could be relatively comfortable, depending upon whether individuals cared little for sleeping in halls filled with scores of other vagrants and their families.

Privacy was very much lacking in the slums of Victorian London. Whether it be in communal sleeping halls or shared dosshouses, a lack of privacy was commonplace and problematic. In cases where whole families shared a single room, cloths and tarpaulin could be hung from the ceiling as makeshift curtains and room dividers. This was particularly useful when individuals bathed or toileted in buckets in rooms filled with family members, and was especially utilized in cases where adults engaged in activities like masturbation and sexual intercourse. Contrary to popular belief, the vast majority of good parents would not engage in intercourse while their children slept in the same bed as them or were awake in the room beside them.[16] Rather, if they felt the sexual urge they would wait until they were alone and away from prying eyes. That did not mean, however, that poor children were entirely naïve when it came to sex and its associations such as pregnancy. In one description of a slum dwelling in the late 1860s, a married couple and their two children lived in the same 14ft by 12ft room with three female prostitutes, who hid (somewhat poorly) their business from their host family.[17]

With so many people crammed into such small spaces, children would have undoubtedly been exposed to some semblance of sex from a much earlier age than children in today's society. Indeed, social commentator Henry Mayhew writes that, due to dozens of individuals sleeping head to toe in the beds of common lodging houses, 'words and acts between boys and girls did take place'.[18] Indeed, considered cognisant of the law when they reached the age of 14, adolescents could begin to legally engage in intercourse at this time for they were considered by Victorian law to be capable of forming their own adult decisions. Although it was illegal for children between the ages of 4 and 14 to be physically exposed to sex or to enter a brothel, many undoubtedly disregarded the law. For instance, high rates of teenage pregnancy indicate that young adolescents were engaging in intercourse, while other shocking statistics of London brothels noted that sixty-six girls under the age of 14 had been employed as prostitutes, with two of them being just 8 years old.[19] Indeed, in a study of London brothels conducted just thirty years later, in 1897, Arthur Sherwell discovered that there were eleven prostitutes aged 16, seventeen aged 15, seven aged 14, five aged 13, two aged 12 and three aged just 11 years old.[20] In response to Sherwell's disturbing findings, the Criminal Law Amendment Act of 1903 finally declared that any man found to engage in sexual intercourse with a female under the age of 13 would be charged with indecency.

Meanwhile, other forms of sexual intercourse were looked down upon by Victorians, particularly in cases where individuals would profit from it. Henry Mayhew describes somewhat scathingly a practice which apparently took place within the slums, whereby men would swap their wives with those of their friends to enjoy a night of pleasure for a fee.[21] Mayhew writes that 'a departure from this fidelity – if it provided a few meals or a fire – was not considered at all heinous' amongst members of the poorest communities.[22] Elsewhere, warnings about enjoying the pleasures of masturbation (known as 'frigging') were issued, particularly to young men and adolescents, which warned that if engaged in frequently, 'you will die in a mad-house; lots of boys do'.[23] Perhaps most troubling to Victorians of all, however, was the issue of same-sex relationships and romance. Homosexuality in nineteenth-century Britain was heavily warned against and frequently looked down upon by members of society, who found it disgusting and against the laws of nature.

Homosexuality

To be homosexual in the nineteenth century was to commit a crime. Declared a capital offence under the Buggery Act of 1533, being found to be a homosexual could result in heavy fines, harsh punishment and even death.[1] Men found engaging in homosexual activities would be arrested; one Thomas Lane, a London coffeeshop owner, was found committing an 'unnatural offence' on the aptly named Love Lane in Eastcheap with his lover, seaman James Mortimer.[2] The men were let off with a warning from the police, but were later caught that evening 'misconducting' themselves at a public urinal. They were then arrested by the same police who had earlier pardoned them, and taken to the nearby police station for questioning.

Both Thomas and James had been lucky; other gay men in nineteenth-century Britain were not so. Between 1806 and 1861, no less than 8,921 men confessing to homosexuality had been prosecuted by their local jurisdictions. Of these men,

404 had been sentenced to death.[4] Despite the law declaring homosexuality to be a crime, however, public opinion was far more empathetic. Many tight-knit families aware of their relative's sexual orientation would hide it from neighbours and the wider community for fear of retribution, and true friends would turn a blind-eye. There did exist safe places in London for homosexuals to meet others and engage in sexual activities away from the prying eyes of the public. So-called 'Molly Houses' were established in almost every city in Victorian Britain, hidden away in plain sight behind uniform-looking houses and establishments such as bars, social clubs and public houses. At these places, men from the richest to the poorest of society could engage in eroticism and sex without prejudice or judgement. Owners of Molly Houses were protective of their 'guests', and kept a watchful eye on any authorities that suspected them. Behind closed doors, activities ranged from the tame to the extreme, and as such secrecy and trust were of the utmost importance to ensure that no reputation would be ruined and no lives lost.

Not every homosexual would hide their true identities in the nineteenth century, however, and there are numerous figures who paved the way for gay rights by expressing their true selves. Famous homo- and bisexuals of Victorian Britain include such figures as the renowned author Oscar Wilde, the poet Lord Byron and the diarist Anne Lister, who was more famously remembered as 'Gentleman Jack'. Anne Lister, a lesbian who recorded her affairs with women in thick monographs of coded diary entries, was known to dress as a man, something that was extremely untypical for women in the nineteenth century, who rarely, if ever, wore trousers. For Anne, dressing as the opposite sex had helped somewhat to emancipate her from the oppressive world in which she had lived. But Anne Lister had certainly not been the only Victorian woman to explore her identity through the way that she dressed; references to other 'cross dressers' can be found in records dating from the time.

Another nineteenth-century lesbian who had assumed the identity of a man was Ann McGaul.[5] McGaul, who went by the name of 'John Jones', had short cropped hair, wore men's clothing and lived with another woman, whom she had considered as her wife. They lived unsuspected for at least six years, until nosey neighbours raised their suspicions and alerted the police. Another was 'Thomas Walker', who was discovered to be a female when she refused to bathe in the communal bathtub in prison.[6] Walker had evaded being noticed for years, her domestic life with her common-law wife convincing the community around them that she had genuinely been born as a male.

Equally, some men would dress as women in order to express themselves. John Challis, a 60-year-old man, would regularly be spotted in public houses across London dressed as a shepherdess.[7] George Campbell, a 35-year-old lawyer, would adorn himself in women's garb; both John and George were charged for 'immoral practices'.[8] So too was Thomas Francis Druce, who was arrested for wearing petticoats, a bonnet, make-up and a long black wig to casinos and gambling parlours.[9] Druce had insisted on being referred to with the pronouns 'him, her or it', and had been imprisoned for an 'impropriety of conduct'.[10] He was released later in the evening on the day of the arrest, having made promises to the police that he would only wear masculine clothing from then on.

Agreeing to the terms of the police, even if they had no intentions of actually abiding to them, was one way in which a Victorian homosexual could lessen their sentence and restore their reputation. One way in which a homosexual could successfully hide their true identity and orientation was through something known as 'homosociality', a term given to friends of the same sex who had a particularly strong relationship. The lines of homosexuality and homosociality were greatly blurred in the nineteenth century; a man could be imprisoned for holding the hand of another in public, for example, but if he pleaded homosociality he would be entirely free to go. As such, homosociality was adopted almost as a mask, which lesbians and gays could hide behind to avoid detection. These 'intense relationships' meant that lovers could own homes together, sleep in the same beds and even be each other's legal executors without raising suspicion.[11] These relationships were even encouraged within schools, universities and social clubs, for they were believed to strengthen ties with others and improve relationships.[12]

Yet no amount of concealing and hiding the truth made life any easier for homosexuals in nineteenth-century Britain. The law was still against them, and one misstep could result in fatality. In somewhat surprising solidarity, some high-profile social reformers like Jeremy Bentham had supported the plight of homosexuals and campaigned for the act's decriminalization. Bentham's involvement, as well as the efforts of other campaigners, had resulted in success; of the 404 men sentenced to death between 1806 and 1861, only fifty-six were actually executed – the rest were all pardoned.[13] The final execution of a homosexual man in Britain occurred in 1835, and although the rights of homosexuals still had much further to go, the efforts of these early radicals and reformists had made the lives of 'all men and women of everyland, who are not afraid of themselves, who trust so much in their own souls that they dare stand up in the might of their own individuality' just that tiny bit better.[14]

What did Victorian paupers look like? What did they wear? Did the poorest members of society wear clothes similar to the wealthy, and were they able to keep up with fashion trends to fit in?

Clothing and Fashion

Fashion took many forms throughout the nineteenth century, with trends continuously changing with the seasons. For the wealthier classes, who were able to keep up with these trends by purchasing new outfits frequently, fashion was a way in which they could express themselves. For the poor, however, who could not afford to prioritize their clothing over other needs such as food and rent, staying up to date with fashion trends was far more difficult.

According to beauty guides of the time, 'men seldom occupy so long a time in the duties of the toilette', whereas 'ladies take a length of time to dress'.[1] For wealthier members of society, getting dressed could certainly take a lengthy time, particularly if an individual was female. Wearing multiple layers even during the hottest months of the year, an outfit typically consisted of underclothes, outerwear and accessories that could be pinned, tied or attached to the wearer. For the poor, such a routine would not be expected to take so long. When Richard Rowe observed one man in the slums of London in 1881, he noted that his clothing consisted of a single layer of worn and tattered fabrics, as well as shoes that were held together by string and missing their soles.[2] His clothing 'was not much better than a scarecrow's', Rowe wrote.[3]

Regardless of one's wealth, however, the basis of a good outfit always started with underwear. For men and children, long knickerbockers would be worn on their legs to preserve their modesty.[4] Women too could wear these knickerbockers, which eventually became shortened to fit snugly above the knee, and later around the groin, to become modern-day 'knickers'. As well as this, most women would wear at least one underskirt known as a 'petticoat' (though some poor women have been recorded as wearing two or more) or a 'chemise', but these appeared to fall out of fashion after the eighteenth century.[5] If they could afford it, some women may have also worn crinolines, stiff underskirts which were made from semi-flexible materials like light woods to resemble a cage and give shape to the outer skirts of a dress. Crinolines were particularly popular amongst the wealthier classes during the first half of the nineteenth century, where a voluptuous silhouette was considered attractive. They were heavy, however, and could cut into the waist and hips of the wearer, and therefore sometimes required spongy padding to prevent sores. They could also be incredibly dangerous near bodies of open water (for they easily became waterlogged and could cause the wearer to drown) and naked flames (they were often so wide that women had to be wary of stepping too close to a lit fireplace), and as such proved to be wholly impractical in daily life.

For the upper part of the female body, 'stays' would be worn for support and modesty. Stays, or corsets, were sold for just 12*s* in the nineteenth century, and were therefore affordable for most women in Victorian society.[6] It is likely that even poor women owned at least one stay, which could be worn for days on end without requiring changing. Stays were supposed to be comfortable for the wearer, akin to a second-skin of sorts. They 'should be flexible to the motion of the body', and allow for movement, breathing and even the swelling of the body during pregnancy.[7] Just like modern bras, stays would be comfortable if worn correctly. It was only when pulled too taut that they could be 'crushing in the ribs, injuring the lungs and heart, the stomach and many other internal organs'.[8] Indeed, if laced too tight, corsets could cause damage to the spine, stomach and lungs, and could result in women fainting from low blood pressure caused by the constriction. Contemporaries warned against inflexible materials such as whalebone and steel in their stays, for 'it destroys beauty' and causes 'abscesses and cancer'.[9] Such was the danger of wearing too-tight stays that some women chose to go without them entirely, considering them to be 'enemies to the female form'.[10] Indeed, according to Isabella Bird, some women went without underwear entirely. In her *Notes on Old Edinburgh*, she mentioned three adult women sitting outside upon the kerb entirely naked.[11] Public nakedness was most likely not commonplace in the Victorian slums, however, for even the poorest members of society preferred to wear at least some semblance of clothing no matter how dirty, tattered or unfashionable it be.

Occasionally, Victorians would sleep naked, though it was more likely that most wore pyjamas if they could be afforded. Men would typically wear a two-piece set consisting of a nightshirt and long trousers, though some slept without any leg coverings. Women and children would typically wear light nightdresses to sleep in, as well as woollen socks if they suffered from cold feet in bed.[12] Some of the poorest members of society would even wear their 'day' clothes to bed, being unable to afford separate articles of clothing intended purely for sleep.

Shoes were relatively simple articles of clothing in the nineteenth century, and were typically plain and black. Versatile black shoes could, and would, be worn by both men and women regardless of their sex amongst the poorest communities of Victorian Britain. However, by the end of the century, gender-specific shoes began to hit the market thanks to the establishment of dedicated cobbler shops and shoe stores such as Clarks in 1825.[13] Many shoes and boots were even purchased in one size, then moulded to the individual's foot over time with natural wear.[14] Shoes could be made from leather, rubber or even elastic, as well as hardened cloth for use by small children.[15] Socks would typically be worn up the length of the thigh, reaching the knee, though some women wore stockings which covered the entire leg and helped keep wearers warm.

Accessories and jewellery could also be worn to complete an outfit, even by the poorest of society. In higher social circles, tradition dictated that jewellery be worn only at dinner and in the evening, but very rarely during the day.[16] For the poor, however, jewellery would be worn with pride regardless of the time of day. To have jewellery of some kind in the Victorian slums was truly a treasure; most had to pawn their valuables to afford even the smallest of necessities to get by. Because of this, poor Victorians found clever ways to bring added flair to their outfits; some wore velvet ribbons of varying colours around their wrists and throats, while others made their own trinkets from metal scraps and items such as coins or thimbles.[17] Buttons formed makeshift medallions, while beads were strung together and clipped into the hair for a particularly eye-catching look. Catherine Eddowes, one of the victims of Jack the Ripper, had been found with apparently fashionable 'strings tied to her head' as well as cuffs made from imitation fur.[18]

Flowers could be worn in the hair or within hats and other headpieces by both grown women and children. Oftentimes, these flowers were genuine, though others were made from silk or paper and could be bought from talented street vendors who made them. Mary Jane Kelly, the final victim of Jack the Ripper, was one such seller.[19] These hair accessories could be tied to the hair with ribbon scraps or hairpins, which could reach around 12 inches long and were very sharp. Indeed, women were encouraged not to wear long hairpins on omnibuses else they accidentally stab other passengers, and they were even later confiscated from arrested suffragettes who used them as weapons toward the end of the nineteenth century.[20]

Like clothing, hair styling took many forms in the Victorian era. Fashionable with young women and girls, loose braids and pigtails were a fun, yet practical hairstyle. So too was the 'Gibson Girl' hairdo, a fashionable style in which hair would be messily coiled atop the head. Inspired by the models of artist Charles Dana Gibson's illustrations, the Gibson Girl was seen as an elegant yet effortless style that women of all ages could emulate, and saw a boom in popularity at the end of the Victorian era and well into the Edwardian age. Achieving the excessive volume of the Gibson Girl could be difficult, however, so faux hair pieces, extensions and wigs, and items called 'hair rats', were employed to help. These hair rats were not made from the animal, but were bundles of shed hair that had fallen to the floor or gathered on a hairbrush. Once a considerable collection of hair had been acquired, Victorian women would pin it to their heads in faux chignon buns.

Other women preferred to wear their hair in coils, ringlets or harsh plaits, but some believed this would 'impart a vulgar appearance, and frequently make a gentlewoman appear like a dressed-up servant maid'.[21] To achieve these tight curls, Victorian women wound papers, rags or pins tightly and evenly throughout their hair, or even used primitive versions of electrical heated curling and straightening irons and crimping tongs if they could be afforded.[22] Children's hair would also be curled in this way, and decorated with ribbons. This was a particularly favoured hairstyle in the nineteenth century, made fashionable in the time of Dickens, and had 'come into vogue again' by the end of the century.[23]

Men too could curl their hair in the nineteenth century, and indeed waves were fashionable for males at the time. Influential figures such as Prince Albert had made short and neat hairstyles that kinked with a slight curl attractive in the earlier reign of Victoria, while Oscar Wilde had made longer hair popular and fashionable toward its end. The quiff also began to rapidly gain in popularity toward the end of the century, while greased, slicked-back hair became fashionable amongst younger men in society.

Though they may not have kept up with fashions at the same pace as the wealthy, poor Victorians still tried their best to look the part. 'They don't look very nice', wrote one contemporary about the poor, 'but they are good, honest working' people who just so happened to have 'stories printed on their faces of hard lives, abuse and poverty'.[24]

Chapter 3

Bone Grubbers, Mudlarks and Matchstick Girls: At Work in the Slums

> 'None but God and ourselves know how hard my wife
> here has fought against the workhouse, how hard
> we have all lived to keep out of it.'
>
> Thomas Wright, *The Army of London Poor, by the River-Side Visitor* (1882)

Life in the slums of Victorian London would not have been possible without an income of some kind. Men, women and even children were forced into employment to support their families, yet even when their earnings were accumulated, many still struggled to scrape by. There was no such concept as retirement for the poorest of Victorians, nor were provisions such as sick and maternity pay introduced until the close of the nineteenth century. The average wage for a labouring man in Victorian Britain was just thirty shillings a week, which he would be paid every Saturday unless he had been absent through illness or other means during that time.[1] It was by no means a lucrative wage, yet was still marginally better than the vast majority of earnings of dwellers in the slums of Victorian London. A laundry maid, for example, would make just 8*s* a week if she was lucky, while 'sandwich board men' (who carried heavy advertising boards over their shoulders through urban areas) would make just 5*s*.[2]

Some jobs in the Victorian slums fared slightly better. According to Henry Mayhew in a letter to the *Morning Chronicle* in 1849, a sewer-flusher (a man who would quite literally 'flush' sewer systems of its waste) would earn around £1 4*s* per week, a relatively comfortable wage that could quite easily support life in the slums.[3] An ironer, who would be hired to iron the clothes of wealthier patrons, could expect to make 3*s* 6*d* per day, which could quickly mount up if she was lucky in finding available work.[4] Other types of domestic employ available to the working class in Victorian London included kitchen maids, which could make anywhere between £10 and £25 per annum, 'maids of all work', who averaged a meagre £6 to £15 annually, and nursery maids, who fared slightly better and made around £30 per year on average.[5]

Domestic work was particularly favoured by females in the Victorian slums, who could begin their careers as lowly chambermaids tasked to perform the most menial of chores, before slowly graduating to other forms of housemaid (such as lady's maid) if they performed particularly well and had a good rapport with the family that employed them. Wealthy homes in the Victorian era could afford to employ domestic help if they so desired, with households even at the lower end of the middle-class wealth bracket being able to hire at least one, if not two, maids of all work. These girls, typically adolescent and embarking on their first job, would often live with the host family. Beginning their days as early as five in the morning, maids of all work were expected to carry out every chore in the home, from scrubbing floors to beating carpets, washing the exterior of the home and shining the crockery in the kitchen.[6] Maids of all work would often work in conjunction with the kitchen, their roles merging with that of a scullery maid. Typically earning around just £9 per annum (around £532 today), kitchen maids would assist in the cooking of dishes and the cleaning of the kitchen, their role being typically considered as a rudimentary form of work experience for young women.[7]

Wealthier families in the nineteenth century who earned at least £300 per annum could afford to widen their employ of domestic help. As well as maids of all work, families in this fiscal bracket would typically employ nursemaids for their children, cooks and 'upper' housemaids, who typically tended to the family rather than the home.[8] These maids would light the lamps and fires of the home, help serve the family at mealtimes and answer the door to visitors enquiring about business or delivering goods.[9] Upper housemaids would also ensure that their younger charges kept in line and performed their duties to a high standard.

Despite sometimes referred to as 'slaveys', being a housemaid in the nineteenth century was a job that surprisingly earned much admiration.[10] To become a domestic servant, writes Isabella Beeton in her *Household Management*,

> 'presents no degradation, but the reverse [...] they are initiated step by step into the mysteries of the household, with the prospect of rising in service, if it is a house admitting of promotion, to the respectable position of butler or house steward [...] can there be any stronger security?'[11]

Further, some families forged strong and friendly relationships with their domestic staff, which lasted even after their service had ended. Indeed, host families were encouraged to be kind to their staff, knowing that 'if servants depend on them for their means of living, in their turn they are dependent on their servants for very many of the comforts in life'; staff should therefore be treated with the utmost kindness and respect, no matter their social position.[12]

So too were household staff directed to show their respect to their employers. Although Isabella Beeton wrote disparagingly that,

> 'the race of good servants has died out, at least in England [...] there is neither honesty, conscientiousness, nor the careful and industrious habits which distinguished the servants of our grandmothers and great-grandmothers [...] domestics no longer know their place.'

Maids in the nineteenth century were still expected to abide to 'polite manners, modest demeanour, and a respectful reserve', as well as a 'good sense, good temper, some self-denial, and consideration for the feelings or others, whether above or below them in the social scale'.[13] Some mistresses were so fond of their staff that they encouraged their friends to also employ their services, and indeed many domestic servants found their position thanks to networks of wealthy women who recommended them personally to others.[14]

Male staff were often treated in the same way. Butlers, valets and footmen were all attractive jobs for the poorest of Victorian society, who would earn the opportunity to leave behind their lives in the slums and reside within grand homes for nothing but their work in exchange. Arguably closer to the family than their female counterparts, the duties of male servants ranged from serving meals to paying household bills and personally waiting upon the family.[15] As such, male servants were expected to be discreet, loyal to their masters and trustworthy, such was the importance of their roles within the home. They were also expected to be punctual, reliable and respectable, as they would represent the family while running errands and in answering calls made to the house.[16]

Domestic work was not the only form of employ available to women who hailed from the slums of urban spaces. If they could write, or at least read to some degree, a working-class woman could find work as a clerk or registrar, particularly within the Church. She could also become a nanny, childminder or teacher of younger children, whether it be in a brick-and-mortar school or in makeshift places of learning erected for children throughout the slums of cities. But perhaps the most infamous of jobs available to women in the slums of nineteenth-century Britain was one far removed from the honourable duties of servitude and childcare. It was a job which many desperate women turned to, and many lusty men took advantage of: prostitution.

Known as 'women of the night', 'painted ladies' and even 'skinwalkers', prostitutes were common sights all across Victorian Britain.[17] Some prostitutes and sex workers in the nineteenth century even hid the true extent of their employment behind the disguise of other jobs, referring to themselves as 'seamstresses' or 'semptresses' to avoid the labelling of a bad reputation.[18] Indeed, despite the fact that their services were often sought out by men – even those who hailed from better social standings than their own – prostitutes and their work were largely treated with disdain amongst their peers. 'I could not get out of that life,' confessed one former prostitute to journalist Henry Mayhew in 1850.[19] She continued, painfully remembering the time in which she had spent in brothels, that '[you] get used in there, indeed, and you are life-ruined'.[20] The mistreatment of prostitutes was a fact corroborated by other women who had formerly turned to the trade in order to support themselves. One woman, for example, had testified that she had been 'treated like a toy, a plaything, an animated doll', not as a human at all.[21]

One particularly harrowing story of the mistreatment of prostitutes comes from Aldershot, where a 15-year-old girl who had come from a poor but respected family fell into the pit of prostitution.[22] Leaving her job as a nursemaid due to an abusive mistress, the girl had befriended a young woman on the street who convinced her to travel to Somerset on a jaunt. The girls began their journey, yet eventually the elder of the two lagged behind, claiming pennilessness. As she continued her journey alone, the 15-year-old girl soon found that she had spent all of her money on food and had been forced to pawn her clothes to pay for provisions. At some point she had met with an older man, who had convinced her to travel with him on the offer that he would sustain her with food and money. Graciously accepting the request, the pair travelled onward to a pub which was full of soldiers, mariners and labouring men. It was there, the girl later admitted, that she had been coerced into sex by the men, to whom she 'became a toy'.[23] After weeks of languishing in the pub as a helpless, pimped-out prostitute, the girl's family finally found her and rushed to take her home, discovering that she was suffering from the effects of numerous venereal diseases and was heavily pregnant.

When the going rate for an average poor prostitute in London was just 3*d*, or the equivalent of one loaf of bread, it was no wonder that they were amongst the most exploited of workers in Victorian Britain.[24] Only a select few of London's poor prostitutes had been lucky enough to earn a decent wage from their trade, enough to support their lifestyles considerably. Mary Jane Kelly, the final victim of Jack the Ripper, for example, had travelled across Europe with her lovers as a high-end prostitute.[25] Yet even then, prostitution was a dangerous profession, one which saw women frequently get abused and mistreated. At one of the more sophisticated of London brothels, for example, where the prostitutes were described as 'strong, hearty healthy girls, and keep clean rooms', they were still 'beaten for other things too, or for nothing at all'.[26]

Prostitution was not the only profession which could endanger people in the nineteenth century. For men, a life as a miner could be a relatively short one. Threatened by collapsed mine shafts or the development of diseases such as asthma, mining was among the most dangerous jobs of the Victorian era. Working in a colliery meant long hours spent entirely in darkness, or with a sole, flickering oil lamp to guide the way. Mining could be lonely and isolating, cold and depressing. It could also be injurious to men, particularly if their legs got caught in the tracks of minecarts and they had been too slow to move them before impact with the heavy wagons occurred. Mining even caused health problems such as bone malformation and muscle aches, due to the unnaturally bent posture required of miners as they slowly picked away at the tunnels of iron ore, coal and stone below the earth's surface.

Mining was also a dangerous job for children, particularly young boys who were employed as colliery hands and subjected to long hours picking lumps of coal that their elders had dislodged from the cave walls, as well as opening and closing trap doors and hauling stone.[27] Like adults, the wellbeing of children suffered from a life underground. Reports of terrified children sat crying alone as they awaited the rumble of a minecart abound from the nineteenth century, particularly from areas where the mining industry was particularly heavy like in South Wales and Northern England. It was little wonder; many of these children were below the age of 10, and had had to accompany their older siblings and male relatives into employment in the mines to help support their families. It was not until 1842 that the Mines Act officially raised the working age of children in mines to 10, gradually continuing to rise with each subsequent act, aimed at eventually phasing children out of the workforce.[28] Despite this, the 1851 Census revealed that more than 24,000 boys under the age of 15 were still being employed in the mines, with many undoubtedly having already been stationed in their roles for years before the survey had been taken.[29]

Another dangerous job typically carried out by children in Victorian Britain was chimney sweeping. In his *London Labour and London Poor*, Henry Mayhew estimated that there were at least a thousand child chimney sweeps in London during the mid-1800s, and a thousand more working as 'turncocks' (street lamp lighters).[30] Children had been employed in the sweeping of chimneys for centuries, ever since chimneys had been introduced to houses on a mass scale during the reigns of the Tudors, for they were lithe, small and agile enough to climb up the breast of the chimney and into its flues.[31] Despite the Act for the Better Regulation of Chimney Sweepers and their Apprentices being passed in 1788, which sought to improve the dangerous working conditions of chimney sweeps, many boys still found themselves lodged within flues and suffocating to death.[32] Breathing in the cinders and coal dust would choke the boys, who would struggle in their efforts to take a deep breath. In their struggle, they would twist and turn, their movement limited by the incredibly tight nature of the chimney, which was purposely designed to taper to allow the expulsion of smoke from the fire. Some chimney sweeps even found themselves catching light when flames beneath them were lit, causing horrific burns and injuries if not death. Such were the dangerous conditions of chimney sweeps that a number of acts were passed (in 1834, 1840, 1864 and 1875) which aimed to limit the amount of time boys could legally work within a chimney breast, as well as raising the minimum working ages, as in the case of mining boys.[33] As a result, chimney sweeping became relatively obsolete in the decades following the Victorian period, with adult men instead taking up the roles from the safety of open rooftops, where they could breathe fresh air without the restraint of the flues. For many families, however, it was too little, too late.

Perhaps the most infamous of jobs in Victorian Britain was one that has become synonymous with the period. Often represented in contemporary literature, employment in these institutions could lead to injury, disability and death, and were often a last resort for even the most desperate of Victorian paupers. It was a place which no Victorian had wanted to enter: the workhouse.

The Workhouse

Dating back as early as the Middle Ages, the workhouse saw a resurgence in popularity in the eighteenth and nineteenth centuries thanks to the efforts of Jeremy

Bentham, a political reformer whose establishment of 250 such institutions across Britain aimed to alleviate homelessness and incentivize people into getting off the streets and into work. Often seen as the last resort of employment, desperate Victorian paupers would reluctantly enter into its halls in an effort to earn a meagre living. Employment in the workhouse was designed to be temporary, providing bed and board for workers until they were established enough to pursue employment elsewhere. Earning a reputation for desperately long working hours, in which labour was 'most wearisome and monotonous', the workhouse has come to be considered by modern historians and contemporary Victorians alike as 'one of the dark sides of this age of machinery'.[1]

Heavy industry in Britain first made its impact in 1770, when Arkwright's spinning frame led to the birth of mass production and machine manufacturing amongst the working classes.[2] Some traditionalist historians believed that the emphasis and reliance on heavy industry within British trade led to working-class families growing fearful about the possibility of human obsolescence within the workforce. Previously, factories and workhouses had been full of hard-working people, who produced anything from boxes and shoes to cigars, lace and even sporting goods (such as tennis balls) on a mass scale.[3] Yet despite initial anxieties that machines would replace human labour, the opposite effect entirely occurred. As demand for mass-produced goods grew to a height never before experienced in Britain, machines began working overtime. Still in their infancy, these machines required human intelligence to ensure that production was steady and up to standard, creating hundreds of thousands of jobs for working-class men, women and children throughout the Industrial Revolution of the nineteenth century.

In 1800, there were an estimated 20,000 youths employed in cotton mills alone across Britain, and thousands more in factories and workhouses that specialized in the production of other materials.[4] Indeed, children as young as 6 were regularly employed in workhouses, with the average age of a child workers just 8 years old in industrial areas.[5] Even Dickens had worked in a factory as a child, wherein he had produced 'blacking' ink for printers and publishers.[6] In his reflections of his childhood, Dickens described the factory in vivid detail:

> '[I]ts rotten floors and staircase, and the old grey rats swarming down in the cellars, and the sound of their squeaking and scuffing coming up the stairs at all times, and the dirt and decay of the place, rise up visibly before me as if I were there again.'[7]

It is believed that Dickens's experience of life as a child in the workhouses of the dark and dingy slums of early nineteenth-century Britain went on to inspire his future works, most notably *David Copperfield* and *Oliver Twist*, which outwardly criticized the treatment of children in these institutions. Along with other campaigners of the time such as Elizabeth Barrett Browning – who wrote *The Cry of the Children* in 1844 in response to the horrific conditions to which working-class children had been exposed in factories – Dickens helped to influence

Parliament to end child exploitation in the workforce. In 1842, the Children's Employment Commission Report was delivered to Parliament, which detailed the jobs of children across Britain, the extent of their exploitation and the dreadful conditions that they endured while employed. In response, Parliamentarian Lord Shaftesbury advocated for the passing of the Ten Hours Act, which limited the working hours of children in industrial settings. It was a small, yet nevertheless impactful reform, which directly led to the passing of numerous Factory Acts throughout the nineteenth century, beginning with one in 1833 which banned the employment of children under 9 in workhouses.[8] The 1833 Factory Act also limited the working hours of children aged between 9 and 13 in factories and labouring jobs, setting a precedent for other reforms concerned with the exploitation of children throughout the century.

Although they accepted the employment of children, workhouses had harsh rulings concerning babies and infants. Deemed a 'distraction' for other employees, babies were removed from the custody of mothers within workhouses and either sent to orphanages, children's homes like The Foundling Hospital in Bloomsbury or back to any relative available outside of the institution.[9] Many mothers could not bear the thought of handing over their babies, however, and so, despite their desperation, they remained firmly upon the streets, hoping to make whatever pittance they could to support themselves and their infants. This treatment of mothers and their children in workhouses across Britain had tugged at the heartstrings of early reformists and suffragists, who campaigned for improved attitudes to single working mothers. One particular reformer, Clara Collett, who had been one of the first female graduates of the University of London, had seen at first hand the effects of separation upon mothers and their children. In response, she had tirelessly campaigned for provisions for working mothers in factorial environments, including nurseries where they could leave their infants while they were engaged in labour, as well as an increase in wages.[10] Drawing upon her own education, Clara had also campaigned for the establishment of institutions that provided schooling for adult women, as well as the right for women to found their own businesses and enter the world of industry without the assistance of men.[11]

As an ancient institution (that dated from at least 1388), the workhouse required much overhaul.[12] Many laws and regulations upheld within them had been established during the reign of the boy king Edward VI, and were greatly outdated for the modern Victorian society. The interiors of workhouses also needed renovating, for many had already existed for centuries by the nineteenth century. William Crooks, the Mayor of London and later Labour Member of Parliament, was one of those pressing for the revamping of workhouses in Victorian Britain. Crooks, who had grown up in a workhouse in Poplar as a child, had stressed to his fellow Parliamentarians the importance of improving conditions within these institutions for the benefit of public health. Crooks could vividly remember the dirtiness of factories and workhouses, and that its inmates would wear soiled uniforms without socks or shoes.[13] Issues of safety aside, Crooks also spoke of the provisions given to labourers within the workhouse, from flea-ridden beds to waste-tubs filled with inedible and rotten food that the inmates were expected to eat.[14] It was no wonder that working-class people were reluctant to enter the workhouse. One man named Jim, interviewed by Thomas Wright in 1882, had confessed that

> 'none but God and ourselves know how hard my wife here has fought against the workhouse, how hard we have all lived to keep out of it.'[15]

It was a sentiment shared by another of his contemporaries, who had told journalist Richard Rowe of his hesitancy to enter the institution in 1882: 'I suppose I shall have to go into the workhouse at last, if I don't die first – and I can't say I should be sorry if I did.'[16]

With such unpleasant conditions in the workhouse, many Victorian paupers instead preferred a life of unemployment on the street. A person could be unemployed in the nineteenth century in numerous ways, and it did not necessarily indicate that an individual was workshy or slothful. Although the practice of retiring did not exist in the Victorian period as it does today, many elderly people chose not to work due to their age or infirmity. Provisions for pensioners would not be issued in Britain until 1893, when social campaigner Charles Booth established the Royal Commission of Aged Poor to assist in their sustainment. The work of the Commission led to the eventual passing of the Old Age Pensions Act in 1908, which finally awarded elderly people monthly monetary payments in recognition of their work earlier in life. Pensions were also available to injured military personnel in the nineteenth century, thanks to the efforts of campaigners such as Martha Webb who pressured Parliament into providing for their care.

People could also be unemployed due to illness and disability in the nineteenth century, something which was particularly prolific in the slums of Victorian London, which were hotbeds of infection and disease. This lack of sanitation grew increasingly worse as many working-class paupers entered into occupations which greatly threatened their health. Relatively popular in urban areas for they required no experience and could allow individuals to easily earn a few pennies, jobs such as rat-catching, bone-grubbing and sewage-hunting were available to men, women and children alike. As the name suggests, rat-catchers would set traps at the bequest of local businesses who found themselves plagued with the vermin. Upon catching their prey, the rat-catchers would be paid by the owner of the business in reparation for their work. Bone-grubbers, who would sell old bones and other waste scraps such as rags to merchants, would spend their days wandering the mudflats of rivers and buried in refuse heaps. The occupation of bone-grubbing was so surprisingly lucrative that it survived throughout subsequent generations, and even exists in modern societies under the term 'rag-and-bone men'.

Henry Mayhew estimated that there were around a thousand bone-grubbers in central London alone in the mid-nineteenth century, as well as around a thousand street sweepers and scavengers.[17] Scavengers, typically consisting of children and adolescents, would clean machines of dust and cotton within factory settings, as well as 'scavenge' for materials such as metal and even lace upon the street.[18] Their job was similar to 'toshers', who would dredge sewers and open cesspits for any valuables that may have been washed away with human waste.[19] Another occupation requiring the scouring of faeces was 'pure finding', where individuals would collect dog waste left upon pavements and sell them to tanneries for use in the trade.[20]

One of the most popular of unhygienic jobs in Victorian London was the practice of 'mudlarking', where men, women and children would climb down onto the foreshore of the River Thames at low tide and dredge its muddy sands for valuable treasures. 'Those poor creatures may be seen of all ages, from mere childhood to positive decrepitude, crawling among the barges at the various wharfs,' wrote Henry Mayhew upon watching a group of mudlarks busy at their work.[21] If their day had been particularly lucrative, mudlarks could hope to find such riches as historical coins, jewels and beads, as well as a multitude of glass bottles, rags and scraps of metal which could equally bring in a fair wage when sold. Indeed, street buyers in the slums of Victorian London seemed indiscriminate in what they purchased from individuals such as mudlarks, toshers and pure finders, who earned money for items such as animal skins, broken glass, dismantled umbrellas, ashes from fireplaces and even the dripping produced during the cooking process of meat.[22]

Retail was a profitable business in the nineteenth century, even in areas of great deprivation. Urban districts thrived on trade, which helped keep local economies afloat and residents provided for. There were believed to be around 30,000 men, women and child traders throughout the street markets of London, with some 2,500 of them dealing in Covent Garden each day during the summer months.[23] London and other dense urban areas of Victorian Britain were replete with market stalls that were either permanently in position or erected every week within common areas. Residents of London, both the wealthy and the poor, attended these markets every day, no matter the weather. The largest of the London markets was Billingsgate, which had almost 4,000 individual traders operating within its quarters in the mid-nineteenth century.[24] Henry Mayhew estimated that there were at least fourteen stalls per mile at Billingsgate, with five out of every six selling foodstuffs like fish, meat or fruit.[25] He also reckoned that there were at least 8,000 permanent individual stalls at Billingsgate which sold goods ranging from stationery to children's toys, clothing and pet care items.[26] Similar scenes, though on a much smaller scale, could be found at Rye Lane in Peckham, Chrisp Street in Poplar and Old Kent Road in Islington, all areas which had a notably large populus of slum dwellers.[27]

In his memoir of his visit to London, Max Schlesinger reported with glee on the

> 'furious, rattling, ceaseless crowd of vehicles, the moving and pushing of the foot-passengers, women hunted over the crossings;

> walking advertisements; street-sellers; red Post-Office carts; the dusky-streets, and the heavy leaden sky – the City in it's [*sic*] working dress!'[28]

Indeed, there was no better microcosm of Victorian Britain than in the midst of these markets, which brimmed with noise and fervent excitement. Stallholders, shop owners, bakers, grocers and street pedlars would all wander the streets of Victorian cities hoping to shill their wares to intrigued customers, all the while avoiding horse-drawn carriages operated by 'car men' which delivered goods throughout the metropolis. To advertise their trade, business owners could employ the use of 'walking advertisements', or 'sandwich men', who would wear two painted wooden boards suspended by straps over their shoulders which promoted goods and wares. Advertisements also came in the form of newspapers, printed on the side of vans, trams and carriages, and in fliers, or painted and chalked upon pavements to catch the eye of wandering customers.[29] Many Victorian shops also erected shop signs above the doors of their establishments, which frequently took the form of large objects relating to their trade. Not only did these signs serve as eye-catching designs intended to entice patrons, they also aided in helping the illiterate locate shops which sold the items that they required. Mr Rose's Teashop in Central London, for example, had a large red teapot suspended from its exterior beams, while the Elephant and Castle Tavern on Old Kent Road had a wooden replica of an elephant, much to the delight of passers-by and their children, who mirthfully noted its existence as they walked past.[30]

For those without the luxury of a brick-and-mortar store, they could sell their wares carried upon their backs or shoulders. Costermongers, for example, were merchants who would sell bulky items such as door mats, ladders, brushes, buckets, clothes, shovels and fishing rods, which they slung over their shoulders and carried about the city.[31] Costermongers could be male or female, adult or child, with many younger merchants selling items such as children's toys, cut flowers, soap bars or fresh fruits. One form of costermonger in the nineteenth century was matchstick sellers, who carried their precious but tiny goods in boxes suspended around their necks. Hans Christian Anderson's *Little Match Girl* has long served as an enduring image of Victorian matchstick sellers, an allegory of desperation and child exploitation, for – like many other children of the Victorian slums – the young protagonist succumbs to the cold of the street when no one purchases any of her matches.

'Picking up a crust' (colloquial slang for 'earning a wage') in Victorian London was a principle hammered into even the youngest of slum dwellers. Well aware that they would need to earn their own keep to help assist in the family's household economy, children entered into apprenticeships from a very early age. Despite concerns of child exploitation expressed by contemporaries, attitudes toward apprenticeships were far more lax. Children as young as 10 could become an apprentice, often lodging with distant relatives or family friends as their first foray into employment and independence.[32] Unlike many children employed in institutions such as workhouses, child apprentices could earn and keep their own 'bunts' (wages). These wages averaged around 7*s* per week, a remarkably high salary, generating more income than many low-paid professions available to adults at the time.[33] As well as this, apprentices need not worry about bed and board, for they typically lived with their masters or in accommodation with other apprentices of a similar age which was entirely subsidised by their employers.[34]

A healthy and pleasant life in Victorian Britain would be impossible if not for constant employment and the promise of money. Yet despite this, paupers and the poorest of working-class citizens in the nineteenth century made the best of their abilities and opportunities, working hard for the promise of a better future even if it came at a detriment to themselves, instilling a sense of pride and work ethic in the generations to come.

Chapter 4

Health, Hygiene and Medicine: Keeping Clean in the Slums

'Tenement blocks [are] singularly well adapted for the purpose of destroying health.'
Godwin, *A Glance at the 'Homes' of the Thousands* (1854)

There are preconceived notions that the people of the past, particularly the poor and the impoverished, had no standard of cleanliness or hygienic decency. We are often led to believe in modern-day reconstructions of Victorian worlds in film and writing that the Victorian poor were shrivelled, wrinkled little people, their bodies unwashed, their hair lice-ridden and their cheeks dusted with soot. When conceiving images of pauper boys and matchstick girls, we tend to picture them clad in moth-eaten clothing, their shoes full of holes from over-wear. We picture street beggars in tattered rags, their hair running long and straggled about their ears. Toothless crones and pimpled prostitutes greet us as we walk our imagined streets of Victorian Britain, while skin-and-bones infants in soiled napkins play at our feet.

But how true is this picture of the disgusting and dirty underworld of the Victorian slums? How can we definitively know for sure that these urchins, beggars and work-worn labourers shunned bathing and cared little for their health and wellbeing? Were the Victorian slums really as revolting as we are led to believe?

In her 1869 exposé on the living conditions of slums in Edinburgh, journalist Isabella Bird wrote that 'more dirt, degradation, overcrowding, and consequent shamelessness and unutterable wretchedness, exist in Edinburgh than in any town of twice its size'.[1] The vast majority of slums in Victorian Britain had been built in areas already decrepit and uninhabitable for human life. By building cheap houses near to open cesspits, slaughterhouses, tanneries and other foul-smelling places, poor people could occupy living spaces that no other class would find at all attractive. In a memoir written late in life, a Mrs Panton reflected on her early childhood spent growing up in the Victorian slums, painting vivid pictures of dirt, grime and disease, and appalling living conditions. Her most enduring memory of her early life in these slum dwellings was the dead cats and dogs that would regularly float down canals near houses.[2] The construction of decrepit dwelling houses in these less-than-admired areas allowed for local authorities to tackle the issue of overcrowding by forcing poorer citizens to live on the outskirts of society in houses otherwise considered unfit for inhabitation. Through these dirty and disgusting living conditions, the gap between wealthy and poor was made wholly visible, with contemporaries even commenting that the lack of cleanliness in hovels had been 'the result of a struggle to hide [...] extreme poverty from this world'.[3]

When we consider that whole families, sometimes even with extended family members, crowded into these often single-roomed dwellings, it is not hard to understand why dirt and degradation reigned supreme. Not only did these rooms serve as living quarters, but also sick rooms, kitchens, bedrooms and bathrooms. They were places of employment, where people employed in a cottage industry could work from home, employed in jobs as wide ranging as tactile skill-based work like carpentry and needlework to prostitution. Additionally, these rooms served as birthing chambers, saw its inhabitants take their final breath, and even acted as morgues, where dead bodies lay silent in the wait for burial. It was no wonder that these places had been hotbeds of disease. 'It is impossible for these people to be clean in their dwellings, clothes, or persons,' wrote Isabella Bird, complaining about the lack of ventilation and privacy, sanitation and basic hygiene necessities like running water and working sewage pipes.[4] However, was Bird's analysis of the Edinburgh hovels a true reflection of the living standards of poor Victorians, and were they truly as dirty and disgusting as their dark and dingy slums?

The belief that our ancestors paid little emphasis to bathing or maintaining hygiene routines is one that has endured throughout much of historiography. We have been led to believe through books and through the screen that the past was a dirty place, that people were riddled with diseases or ailments, or suffered from poor body odours and lack of hygienic awareness. However, we must remember that these Victorians, despite being separated from us by more than a hundred years, were people just like us. They too felt uncomfortable if they had not bathed for durations of time, and were acutely aware of the condition of their hair, skin, teeth and clothing when out in public. If we are to compare the wealthier members of Victorian society, then we picture upright people dressed in sophisticated garb and sporting beautiful updos or perfectly groomed facial hair; why do we think that the poorer citizens of Victorian Britain were any different?

The art of bathing has been perfected by generations, and it is still often the first thing we think of in order to get clean. To bathe is to effectively 'reset' the body, to wash away evidence of labour and toil and to restore our bodies to perfection. In the nineteenth century, there was a belief that those who did not regularly bathe would develop 'crusts of epidermal scales saturated with old and putrid perspiration', and that the individual would become an 'offensive carcass, in short, that taint the air'.[5] Victorian society was not quiet in voicing its disapproval toward those who forwent bathing, calling women in particular 'dirty Salls' if they had not recently washed.[6] On the whole, there existed an unspoken belief that those who did not bathe were total social rejects, and as such even the poor made sure to clean their bodies 'so that not an atom of dirt remains'.[7]

But how did the poor bathe in their hovel-like homes without running water and central heating? For the vast majority of people in nineteenth-century Britain – even the wealthier members of society – baths were taken in free-standing tubs that would be filled with basins or jugs of water and heated in front of a fireplace or oven. Though 'shower baths' (the precursor to our modern-day shower heads) would become popular amongst the wealthy toward the end of the century, the vast majority of Victorian Britons washed their bodies in these tubs.[8] If a poor person could not procure enough water or afford to light their oven for long enough to take a full bath, then they were encouraged to instead take 'hip baths', which were assured to get the job done in a manner most satisfactory.[9]

Contrary to popular belief, bathing was a daily routine for most people in Victorian Britain, particularly if they worked manual labour jobs and returned home from work covered in the toil of the day. 'Cold or tepid baths should be employed every morning' unless unwell, instructs Mrs Beeton, with warmer baths reserved for evening relaxation.[10] Lola Montez, an eminent figure in the Victorian beauty industry, also called for tepid bathing, recommending it be undertaken twice per day.[11] Once a week, a hot bath with steaming water was encouraged, with bathers sitting in the water for fifteen minutes to soften their skin. During these luxuriously hot baths, individuals would be encouraged to scrub at their bodies (starting with their feet) with a bar of soap and a rough rag or natural sea sponge, or use homemade exfoliants such as ground almonds to buff away at their skin.[12] The bather would then sit in the bath for a further thirty minutes, before soaping their body again and ensuring that every nook, cranny and crevice was spotless. Another half an hour would go by before the bather would finally rise from their tubs, their fingers and toes wrinkled and pruned by the heat of the water.[13]

Alternatively, if the long process of sitting in a steaming bath seemed too arduous for busy Victorians, they could instead employ other methods to stay clean. Upon waking, Victorians were encouraged to completely undress before washing themselves down with a linen or flannel cloth soaked in freezing water.[14] This method, though far from relaxing, was believed to shake an individual from their sleep, as well as protect them from 'nerves, delirium and fever' that they may have been subject to.[15] Bathers would be instructed to take their cloths and begin at their head, carefully washing their faces, necks and behind their ears, before leading down toward the body and finally the feet.[16] For an added 'zing' of freshness, bathers could add vinegar, salt or even sodium chloride to the water in order to feel cleaner.[17] To some degree, these additions did their job rather effectively, thanks to the antibacterial and antimicrobial nature of the ingredients.

For those who had no time to engage in full bathing routines, simple rubbing of the skin with rough towels would be enough to stimulate blood flow and bring colour to the body.[18] This was a method employed in the hygiene routines of people dating back to the Middle Ages, where 'body scrubbing' was known to effectively remove surface-layer sweat, rough skin and smells from the body, and made a fair substitute if water was otherwise unavailable.[19] Indeed, not everyone in the Victorian slums could afford such a luxury as bathing tubs long enough to fit their entire bodies, and so made do with simple ewers and wash basins that would be refilled on a daily basis and used for the washing of hands, faces and body crevices.[20] Bathing in some form or another was an expected part of life for the Victorians, just as it is now, and was particularly employed after periods of work or before the commencement of meals and socialization. Even paupers were expected to wash themselves to some degree before leaving the house.

Not everyone had skin that suited regular bathing. Many Victorians, just as now, suffered from skin complaints like eczema and acne, and as such took caution with the rigorous routines of daily bathing. Oil-skin shower caps would be worn to keep the scalp dry if one was suffering from dandruff or flaky skin, while those suffering from red-raw extremities such as fingers through work or illness washed themselves only in cool, fresh water with no added ingredients.[21] Sufferers of eczema would bathe in barley and bran, or would boil poultices and apply it directly to their affected skin to relieve sores and itching.[22] Lola Montez dismissed the recommendation for sufferers of dry skin to bathe in milk, calling the practice 'ludicrous' and 'expensive'.[23] Instead, she devised a more cost-effective solution that even the poorest members of society could benefit from, by washing in water in which rice had been soaked for hours (with the addition of five egg yolks if one was feeling particularly luxurious).[24]

Bathing, then, was considered a daily necessity, or at the very least would have been employed at least twice per week. However, more important still was an emphasis on hand-washing, which even contemporaries understood to be beneficial to health and stopped the spread of disease and illness. One homemade handwash of the time was made with 3 ounces of lemon juice, 3 ounces of vinegar and half an ounce of brandy, and was believed to be an effective way to stave off dirt and bacteria.[25] It worked; both lemon juice and vinegar have properties capable of repelling bacteria, while the alcohol in the brandy further sterilized the hands.

The Victorians were particularly vain about their hands, even those who worked in tactile jobs like in manual labour or the textile trade. Females in particular took care that their hands looked soft, supple and youthful by maintaining a variety of methods. Nail biting and hand picking were considered to be 'vulgar and disgusting practices', and as such nails were filed short and regularly maintained.[26] If a female particularly wished to show off her nails, she would polish them with emery sand and colour them with a powder of red lead sulphurate of mercury, an early predecessor of modern-day nail varnish.[27] This dangerous powder would be brushed onto each nail and left to sit for a few minutes, before being washed away in cold water. The resulting look was subtle pink nails, which were believed by Victorians to exude health and vitality in a person.

Women would also typically wear gloves, no matter their social standing. Not only a social expectation of the time, by 'constantly wearing gloves or mittens' a woman could hope for white hands free from the chafing of the elements.[28] 'No lady who wishes to be particular about her hands, will ever go out into the open air without her gloves,' wrote Lola Montez, who encouraged women to slather their hands in cold creams, oils or thick pastes to keep their skin soft.[29] Pomades made from an ounce of mutton tallow, salad oil (a condiment dressing for leafy greens) and half a pound of soap would be boiled in cheap wine, then slathered on the hands as women slept at night.[30]

When reading authentic recipes for beauty products in the nineteenth century, one may be struck by the amount and variance of ingredients which went into a particular concoction. That these recipes were afforded only by the wealthiest of society is incorrect, for there are numerous references to poor women having access to cheap ingredients like tallow, oils and soaps from local chemist shops or market traders. Even the poor could purchase soap for themselves for just a pittance, and cakes of solid bars were sold in portions starting at the price of a half-penny. Indeed, Annie Chapman, a victim of Jack the Ripper, was found with one of these penny-portions of soap on her body at her murder scene, as was Catherine Eddowes, another of the Ripper's victims, who had stashed the cake within one of her coat pockets.[31] When sold in these portions, soap was known as 'wash balls'.[32]

Soap was sold in two forms in the nineteenth century 'hard' (made from fats) and 'soft' (made from potash or other oils).[33] Hard soaps were particularly employed within the household, and could be used as cleaning products around the home, whereas soft soap was intended solely for the body and for the maintenance of personal hygiene. Soft soaps could be made from ingredients such as coconut and olive oils, or lard, tallow or suet.[34] They were also regularly made from ingredients such as sweet almond and castor oil, all ingredients which are known to be beneficial to the skin in keeping it both clean and moisturized. Despite ingredients deriving from animal products such as suet, these additives would be melted together along with fragrance oils and artificial colourants to mask any unpleasant smells, and were marketed to the poor as cheap 'toilet soap'.[35] This form of toilet soap was the most common amongst Victorian slums, and would have been most used in the hygiene routines of the poor. For those who wanted to spend a little more, they could purchase cakes of 'pearl soap' from vendors, which left delightful scents upon the skin and moisturized the skin through the addition of *crème d'amandes* (cream of almonds).[36] Major companies like Pears Soap, established in 1807, sold varieties of pearl soap, including cakes of large, moulded, rose-scented soaps for just 2*s* 6*d*.[37] Lilly Langtry, the mistress of Queen Victoria's son, Albert Edward (the future King Edward VII), endorsed this particular soap sold by Pears and demanded £132 in returns; the exact figure of her weight in pounds.[38]

The Pears company was followed by other soap-making giants such as Avon in 1866 and Johnsons in 1886, which also marketed affordable bars of sweet-smelling soaps to the poorer communities of Victorian Britain. In 1837, William Procter and James Gamble launched their first prototype of soap which they supplied to the US Army, becoming the incredibly popular Ivory Soap which was favoured by Victorians from 1879 onwards.[39] In 1885, William Hesketh Lever launched Sunlight Soap, which lathered well and was scented, much to the delight of working-class Victorians, who used it principally to wash their laundry. It was an immediate hit and was even used on board the *Titanic*.[40] William Hesketh Lever also launched the carbolic soap Lifebuoy, which is still used today, laying the groundwork for the establishment of the Unilever brand, which still oversees the production and manufacture of hygiene products to this day.[41]

Hard soaps, meanwhile, were intended not for the body but for the home. Typically made from more harmful and stronger ingredients such as bone marrow, horse fat, resin and 'rancid palm oil', household or 'common' soap was used in the washing of dishes and floors. Clay was also used in cakes of household soap, as was cod-liver oil and lard derived from the melting of hog fat.[42] As one can imagine, these soaps smelled particularly offensive, and as such required additives of sweet scents like citrus and flora to alleviate their unpleasantness.[43] 'Windsor soap', made in Windsor, was made from mutton suet, and would turn yellow, crumbly and rancid after days of use.[44] It was used in the cleansing of bathing areas, such as latrines and basins, in conjunction with soaps created from melted butter or 'sperm oil' (melted sperm whale fat, which reportedly smelled fishy). There was also 'marine soap', for washing laundry in salt or sea water, and 'beef marrow' soap, which was advertised as 'good to eat'.[45] Just how many *did* eat this beef marrow soap, however, is not recorded!

Another soap used in the cleansing of living areas was 'human fat soap', which, despite its name, did not derive from human origins, but was instead animal-product-based and was particularly oily.[46] It was used to scrub floors and cinder pails, wash down steps and scour chamber pots. In the nineteenth century, toileting was an affair far more public than it is today. Now, safe in the privacy of our own dedicated bathrooms, we can use the toilet without any issue and flush away any waste that our bodies produce down sophisticated twisted networks of pipes and drains, safe in the knowledge that it will reach its final destination in sewers and waste water treatment plants far away from our homes. In nineteenth-century Britain, however, going to the toilet was far less sophisticated. It was estimated that in the mid-1800s, more than 100 houses in London slums shared communal latrines.[47] These latrines, set outside in dark alleys or at the end of gardens and green spaces, were small, enclosed areas that had no lighting and no drainage system. Many of these latrines would be emptied either by a bucket, which would be thrown into rivers or disposed of by what other means may have been available to individuals, or fell down into open cesspits that had been in existence for many decades or even centuries. In London, for example, many Victorian slums had been built upon pre-existing areas of inhabitation that had existed as early as the Middle Ages, and sometimes even earlier.[48] The extent of these cesspits can only be imagined. They posed not only a health hazard to those who were forced to come into close contact with them, but were also dangerous for children, animals and even adults who found themselves falling into them.[49]

Once a person had waited their turn to use the communal latrine, and had carried out their important business, they could clean themselves with rags, scraps of crumbled brown paper or strips of newspapers, which would often leave inky-black streaks from the print upon the individual's skin. Toilet paper would not become commercialized or marketed until the mid-1800s; indeed, many communities still shared communal latrines and utilized these makeshift rags to clean themselves until well into the twentieth century. It was an issue not only in terms of smell and sanitation, but also due to the fact that build-up would occur if rags had been improperly disposed of. In the nineteenth century, records of sewage and waste can be regularly found as offending tenants of shared living areas. Isabella Bird wrote that one particular tenement building was plagued with sewage seeping into hallways and gutters until 'scavengers' removed it at night.[50] Such an effort was not always successful, however; after all, once liquid sewage had seeped into living quarters, there was very little someone could do to alleviate lingering smells and harmful bacteria but to destroy the area entirely.

One particular issue when it came to sewage collection was menstruation. In the nineteenth century, rich and poor women alike would wear menstrual belts to protect their clothing from staining and to collect blood. These belts would often clip onto the underskirts of women, suspending thick rags between their legs, or would be hoisted around their waist. They were uncomfortable and shifted throughout the day, and caused more problems in keeping women dry and free from leakages than they were worth. Many of these rags would be reusable, particularly if the individual had come from a background of very little wealth. Indeed, Catherine Eddowes, Elizabeth Stride and Annie Chapman – victims of Jack the Ripper – were found with muslin cloths within their pockets at the time of their death, all stained with old blood presumably from their periods.[51] Tampons as we would now recognize them did not come into circulation until after the end of the century, when they were marketed as blood stoppers for bullet wounds acquired during the First World War. It was not until women began utilizing these tampons for their periods that the modern-day tampon was born. Until then, women would use rolled-up rags or even sponges to collect their menstrual blood, putting their makeshift tampons into their vagina and removing them whenever required. These inventions served women well; they were at least able to move about and continue with their daily lives without running the risk of leaks and embarrassment.

If a woman particularly struggled with menstrual complaints in the nineteenth century, then she could alleviate them with remedies marketed toward women precisely for their feminine health. Hot water bottles, made from ceramic rather than rubber, were heated and applied to the lower abdomen in cases of menstrual cramp, while other natural remedies like safflower or lavender would be boiled in tea and consumed to alleviate pain and discomfort. If a woman's period was so bad that these natural remedies failed to work, then she could purchase belladonna or opium from her local chemist, and consume a few drops mixed in with her food or drink. However, not only were these particular remedies incredibly unsafe and threatening to life, but they were also highly addictive, launching some women into deep pits of addiction from which they couldn't climb out.

Keeping your genitalia clean in the nineteenth century was a relatively simple task, though many struggled with issues such as overgrowths of bacteria and foul smells developed in part due to the existence of venereal disease. Such afflictions as syphilis and chlamydia were reasons enough to often put people in hospital in the nineteenth century, and hospital records show that treatments of venereal disease were particularly frequent in dense urban areas. If left untreated, venereal disease could cause all sorts of problems, from scarring to intense pains and even pus-filled swellings. Even Prince Albert Victor, a grandson of Queen Victoria, was said to have suffered from the effects of venereal disease, which some believe drove him mad enough to conduct murders under the alias of Jack the Ripper.[53]

Death and Disease

As well as diseases affecting the genitalia and sexual organs of certain sections of the Victorian population, nineteenth-century Britain was riddled with other contagious illnesses not yet treatable with medicines and drugs. In 1871, a diarrhoea epidemic swept London and resulted in thousands of deaths through dehydration. Its cause has typically been associated with the unclean stagnant drinking water of the slums, which was used not only by humans, but also vermin and larger animals such as wild street cats and wandering mangy dogs. So too has the 'Great Stink' of 1858 been attributed to the general poor sanitation of Victorian London's water systems, with politicians forced to finally put an end to the constant foul smell of the city by pouring gallons of quick lime, chalk and carbolic acid into the Thames from the banks of the river.

In the nineteenth century, there existed a belief that disease was spread through bad smells. This belief, dating back to the Middle Ages, placed emphasis on 'bad miasmas', which were believed to be harmful to one's health if breathed in. The Victorians believed that miasmas and foul smells could infect the body and cause grievous illness, so it was little surprise that many doctors prescribed air fresheners in an attempt to stave off disease, instead of tackling the issue at its root. The first consumer market for scented cosmetics and hygiene products emerged in mid-eighteenth-century France, where 'perfumes [and] scented oils' were given to people who anxiously avoided bad miasmas for fear of contracting contagious air-borne diseases.[1] Eventually, this trend reached Britain, where scented oil or water-based perfumes made from naturally derived ingredients such as rose, lavender and orange peel were encouraged to be sprayed around the home in an effort to keep it clean. Even within the hovels of the Victorian slums, scented bags filled with fragrant herbs and flora like clove, jasmine and musk would be hung above doorframes or window panes, or on the walls of living spaces.[2] One contemporary hygiene handbook also recommended keeping vials of distilled alcoholic spirits in the room to draw out any foul smells.[3]

Perfume has long been associated with the wealthier sections of nineteenth-century society, with figures such as Eugene Rimmel (of the cosmetic empire) writing in his *Book of Perfumes* (1867) that 'good taste and breeding may easily be ascertained by the perfume she wears'.[4] That does not mean, however, that it was worn solely by the rich and the affluent; indeed, Pears Soap sold Odoriferous Compound Lavendar Water, which would be applied to the handkerchief and dabbed on the skin, and cost just a small sum to purchase.[5] They also made Oriental Bouquet Perfume, which was designed to be used in rooms to mask smells.[6] Scented perfumes were also marketed to the poor in solid, waxen forms, as well as sprays and liquids. One particularly influential cosmetic product introduced in 1888 came in the form of a highly scented deodorizer cream. This cream, known as 'Mum' (and still in use today), was the first known mass-marketed deodorant to hit nineteenth-century shelves.[7]

Although Victorians could apply as many scented lotions, deodorizers and perfumes as they wanted, the root cause of disease had still not gone away. Perfumes simply masked these bad miasmas, which still threatened human health due to the fact that they had usually been borne from diseased-riddled origins. Indeed, without properly effective medicine and cleaning products, disease threatened the lives of rich and poor alike, no matter their social standing. Some of the most dangerous and contagious diseases of the nineteenth century came in the form of air-borne illnesses or were passed through touch or water-droplets upon the breath. Cholera, scarlet fever, influenza and diphtheria were just a few of the diseases which struck fear into the hearts of the Victorians. Now managed with medication or entirely treatable, it is difficult to truly comprehend the extent of terror these diseases had over nineteenth-century society. From the rich to the poor and everyone in between, disease did not discriminate.

In his patient's notes from Bethlem Hospital, Mr William Reeves Allen had been recorded as suffering from scarlet fever, measles and whooping cough as a child.[8] The fact that he had survived not just one but all of these diseases in childhood was remarkable, particularly considering that he hailed from a working-class background. Some others were not so lucky. When Isabella Bird paid a visit to a young couple and their disabled toddler in 1869, she was horrified to find the young father totally bed-bound upon a makeshift straw bed in the middle of the floor, suffering from a vicious fever that left him shaking with sweat and chills.[9] He had been lying in one position for six weeks without moving, amidst his own excrement and waste, and had developed painfully inflamed bedsores. When Bird enquired about the man's health some weeks later, she was told that he, his child and his wife (who had been heavily pregnant) had all succumbed to the disease and died.[10]

It was not only life-threatening illnesses that had dangerous effects on the lives of Victorians in the nineteenth century. Something as simple (and now treatable) as rheumatoid arthritis could grip sufferers and bring them immense pain. One young man riddled with arthritis in his joints, brought on through heavy manual labour, had been forced to give up work, albeit rather reluctantly.[11] Not only had his employment supported his own living, but also the lives of his elderly father and unmarried sister. Without his meagre income to pay their rents, they were all sent to the workhouse.[12]

Even the simple common cold could have lasting impacts on the health of Victorians. 'There is among the natives of the British isles an almost universal tendency to "catch cold",' complained one contemporary in his *Handbook of the Toilette*.[13] People were believed to catch common colds from having draughts in the house, leaving their doors and windows open, standing upon damp floors, sitting with their backs to an open window and even removing their cap.[14] There was a fear that if a cold had become chesty, it could become a 'disease which frequently ends in death'.[15]

To cure a common cold in the nineteenth century, sufferers were encouraged to drink large quantities of hot spirits such as whisky and brandy mixed with hot water.[16] Menthol cones, purchased from chemist shops and market vendors, would be sniffed to get rid of colds or stuffed into a nostril, given its convenient bullet shape. These menthol cones worked by clearing the sinuses of catarrh and mucus, and thus, alleviated unpleasant symptoms of colds that had affected the head. These cones were the precursor of modern-day camphorated medicinal treatments such as Vicks Vapour Rub, which was established and sold to the suffering masses in 1894.

If a sufferer did not wish to consume or ingest any product which promised to alleviate colds, they could instead employ a rigorous routine of daily skin rubbing with hard cloths, before relaxing in steaming hot baths.[17] To these baths would be added Epsom salts, camphor or menthol, which stung the eyes but proved effective in opening the airways. These were known as 'Aqueous Vapour Baths' and were believed to cure anything from nerves, irritability and epilepsy to asthma, whooping cough, bronchitis, diphtheria, lumbago, arthritis, diabetes, gout, inflamed joints, dropsy and even 'internal haemorrhage'.[18] Truly, these baths appeared to be miracle cures. Other forms of bathing, such as 'electric current' and 'chemical solvent' baths, were believed to cure diseases affecting the body's nervous systems, as well as bone stiffness, skin complaints and ulcers.[19] So-called 'continuous baths', which lasted seven to eight hours and were prescribed as genuine hospital treatments, were believed to cure lung problems.[20] Just how effective these baths were in tackling the underlying cause of illness and disease in the nineteenth century was inestimable; what they did do, however, was cleanse the body, which irrefutably quelled the spread of contagious disease.

Improved hygiene and sanitation conditions did not only alleviate such problems as the common cold. In 1844, epidemiologist John Snow published *On the Mode of Communication of Cholera*, which confidently confirmed that the incredibly dangerous disease that had killed 60,000 people in Britain was transmitted through water.[21] Snow, one of nine children in a poor family, had been born and raised in the slums of Yorkshire. He perhaps knew better than most contemporary scientists and doctors – who had traditionally come from well-bred and affluent families – the dangers of a lack of adequate sanitation in slum dwellings. When studying the adverse effects of London's 'incomplete' sewage systems on the lives of those who lived nearby, Snow noted what no scientist had before: a link between raw sewage and death from cholera.[22] Due to incomplete waste disposal, raw sewage was transported not to the sewers, but to the same areas where poor Victorians gathered their water, like pumps and open sources of water such as streams. Snow recognized this when no one else had, and conducted a study into the health of households that had access to contaminated water and those that did not. His theories were correct. Snow noted major outbreaks of cholera in Vauxhall and Southwark that killed many of the local population, which he was able to trace back to a single water pump on Broadwick Street near Oxford Circus.[23] Indeed, eighteen people had died from cholera on this street alone. Snow braced himself to trawl the sewage-filled water source, and extracted the main culprit: a used nappy disposed of by the mother of an infant who had died from cholera.[24] Upon presenting his findings to the local health board, Snow initially received plenty of backlash from people refusing to believe that they had been ingesting and using water that had faecal matter in it to wash their bodies and clean their homes. Indeed, Snow's germ theories on the spread of cholera would never be accepted until after his death aged 45 from a stroke. Only posthumously, when his good friend Dr William Farr published Snow's findings on a grand scale, did it change the way people thought about standards of sanitation and give him the recognition that he so rightly deserved.[25] Just one man had saved the lives of thousands.

Unfortunately, other diseases ran rampant in Victorian London and threatened the lives of inhabitants. Tuberculosis, also known as consumption, 'stalks like a hideous phantom through the land' and killed thousands across Britain throughout the nineteenth century.[26] Believed to be caused by an 'improper mismanagement of the body' and 'bad habits', tuberculosis was characterized by a difficulty in breathing, a wheezing, chesty cough and the spitting up of bloody sputum.[27] Tuberculosis was a highly contagious disease, and was spread through particles of bacteria found in the bodily fluids of those infected. Once contracted, tuberculosis would slowly kill the individual unless a treatment was sought to cure or stave off the disease. If they could afford it, wealthier Victorians would travel to the coast, believing that the sea air would improve their conditions, or would purchase medicines that were, on the whole, completely ineffective against the rampaging disease. It would not be until 1890 that a vaccine against tuberculosis was proposed by immunologist Robert Koch, though it would take a further thirty years before these inoculations would actually be rolled out to the long-suffering people.

Without the dedication and perseverance of such people as John Snow and Robert Koch, medical thought and germ theory would still have been in its infancy. However, the efforts of some social campaigners in the nineteenth century would go on to improve medical understanding and shape modern healthcare today. None was perhaps more influential in reforming medical care than one of England's greatest social advocates: Florence Nightingale.

Born to a wealthy family, Florence Nightingale registered as a nurse upon the outbreak of the Crimean War, feeling that her time and energy would be better spent caring for wounded and sick soldiers than sat at home. It is important to remember that most hospitals in the nineteenth century were places that people typically went to die, something that was particularly true in makeshift hospital wings constructed during times of war. Upon reaching the hospital where she would be based at Scutari in Turkey, Nightingale was horrified to find that her expectations of clean and sterile hospital wards could not be further from the truth. Instead of clean beds and hygienic surroundings, she found men writhing in agony upon sheets drenched in the blood of fellow soldiers who had already perished from their injuries. Despite having no classical training whatsoever in nursing, and no knowledge of medicine aside from what she had learnt on the job, Nightingale immediately demanded that hot water and carbolic soap be brought into the wards, and that the other women who had volunteered as nurses get straight into deep-cleaning the hospital. Nightingale also advocated for daily loads of laundry, recognizing that the infection passed through bodily fluid-soaked sheets, blankets and towels was much more deadly to the soldiers than their wounds.

Despite bacteria not having an official name until 1854, Florence Nightingale still stressed the importance of keeping it at bay. As such, she advocated for any contagious men suffering from disease and infection to be housed in quarantine wings, so that men who had entered the hospital for their wounds would not be infected. Back at home, Nightingale used her experiences of preventing infection at Scutari by campaigning for improved medical care in British workhouses and infirmaries, as well as improving standards of sanitation. Her treatise, 'Suggestions on the Subject of Providing Training and Organising Nurses for the Sick Poor in Workhouse Infirmaries', aimed to teach nurses to recognize signs and symptoms of deadly infections and disease, and made great strides in improving medical conditions of nineteenth-century Britain. Florence Nightingale, the 'Lady with the Lamp', has been described as an 'angel of the wards' not only due to her gentle and kind care of suffering soldiers, but also her dedication to eradicating infection and improving conditions in hospitals of the time.

Like Nightingale, other social reformers of the time advocated for improved standards of health and hygiene in medical settings. Edwin Chadwick, for example, campaigned for sanitary reforms which included improvements to water supplies and sewage systems, as well as regulations into building methods and living conditions in the slums of Victorian London. Such was his steadfast dedication to his campaigns that he was appointed as the first Medical Officer of Britain in 1847.

Other reformists championed the rights of the less able, such as Thomas Barnardo, whose daughter Majorie had been born with Down's Syndrome, which strongly inspired him to campaign for the rights of infirm children.[28] Martha Webb, on the other hand, campaigned for better provisions of wages for adults with disabilities, particularly emphasizing that they be supported by the government if incapacitated by their infirmity or capabilities.[29] Webb was especially vocal in her campaigns of awarding pensions to men injured in active service, a tradition which is still maintained by the Armed Forces in Britain today.

Having a disability in the nineteenth-century slums did not necessarily mean that your life was limited. In his *Saunterings in and about London*, Max Schlesinger came across a man with a prosthetic wooden leg, who carried out his daily routines as if it had been made of flesh and bone.[30] Elsewhere in London, many popular public places hired out walking sticks, frames and even wheeled chairs, such as the Great Exhibition, which ensured that 'the convenience of visitors is consulted in every possible way'.[31] Charles Dickens described disabled children as

> 'the very dregs of the population of the largest city in the world [...] the children of poverty, misery, and crime; in very many cases labouring under physical defects, such as bad eyesight or hearing; almost always stunted in growth, and bearing the stamp of ugliness and suffering on their features.'

Nevertheless, Dickens helped pave the way for the changing of attitudes toward disability in the nineteenth century, with beloved characters such as Tiny Tim in *A Christmas Carol* endearing readers to the cause and provision of the care of real people who suffered from the same limitations.[32]

Admittedly, without proper medical healthcare and support, caring for a disabled family member in the Victorian slums (much like today) could be incredibly difficult. One man interviewed by Henry Mayhew in 1849 told him: 'We had seven children alive then. We only buried one three months ago. She was an afflicted little creature [...] it was one person's work to attend to her, and we was very badly off for a few months then.'[33] Likewise, one 76-year-old man confessed to Isabella Bird that he and his 63-year-old wife had found it difficult to care for their 'dumb grandson'.[34] The man explained that the young lad was much larger than either of his grandparents, who had both overcome typhus and still suffered from its lingering effects. The grandmother, confined to her bed for twelve months straight without moving, had wasted away, her ribcage visible beneath her taut skin. When Bird later revisited their hovel to enquire about their health, she was distressed to learn that they had all been forced into manual labour in the workhouse.

Physical incapacitation was not the only form of disability that Victorians recognized. During the nineteenth century, provisions for mental healthcare were very much in their infancy, and largely unethical and entirely inhumane. However, despite these provincial beginnings, these practices helped pave the way for a greater understanding of the mind and its afflictions in the Victorian era, which would subsequently be built upon in the later years of the period.

Mental Illness

According to the admission records of patients at the Bethlem Mental Hospital in the nineteenth century, recognized mental illnesses took the form of anxiety, nerves, depression, 'puerperal insanity and melancholia' (now more commonly known as post-partum depression), as well as mania, mutism and dementia.[1] Other mental afflictions controversially included 'menstrual irregulance' (likely a form of menstrual disorder which affected the emotions), as well as bereavement, overwork, travel exhaustion and 'intense heat'.[2] Even 'disappointment' had been considered as a mental illness in Bethlem at the time.[3]

The notes of patients who resided temporarily at Bethlem Hospital and other institutions of a similar kind help paint a picture of life for the mentally disabled in the nineteenth century, as well as the provisions that they may have received. One mother, who had 'fretted herself into decline for two children who had died of the cholera', for example, was left to cope with her emotions without any medical intervention.[4] Another mother, who was suffering from presumed post-partum depression or psychosis, was treated entirely differently, indicating the disparity in the level of care for mentally unwell patients in the Victorian era. Ada Jane Warren was just 28 when she became an inpatient at Bethlem Hospital.[5] Admitted in 1892, only five weeks after the birth of her youngest daughter (of four children), she had been declared a danger to herself and others on account of her being 'insane after childbirth'.[6] Convinced that herself and her baby were dead from an overdose of chloroform, Ada threw bodily waste at nurses who tried to restrain her and threatened to jump from windows, and would collapse into fits of hysterics whenever she tried to communicate verbally. Later confessing that she wished to kill her husband and children, Ada swore that she could see faces beneath her bed and would ingest items such as nails hammered into walls and scraps of fabric, being convinced that the food at the hospital was laced with poison and that her nurses were trying to murder her. Despite attempts at treatment, which included tranquilization and spoken therapy, Ada grew more 'demented' over time, succumbing to such a deep depression that she would no longer talk, dress or wash herself, or face her husband. Despite this, she was discharged from Bethlem Hospital entirely uncured in April 1893, and allowed to live as part of society without ongoing treatment or regular check-ups.

The discharging of patients still very clearly unwell was unfortunately not uncommon in Victorian Britain, for institutions were simply too stretched and under-funded to provide long-term, adequate care for its sick patients. When 18-year-old Hannah Levy Bensusan entered Bethlem Hospital in 1893, doctors expressed little hope in her recovery.[7] Hannah was diagnosed with acute mania and was severely impacted by delusions, hallucinations and fits of 'excitability', wherein she would talk incessantly for hours and refuse to consume food. Hannah was violent, needed to be spoon-fed and would defecate upon herself without warning, yet her discharge papers in April 1894 – exactly one year to the date of her admittance – stated that she was 'sufficiently recovered'.[8]

Similar circumstances occurred when other patients were admitted to the hospital. Thomas George Callaghan, a 17-year-old pauper, had required four men to restrain him, his hands and feet bound to stop him from moving.[9] Thomas, who was agitated and violent, was kept in a padded cell for the safety of the other patients, but was later discharged, uncured, and enlisted in the 57th Regiment of the British Army. Twenty-five-year-old Henry Leotine Gamlen, who was admitted to Bethlem Hospital with schizophrenia at the latter end of the century, would spend hours conversing with 'demons' and 'the Devil'.[10] When medication and therapeutic exercises proved insufficient for his care, Henry was discharged and fell into a pit of self-medication with alcoholic spirits and substance abuse.

It was no wonder that many sufferers of mental illness in Victorian London felt as though they were beyond helping, for if they pursued medical intervention they were often turned away without sufficient treatment or improvement. 'I don't know that there's any institution would help a man like me,' confessed a solemn street urchin in 1881.[11] Although most mental institutions were not wholly prejudicial in the nineteenth century, and instead catered for patients from both ends of the social spectrum, there nevertheless existed a school of thought which dictated that the poor 'should not expect anything and should not complain'.[12] One nurse informed Nellie Bly upon her undercover visit to Blackwell's Insane Asylum that,

> 'you are in a public institution now, and you can't expect to get anything. This is charity, and you should be thankful for what you get [but] you don't need to expect any kindness here, for you won't get it.'

It thus became strikingly evident that the mentally unwell amongst the working classes 'added to a long list which had long since ceased to be of any interest or concern' to local parishes, law enforcement and governments.[13]

But is it a fair estimate to suggest that mental health care provision in nineteenth-century Britain was as shambolic as we are led to believe? Arguably, the very same institutions that discharged sick patients without sufficient treatment plans were also the nucleus of positive change. Bethlem Hospital, for example, was originally nestled within the heart of the City of London, yet was relocated to St George's Field in Southwark in 1815 when it became apparent that its patients were quickly outgrowing the building. At its new location, Bethlem provided care for both males and females ranging from adolescence to old age, the deprived to the affluent. Built over four floors, Bethlem Hospital had wards consisting of communal four-bed rooms, as well as single-occupancy cells for the more disruptive or disturbed of patients.[14] The wings of the hospital were mirrored, meaning that the same number of males and females could be treated without particular bias or discrimination. There was also a 'basement', which housed the most severely unwell of patients in padded cells. These cells were small, capable of holding just one patient at a time; their walls, floor and ceiling were made from a shiny, spongy material to prevent injury to the patient within, and were without windows or access to the outside world.

Doctors and nurses at Bethlem Hospital could keep a watchful eye on patients either while doing their rounds of the wings, or by observing patients in communal areas such as the dining hall or gardens, as well as via a deck built above the 'disruptive' wards of male and female patients, which had been introduced to the hospital in 1888.[15] Glass doors and windows were common throughout the hospital, allowing nurses to diligently watch their patients in case they harmed themselves or others, the largest of these being locked and barred to prevent suicidal patients jumping from them.[16]

Despite the popular belief that mental asylums in the Victorian period were cold, unwelcoming and wholly unsatisfactory for the treatment of the unwell, Bethlem Hospital maintained a reputation for calm and pleasantly decorated wards which were believed to assist in the treatment of its patients. Photographs inside Bethlem Hospital from the nineteenth century depict it as an inviting, almost cosy place, with flowers, oil paintings and soft furnishings decorating communal areas, and even pets (most commonly singing birds) allowed to wander its halls.[17] In 1889, hot water pipes were permanently installed within the hospital, allowing for the enormous building to be fully centrally heated and much more comfortable for the many who lived and worked there.[18] The population of Bethlem was considerably larger than other mental institutions in Britain at the time, with at least three nurses to every patient, further increasing the number of people who traversed its halls on a daily basis.[19]

When not engaging in treatment, patients at Bethlem spent their time socializing at weekly sewing parties, engaged in ball games such as croquet, bowls and tennis, or other pastimes like garden walks, reading, singing and dancing, all of which were recognized as being beneficial to mental wellbeing.[20] Concerts and theatrical productions – professional and amateur – would regularly be hosted at the hospital, sometimes consisting of a cast made up of patients or staff, or attended by classically trained orchestras and brass bands.[21] Card games, board games, quizzes and crafts were also enjoyed by patients and staff alike at Bethlem Hospital, as were lectures and classes which were held on a regular basis and attended by anybody that was interested, regardless of their position within the institution.[21] In 1888, investment in the recreation of patients allowed the hospital to purchase real trees to decorate the halls at Christmas, as well as provide gifts and crackers for every individual.[22] It even allowed for the installation of a seesaw in the expanse of the gardens, as well as frequent excursions to the Royal Mint, the Tower of London and the Royal

Mews alongside Buckingham Palace.[23] A library consisting of books donated by WH Smith provided patients at Bethlem with a chance of respite from the illnesses which plagued them.

When not engaged in recreational pursuits, patients were expected to carry out chores around the hospital, particularly within the wards in which they slept. A typical daily routine for patients at Bethlem began at six in the morning, when matrons would serve each patient a cup of steaming hot tea or coffee from a wheeled cart. Once they had been drained and the cups put away, the doors to the wards would be unlocked and the patients were able to wash and dress within the communal bathrooms. At 8.00 am, patients would file to the dining hall for breakfast, which was served buffet-style and designed so that patients could feed themselves with as much or as little as they desired.[23] They would then engage in cleaning, mending or gardening around the hospital, unless they were called for treatment or occupational therapy. At 1.00 pm, the patients would reconvene for a lunch of soups, fish, pies, sweet puddings and fresh meat, a diet that was purposely designed to be healthy and nutritious.[24] They would receive a further filling meal at teatime (served at 4.00 pm), as well as a final cup of tea before bed at 9.00 pm, when doors would be locked and patients expected to sleep.[25]

That their duration in hospital was surprisingly pleasant was intentional; by observing patients engaged in routines without the use of medication or other treatments, doctors could sufficiently discharge patients who they deemed less demanding of their care. For the vast majority of patients at Bethlem, particularly those who had been admitted for such ludicrous ailments as heat exhaustion, this meant that they could be released efficiently and hastily without causing strain upon the hospital and its supplies. Not every patient was so lucky, however. To be admitted to the hospital, you needed two official medical certificates to determine the severity of your 'insanity', including a doctor's review of your behaviour, as well as communication from family and friends.[26]

'Lunacy commissioners', who were employed to determine the extent of a mental illness, enquired about the patient's symptoms, including the 'duration of "attack"', whether they were a danger to themselves or others, their religious 'persuasion', their sobriety and their degree of education.[28] The status of their bowels and urine would be examined too, along with their appetite and any food aversions, as well as the interpretation of their dreams.[29] Mental illness was apparently further proved by the 'excitability' of the patient, their 'tendency to leave home' and their outward appearance, as well as their ability to occupy and entertain themselves, and even the condition of their tongue and gums.[30] Patients could be quizzed about their family history and whether it contained any instances of incest, their sexual histories and whether they had contracted syphilis, as well as catamenia. It was also determined whether a female frequently menstruated.[31]

Once a mental illness had been diagnosed (no matter how bizarre or far-fetched it may have seemed), a patient was given four possible outcomes of recovery. The first was self-discharge, where patients who convinced doctors that they were well enough to leave following a period of treatment and 'much improvement' were discharged without question.[31] Next came temporary treatment, whereby patients known as 'voluntary boarders', who were not officially declared insane, could be held at the hospital for seventy-two hours but then discharged of their own accord. Then came the 'incurables', who would be housed indefinitely within the hospital, and not discharged typically within twelve months like the majority of patients at the time. These 'incurables' would reside in wards of their own, and, aside from occasional visits from family and friends, did not ever step foot in the outside world again, unless their condition drastically and miraculously improved. The final possible outcome for leaving a mental institution in the nineteenth century, and the least desirable of all, was death. In the vast majority of cases, most patients would be given the prognosis of 'fair', and could either self-discharge or wait until a doctor signed the paperwork which allowed them to re-enter society.

Just how many of these patients had truly been sufficiently cured at Victorian mental institutions will never confidently be established, though with records detailing the often-tortuous methods of treatment given to sufferers of mental ill health, this statistic was undoubtedly slim. Straightjackets and similar full-body restraints had ceased in use by the 1840s, amid complaints that they were ethically and morally unjustified. However, other restraints (some of which are still used in hospitals today) were utilized to keep patients still. Leg and arm 'dresses', for example, would restrict the movement of limbs, while padded gloves, chains and even mechanical apparatus were used in certain circumstances.[32] Additionally, the uniform of patients in mental institutions would be made from strong and often heavy materials, constructed intentionally so that patients could not rip them apart.

Rowdy and 'excitable' patients could also be controlled through the administration of opiate drugs such as chloroform and laudanum, which were used for their sedation. 'Sulphonal' was a tranquilizer introduced to mental asylums in 1889, while heavy sedatives like paraldehyde and hyoscine were introduced in the preceding century to tackle violence amongst patients.[33] These medicines would be administered to the patient either via injection or through 'lavage', a barbaric practice in which a wooden gag would be affixed to the mouth, forcing the jaw to remain open as doctors forcefully fed the drugs to their patients.[34] Nasal tubes, 'feeding cups' and even enemas designed to flush drugs or other supposed medications such as bicarbonate of soda and carbolic acid through the rectum and into the systems of patients were also used.[35] Somewhat less tortuous, but still inhumane, treatments such as 'continuous baths' (where patients bathed in warm water for upwards of eight or nine hours) and cold water therapy were believed to be therapeutic.[36] So too was the shaving and blistering of the head, which would then be covered in iodine, which was used principally in treating the mental disturbances of men.[37]

Mental health care still had much to achieve by the close of the nineteenth century. However, institutions such as Bethlem Hospital demonstrated to some degree that patient wellbeing and satisfaction was a priority to doctors at the time, and that, despite unethical (and inefficient) therapies, strides were still being made in the right direction in the reform of care of the mentally unwell.

Medicines were readily available to consumers in the nineteenth century. Available to purchase from chemist shops and apothecarists, even the poorest of society could afford to cure their common ailments. The chemist store Boots, established in 1849, prided itself on affordability and a wide range of products. By 1900, Boots had established 180 shops across Britain, which would raise to an enormous 560 stores in 1915.[38] As well as this, street doctors would shill medical advice and treatments to desperate patients, their services being particularly employed by the dwellers of the London slums.[39]

Typically distilled and extracted from plants, medicines and drugs could also be dispensed from hospitals, health clinics and even workhouse infirmaries.[40] However, these drugs were very rarely regulated, meaning that Victorians could purchase as much of the drugs as they desired. Contemporary references to home medical kits mention remedies ranging from the harmless, such as castor oil, to the downright dangerous, like chloroform, laudanum, morphine, opium and cocaine.[41] Laudanum, for example, was used to cure diarrhoea and teething pain in infants, and was particularly popular in the slums, where mothers used it to help their children sleep. One product consisting of laudanum, Mrs Winslow's Soothing Syrup, even targeted exhausted mothers who gave it to their children in large quantities to keep them quiet.[42] As can be expected, this led to overuse, addiction and even overdose in adults and children alike, and is widely believed to have been the preferred method of murder adopted by baby-farmer Amelia Dyer in the 1870s (see 'Cold-Blooded Killers' below).[43] Laudanum was also a preferred method for suicide in the nineteenth century, as it allowed for a painless death that could occur in the sleep.[44]

Another addictive and highly dangerous drug, opium, was made from the distilled seeds of poppies and could be purchased for less money than alcohol in the nineteenth century.[45] Continuing to be sold in pharmacies and chemist shops until the Dangerous Drugs Act of 1920 officially outlawed its sale, users began to experience so-called 'morpinomania', a term coined in the 1880s after Morpheus, the Greek god of dreams and sleep, such was the effect of the drug upon the body.[46] Used as a painkiller, sleep aid and hangover cure, opium use would result in horrific side-effects, including red, painful welts upon the skin, blue fingers and lips, and pink frothy sputum, and often led to coma, fits and death.[47] Even contemporaries were aware of the dangers of opium, coining it appropriately as a 'poison' and calling for its regulation in the Pharmacy Act of 1868. Despite this, opium use was not declared a public health crisis in Britain until 1916 and continued to have long-lasting effects upon those who had used it, changing their lives forever.

Drugs were not only used to sedate or cure patients in the nineteenth century. Some drugs were utilized entirely for cosmetic purposes, such as belladonna, which was also known as 'deadly nightshade'. Belladonna, which could be purchased for relatively little money in the nineteenth century, was used principally by women, who dripped the essence directly onto their eyeballs to cause the dilation of their pupils and give the appearance of wider, brighter and more youthful eyes. Even Queen Victoria was rumoured to employ the use of belladonna to help break apart the cataracts which plagued her in old age.[48]

Beauty

The nineteenth century was a notoriously patriarchal period, a time when women were controlled in everything from their legal rights to the way that they dressed. 'Every woman owes it not only to herself, but to society, to be as beautiful and charming as [she] possibly can,' wrote one contemporary handbook, emphasizing that a woman's looks were not solely her own in the nineteenth century, but were also intended to please those around her.[1]

Standards of beauty in Victorian England varied with culture and class, though most could agree that a petite, yet curvaceous woman was the ideal. In her *Arts of Beauty*, Lola Montez wrote that women should strive to have wide hips, narrow shoulders, small ankles and medium-sized, round and firm breasts.[2] She must possess a small chin, a long 'flexible' neck and delicate, soft hands with perfectly rounded nails.[3] Her eyes must be large, bright and either brown or blue, and her hair dark, as it would make her skin look whiter.[4] Women must have semi-circular eyebrows, a high 'intelligent' forehead, plump cheeks, a straight nose and even small ears that reddened when the woman blushed.[5] Other handbooks of the time emphasized that English women, no matter their social standing, should resemble an 'English rose'; they should have lips 'plump, and of a rich ruby colour' and delicate, blemish-free skin.[6] Beauty standards of the time even called for women to have narrow ankles, as swollen ones betrayed a 'want of exercise and sitting indolently in over-heated rooms'.[7]

However, very few women could achieve these highly specific standards. Unless blessed with the 'perfect' figure, most Victorian women had to settle for accepting the bodies they had. There were, however, routines that women could follow in the nineteenth century to improve their figure and complexion, or even drastically change their appearance altogether. 'You must rise early', instructed Isabella Beeton, who stressed the apparent dangers of lounging about in bed; 'the country lass goes to bed with the robin and is up with the lark; the city belle's life is by gaslight', much to the detriment of her appearance and health.[8] Other beauty manuals of the era recommend healthy diets of fruit, vegetables and lean meat, as well as a daily regimen of light exercise. 'To despise the temple is to insult its occupant', offered Lola Montez, who thoroughly recommended that women practice temperance and cleanliness, and that they should have no late nights or 'high living'.[9] Some guidebooks went one step further, advertising unsafe or wholly ridiculous ways to improve one's appearance as quickly as overnight. To encourage the breasts to grow, for example, a recipe of 1 ounce of myrrh, 4 ounces of pimpernel water, 4 ounces of distilled elderflower essence and 6 ounces of wine would be slathered on to the chests of women anxious to live up to the beauty ideals.[10]

Recipes were particularly employed in the care of the skin, providing a relatively cheap (though often precarious) way for the poor to maintain a semblance of a hygiene routine. Other more affordable items were available for purchase from local chemist and druggist shops, which sold pre-made skincare products for varying prices. In 1897, for example, lavender lotion and 'almond nut cream' were sold for pennies; they were particularly fashionable and desired by Victorian women who had been drawn into advertisements promising beautiful supple skin.[11] One form of the almond nut cream was even endorsed by Lilly Langtry, actress and mistress of Albert Edward, the son of Queen Victoria and later King Edward VII, who propelled it into the height of fashion.

Another product sold relatively cheaply was Secret de Ninon, which enticed British Victorians with its elegant and sophisticated French name. This product, which promised to remove freckles and age spots from the skin, was sold for just one penny in 1897.[12] Kalydor cream was sold in chemist's shops for just 4*s* 6*d*, making it an affordable, if unnecessary, product that even the poor could hope to purchase.[13] Kalydor, made from an incredibly dangerous mix of rosewater, almond oil and liquid mercury, was marketed as a cream that removed pimples, tan, sunburn and freckles. It certainly worked, though only because it entirely took off the layer of skin on which it had been applied.

Much less dangerous were products introduced in the nineteenth century that found such widespread acclaim that they are still used by many today. Pond's Cold Cream, established in 1846 by Theron T. Pond, was produced in collaboration with the Native American Oneida people, who used aloe vera and witch hazel for sunburn.[14] Upon noticing that the Oneida people's skin was beautifully supple and clear, Pond bottled the recipe and sold it to women as a cleansing balm which effectively (and safely) removed all traces of dirt, sweat and make-up upon the face. Vaseline was initially marketed as a similar product used to remove build-up upon the skin. Established in 1870, Vaseline was produced on a mass scale by Robert A. Cheeseborough, who discovered it while extracting oil at work.[15] Cheeseborough had noticed that the waxy byproduct of the oil extraction process had left his skin moisturized and protected from chafing and chapping. Upon its release, Vaseline proved to be an immediate hit amongst women and men of all social strata, who used it not only for cleansing and moisturizing their skin, but also as a pomade for their hair and even a perfume when mixed with essential oils.

For those who preferred to make their own beauty concoctions, recipes and pamphlets were available to service literally any need. To remove sunburn, for example, a common ailment of those working-class members of society who spent much of their working day outdoors, recipes called for a half-pint of milk and a quarter of an ounce of lemon juice, which would be slathered atop the skin and left to settle like a mask.[16] Alternatively, people could take the juice of a lemon and mix it with egg whites until resembling meringue; it would then be applied to the face and left until it became sticky (and no doubt incredibly uncomfortable).[17]

The Victorians considered the skin of the working classes to be more prone to complaints. It was said that 'workmen who are in the habit of handling acrid or mineral substances are liable to various eruptions', for example, while those who worked menial jobs in the direct gaze of the sun would more likely be prone to wrinkles and aging spots.[18] Of course, now that we fully understand the harmful effects of direct sunlight upon bare skin or the handling of dangerous chemicals without sufficient protection, our skincare routines and advice have evolved considerably. The Victorians (although by no means completely ignorant) fought skincare complaints with methods and products proven to have caused far more harm than good. To treat 'nettle rash', for example, a Victorian would drink laxatives dissolved in still lemonade.[19] It appears that the Victorian understanding of 'nettle rash' was not, as the name suggests, a rash procured from stinging nettles, but instead, the term used for an allergic reaction and the production of hives and welts upon the skin. Nettle rash was particularly said to be brought about by people who ate shellfish or nuts, and was accompanied by wheezing and 'mental excitement'.[20]

Acne, which was believed to attack those of a 'nervous and irritable temperament' was also known as 'lichen' in the nineteenth century, and frequently occurred in people of a 'strong mental emotion', causing the skin to go 'from a healthy to a diseased state'.[21] Remedies for acne included lemon juice mixed with water and vinegar, as well as frequent bathing. Pimples were expressly *not* to be picked at or popped, but rather left to heal by themselves. However, in the *Arts of Beauty*, Lola Montez outlined what must have been a painful and unquestionably dangerous solution for acne, which was particularly adopted by teenaged and young adults of the time. By mixing 1 ounce of sulphur, half an ounce of ammonia, 1 gram of potassium and 2 ounces of white wine and water, the solution would be poured onto a rough towel and vigorously rubbed onto the skin until the 'fleshworms' (the pus from the pimple) had been extracted.[22]

Another toe-curling recipe for skin complaints came in the form of remedies for warts and moles. Francis Pears of the Pears soap corporation recommended that sufferers of these raised bumps should skim them first with a mercury-soaked cloth before lancing them or cutting them off entirely with a knife or scissors.[23] The result would cause excessive bleeding, and often resulted in infection that threatened the health of the sufferer. If a person had cut or grazed themselves in the nineteenth century and hoped to avoid blood-borne infections, homemade antiseptic washes could be employed to minimize risk of serious illness. Straight vinegar, made popular in France as a way to remove wrinkles or drunk in the hope of achieving a slim figure, would be poured onto wounds, much to the agony of the afflicted.[24] So too would lemon juice or hydrogen peroxide be utilized, which would cause skin to literally bubble and fizz before crusting over with a thin epidermic scab.

Burns would be remedied by rubbing dry flour on to the wound or smearing butter over the afflicted areas.[25] Indeed, butter as an ingredient makes regular appearances in beauty manuals, being used in anything from cold creams to body lotions and even hair conditioners. The *Handbook of the Toilette*, published in 1841, encouraged butter to be slathered upon the face, hands, neck and arms 'after the morning's ablution' of washing the face and scrubbing it dry with a rough facecloth.[26] For a nicer scent, the *Handbook* recommended people to mix essential oils such as citrus or floral scents in with the butter (and advised it to be kept well away from use in the kitchen).[27]

Other face creams of the nineteenth century could be made from rose, almond, elderflower, sugar and oatmeal, which would be soaked and made to resemble a kind of face mask which would be rinsed off after sleeping with it on overnight.[28] One recipe even called for the use of melted deer fat.[29]

Compared to women, 'the skin of men [...] being never exposed to view, its appearance is of little consequence', believed the Victorians.[30] A male's appearance was therefore 'not so much cared about' in the nineteenth century.[31] Despite this, men were encouraged just as much as women to keep their faces and skin clean and free from blemish as best they could, thus challenging the belief that Victorian men cared little for their appearance and that they placed no particular importance upon keeping clean. Even the poorest of Victorians were ençouraged to wash 'the face every night in hot water', and cold water in the morning.[32] Men were also told to groom and regularly trim their beards or else run the risk of looking unwashed and unruly. Men were particularly targeted to ensure that their ears and noses were free from build-up and hair, and encouraged to used 'ear-pickers' or even sewing pins to remove wax (which received numerous reports of resulting in deafness).[33]

Health and wellbeing manuals in the nineteenth century also targeted men by focusing on typically male-centric features. Authors urged men to go to professionals if they wished to be tattooed, as the alternative of poking one's skin with a needle and ink could result in dangerous blood poisoning and infection.[34] Tattoos and even precursors to modern tattoo parlours existed in Victorian Britain, with fans ranging from the wealthy to the very lowly of society. Albert Edward, the Prince of Wales and later King Edward VII, had tattoos, and so had one of his mistresses.[35] Even Catherine Eddowes, a victim of Jack the Ripper, had tattoos inked upon her skin, proving that they were not favoured entirely by the male sex.[36]

Smoking, its effects and its peculiar set of rules were also targeted at men in handbooks of the time. For example, a man was instructed never to smoke in the company of women or children, for whom it was considered to be 'the worst enemy'.[37] Cigarettes, cigars and even simple strips of paper stuffed with a sorrowful semblance of foraged herbs, which was commonly referred to as 'weed' (which did not mean then what it now does in modern contexts), were smoked by men in the nineteenth century.[38] Chain-smoking was an expensive, but male-centric hobby in nineteenth century Britain, with figures such as Edward VII smoking upward of twelve cigars and twenty cigarettes per day.[39] Edward had even managed to get one of his mistresses, Alice Keppel, to take up smoking. Alice had made it fashionable for women to smoke in the nineteenth and twentieth centuries, where it slowly began to emerge as a sophisticated and urbane activity well up until the 2000s, when attitudes drastically changed.

To combat the lingering smell of cigarette smoke upon the breath, Victorians would employ the use of 'cachous pills', small lozenges typically made from mint or liquorice and carried in small tins. Cachous pills could be bought from market traders or chemist shops, and were a cheap and relatively effective way of ensuring that the breath stayed sweet. Having bad breath in the nineteenth century was also believed to come about from the 'speedy loss of a dear friend, of a beloved child, or of a tender and devoted partner in life'.[40] To alleviate bad breath, the Victorians believed in somewhat ridiculous remedies such as the stimulation of the bowels, conducting 'exercise on horseback' and undertaking boat trip 'excursions on the water'.[41] For those more realistic Victorians who were less inclined to employ such bizarre methods to rid themselves of sour breath, thankfully other remedies were available.

Mouthwash became popular in the nineteenth century as a way of keeping the breath fresh long after brushing of the teeth. Until the introduction of brands such as Listerine in 1879, making mouthwash more readily available to the masses, people could make their own from a mix of spring water and sodium chloride.[42] Alternatively, simply swilling the mouth with fresh water was also supposed to work well.

Oral hygiene was taken seriously in Victorian Britain, with even the poorest of society encouraged to keep their teeth clean. 'Good teeth are a gift to many,' wrote one handbook, 'but few have the art of preserving them.'[43] Toothbrushes did exist in the nineteenth century (they had been mass produced in Britain since the 1780s), and many paupers even owned one of their own. If they did not have a traditional toothbrush, however, poor Victorians used their ingenuity to make ones of their own, which were by all accounts effective and kept the mouth as clean as brushing. One record particularly notes the use of splayed twigs used by paupers to scrub at their teeth.[44] Some used the tips of their fingers to smear tooth pastes and powder over their teeth, while others employed toothpicks or cloths. Some Victorians even used the tips of their quills and pens, as well as sewing pins, celery sticks, sugar cane and even thorns to pick at their teeth![45]

To brush your teeth in the Victorian era was to undergo a relatively long-winded routine. Firstly, you would floss or pick at the teeth to remove any lingering pieces of food stuck between them. Following this, a toothbrush and some form of toothpaste would be used to brush the teeth as we do today. Victorians would then rinse their mouths and scrape their tongues to remove any 'fur', then repeat the whole process again. Once finished for the second time, Victorians were encouraged to use a 'tooth tincture' (marketed as 'eau de cologne' for the mouth and made from myrrh) or mouthwash, which they did not need to spit out but instead could swallow.[46] Adults and children alike were encouraged to follow this process at least twice a day, 'every morning on rising, and every-night at bedtime', or following every meal.[47]

Toothpaste or powders were sold to every social strata in Victorian England, being common possessions of those living in the slums. Indeed, so mass-marketed were these products that very small numbers of Victorians actually made their own tooth cleansers. Some of the most popular toothpaste brands of the day included Jewsbury and Brown's Oriental Toothpaste, which promised to keep the teeth and gums healthy and white 'til old age', and Rowland's Odonto, which was sold for just 2*s* 9*d*.[48] Pears (better known for their soaps) launched their own tooth powder, Quinne Dentrifice, in the later part of the nineteenth century, which effectively whitened the teeth and left the mouth feeling clean and fresh.[49] Even one of the most enduring and favourite brands of toothpaste used in our society today, Colgate's Ribbon Dental Cream, was employed by Victorians as early as 1870.[50]

On the rare occasion when Victorians preferred to make their own tooth cleansers, either out of necessity or because they could not afford commercial ones, recipes were readily available. One of the less-dangerous recipes comes from *The Arts of Beauty*, in which Lola Montez recommended mixing 6 ounces of chalk with 1 ounce of orris root and either charcoal or cream of tartar.[51] Some of these ingredients are found even in today's modern toothpastes, and are surprisingly effective at not only keeping the mouth and teeth clean and white, but also the breath fresh and gums healthy. Another recipe came in the form of mixing an ounce of charcoal with the ground-up bones of a cuttlefish, which was bound together with honey or resin.[52] A similar one called for half an ounce of sugar, 1 ounce of camphor, 2 drachms of ammonia and 2 drachms of tree sap.[53] These particular toothpastes were not recommended by dentists of the time, however, who warned against the effects of such ingredients as camphor, which could cause breathing difficulties and even death if accidentally ingested.

Dentistry in Victorian Britain was a far cry from the practices of today. Often dangerous and unsafe, dentistry procedures included curing toothache with lint dipped in creosote and using muriatic acid to fill cavities.[54] Creosote, typically used in the lining of fireplaces and preventing wood from rotting, could cause respiratory problems, skin irritation, and confusion in patients inflicted with aches and pains in their mouths. Muriatic acid, a highly dangerous and corrosive substance, was used to scrub away tartar and other build-up upon the teeth. Muriatic acid was known to corrode tissues and sensitive mucous membranes, and its fumes could be fatal if breathed in. Now commonly used to sanitize swimming pools, remove rust and even to corrode stone and cement, the practice was highly dangerous and often made problems worse for ailing Victorians. If a tooth needed to be pulled, nitrous oxide would be given to the patient so that they would fall into a hazy, dream-like state and not feel the full extent of the pain. One London dentist claimed to remove teeth without depending on nitrous oxide but entirely with the help of electricity, so that the process would be 'without any pain, [...] little or no bleeding'.[55] His patients would vouch otherwise.

Unsafe products and ingredients were not only used by Victorians to clean their teeth or skin, however. Indeed, women were particularly exposed to dangerous chemicals in the nineteenth century, with so-called 'nostrum' cosmetics (hazardously made products which resulted in dangerous consequences) marketed for their daily use.

Cosmetics

Like skin and tooth care products, cosmetics could be bought in chemist shops, made at home or even purchased via mail order. For the vast majority of poor women in Victorian London, making your own cosmetics was much cheaper and often, ironically, far safer than purchasing commercial products. In recipes made at home, Victorian women could control what ingredients went into their make-up, which were often naturally derived and entirely plant-based. Lips, for example, would be coloured with beetroot juice mixed with cocoa butter as a makeshift lipstick, while face powder could be made from ground rice.[1] In the nineteenth century, regardless of your social standing, make-up was only intended to be minimal and to highlight the natural beauty of a woman. As such, delicate colours and tints derived from natural sources were often far more flattering than commercial cosmetics, which would often be targeted toward actresses and prostitutes.

Indeed, despite the male emphasis upon women looking perfectly made-up in the nineteenth century, natural beauty was deemed to be more attractive, and the less obvious the make-up the better. 'A violently rouged woman is a disgusting sight', wrote one handbook of the time, for 'it transforms the elegant lady of fashion into a vulgar harridan [...] a distortion of nature's harmony'.[2] Even Parliament under King George III had passed an act in 1770 which decreed that any woman

> 'who sought to betray one of his Majesty's subjects into marriage by scents, paints, cosmetic washes, artificial teeth, false hair, Spanish wool (rouge), iron stays, high-heeled shoes, bolstered hips and like misdemeanours shall incur the penalty of the law in force against witchcraft and that marriage shall stand null and void.'[3]

Victorian women were truly set between a rock and a hard place. Expected to look perfect but without the application of beauty products, it was no wonder that some went to great lengths to hide cosmetic use from their husbands. Many women, particularly anxious that their loved one might see them without a ready-made face, would ensure that they rose before him to apply make-up every morning, and took it off at night once he had fallen asleep. Some women even slept all night in their make-up, simply adding to it in the morning to maintain a constant look of beauty.

Compared to today, Victorian make-up routines were relatively simple. The face would be washed with soap and water, then moisturized, powdered and rouged. Mascara, eyeliner and lipstick could be applied if desired, and eyebrows brushed and pencilled. These pencils were commonly made from lead, a dangerous ingredient, and came in numerous colours to suit the natural hair of the woman using it.[4] So too would mascara be sold in colours suited to the natural hair tone of a woman, in blonde, brown or black. Mascara was typically sold in small tins of a waxy substance and applied to the eyelashes either with a small brush or the tips of the fingers. Alternatively, women could make their own mascara out of burnt charcoal or soot and wettened with oil for easier application to the lashes, or even use ink which would be applied with a fine hair brush.[5] Eyeliner was typically applied using the same products used to pencil the brows, or could be made from castor oil and soot acquired from burning a metal spoon over a lit candle.[6]

For the face, an early form of foundation (known in the nineteenth century as 'white paint') would be made from a nitrate of bismuth, the same ingredients found in modern-day indigestion tablets.[7] It could also be made from stirring together 4 ounces of talcum powder and vinegar, which would be left to dry and applied atop the skin following a cold cream, either with the fingertips, a sponge, a soft-bristled brush or even the foot of a hare![8] Other ingredients called for starch, chalk, rice powder, milk of magnesia and even ground zinc oxide or slate.[9] If a woman instead wished for a creamier product, she could purchase a stick of greasepaint for 6*d*, which was made from lard mixed with white zinc, yellow ochre and vermillion.[10] Greasepaint was particularly high-coverage and incredibly sticky, as well as prone to melting upon the skin. It was, however, the favoured product of 'painted ladies' in the nineteenth century, like actresses and prostitutes, who favoured heavy make-up and concealed (if somewhat ineffectively) their facial flaws. White paint could be dangerous if made incorrectly, however, particularly if harsh chemicals were used in its manufacture. Lola Montez warned women against using it, calling the product 'destructive to the skin' and capable of causing 'paralytic affections and premature death'.[11]

To bring colour to the faces of the pale and sickly-looking poor Victorians, rouges and tints were favoured as they gave a subtle yet still noticeable appearance. Blusher could be made from safflower, a harmless ingredient that was often found in tea in the nineteenth century.[12] Other relatively safe forms of blusher came in pressed compacts of pink tinted talc, as well as beetroot-stained sponges which would be dabbed upon the skin. However, just like the other cosmetics of the time, rouge could be incredibly dangerous. One recipe, for example, called for a mixture of red sulphur, mercury and lead oxide.[13] It was only when beauty moguls such as Alexander Napoleon Bourjois and Eugene Rimmel launched their safer, pressed powder blush alternatives that rouge was sold to the masses for less risk.

No look would be complete without lipstick. Surprisingly safe considering the time period in which they were made, lipsticks typically consisted of wax and naturally derived oils such as from almonds or castor, as well as colourants made from ground cochineal beetles.[14]

Hair

Once a Victorian woman had finished making up her face, thoughts could turn to her hair. Hair was typically worn long for women in the nineteenth century, and shortly cropped for men. Beauty guidebooks of the time recommended that hair be brushed at least three times per day: once upon waking (for thirty minutes), once at dinner (for five minutes) and once before bed (for ten minutes).[1] If the poorest members of Victorian society could not afford to own a hairbrush, they would be encouraged to massage their scalps with their fingertips and comb through their hair with their fingers. Hairbrushes were relatively cheap in Victorian Britain, however, and the working class and paupers could, for the most part, buy their own. So too might they have owned wooden combs, pins or other ephemera relating to the care of hair. Indeed, every one of Jack the Ripper's victims had been found with some semblance of a comb upon their bodies, even if these had been broken or had missing teeth, indicating just how important they were to Victorian society.

Contrary to popular belief, hair would be washed at least once a week in the nineteenth century, regardless of one's social standing. In fact, men would wash their hair more often than women, typically because they worked more laborious jobs in dirtier areas (such as mines), and due to the fact that their shorter hair was far more manageable than the long hair of their wives, mothers and sisters. One product particularly used by men in the nineteenth century was macassar oil, a form of conditioner which was made from olive or castor oil.[2] That it was favoured by men was in part due to the fact that it left the hair stiff enough to shape, similar to other products such as pomade or hair wax. It certainly beat the alternative, which was to mix together a disgusting selection of sticky, gooey ingredients and slather it upon the hair for styling. For example, one recipe called for half a pound of lard, castor oil, spermaceti (a white waxy substance found in the heads of sperm whales) and beef tallow, as well as scent to disguise the unpleasant smell.[3] The ingredients would be whipped together until white and creamy, and then melted in the palm of the hand before being applied to the hair and set with a stiff brush.

Removing hair products like macassar, pomade and bandoline (another waxen product available at the time) would undoubtedly have been a struggle, considering the greasy nature of the ingredients. However, men, women and children alike regularly washed their hair with rather effective shampoos or soap bars, and thus their hair would not have been as dirty or greasy as we may be led to believe. Although liquid shampoo as we now know it was not introduced to Britain until the 1930s, other commercial or home-made versions were available. Lola Montez called for one recipe to be made from half a pint of lemon juice distilled in water, which would be applied to the head every morning and used particularly to alleviate symptoms of dry scalp and dandruff.[4] Another recipe favoured by Montez was made from frothing the whites of four eggs with rum and rosewater. It would then be massaged into the hair and rinsed out once allowed to harden.[5] Though appearing rather bizarre hair washes to us today, many Victorian shampoos actually proved beneficial to the hair and scalp, with ingredients such as castor and rosemary oil promoting growth and thickness, and eggs much-needed protein for frizzy and dry locks.

Once washed, Victorians needed to dry their hair. Many would have allowed it to dry naturally, or would use towels roughly upon their scalps to speed up the process. *The Handbook of the Toilette* also recommended women sit next to the vapours of 'balsam', which was believed to dry the hair in little time.[6] According to the *Handbook*, the woman must recline with her head above a hot pan of lit charcoal, upon which powdered balsam would be sprinkled. 'In a few seconds the hair is perfectly dry, beautifully perfumed, and ready for the operation of the brush,' it claimed, somewhat unconvincingly.

Hair was not always natural in the nineteenth century. Even those of the lowest strata of society would purchase wigs, toupees and even hair extensions in order to give the impression of a thicker head of hair. These would typically be made from genuine human hair, donated by women who had their hair professionally cut. Despite some myths perpetuating that false hair would be made from strands taken from the corpses of the deceased, no record of such practice exists. What was recorded, however, was the use of 'hair rats', an unnervingly named process in which women would take fallen strands of hair that had been loosened by hairbrushes and roll them into balls, saving them until enough had been acquired to form a convincing chignon bun or plait.

Hair loss was believed to occur in both men and women who adopted particular lifestyle choices. For example, men were believed to go bald due to 'the greater excitement of the brain which their pursuits occasion'.[8] According to nineteenth-century thought, women, children and those men who worked in menial jobs had thick hair, for they had not needed to exert themselves intellectually; if a man was prone to balding, it was believed to be a sign that he was 'over-exert[ing] the intellectual powers'.[9] In cases where the hair of women would fall out – something which was hardly surprising, given the lack of nutritious diet, stress and such things as hormonal changes to the body in childbirth – it was believed to be due to 'intemperance'.[10] Hair loss in women was also thought to be a sign that 'the stomach be habitually over-loaded with food [...] especially of diet and strong drink', as well as 'excitement', worry and anxiety, and a lack of exercise.[11]

For those men and women particularly insecure about the thinning of their hair, products were sold which promised to cure it. O.E. Horn's Hope for the Bald Hair Solvent, sold in the 1890s, reportedly cured anything from baldness to greying hair, thinning hair and hair fall, and could be purchased in sizes costing 3*s*, 5*s* or 10*s* depending on the treatment required.[12] Another solution came in the form of a liquid made from olive and rosemary oils, which would be applied to the roots of the hair every morning.[13] Caustic potash could also be used by those desperate enough to regrow their hair that they would risk chemical burning and the peeling of their skin.[14] When this method was employed, it was best that the individual 'remain out of sight during a few weeks' to avoid the public gaze.[15] One barber on Oakley Terrace, London, even convinced his customers that the bear which he kept in his cellar was destined to be turned into 'bear grease', a product made from boiled bear fat and applied to the head to encourage hair growth.[16] Thankfully, the bear was spared from such a fate, though numerous others across the globe (particularly in Russia) were slaughtered for this apparent miraculous product.[17]

Once hair had grown to a desired length, it could be regularly cut to maintain its healthy appearance. Even paupers in Victorian Britain have been recorded as receiving haircuts, either from professional barbers, by their own hands or thanks to the kindness of their family, friends and neighbours. For men and children, it was recommended that the hair be cut every two to three weeks, and for women every two months.[18] However, hair would also be cut more frequently when cases of 'vermin' (headlice) were known to be running rampant through the slums. It was believed that lice 'are seldom found except in the heads of children who are not properly kept clean, or in those of the filthiest among the very low classes', according to a contemporary.[19] When the tiny creatures were found crawling amongst the strands of the hair, a thin tooth comb and a bowl's worth of bichloride of mercury would be raked painfully across the scalp to remove them.[20]

For some inhabitants of the dark and dingy slums, entirely removing hair from the body greatly reduced the chance of attracting these vermin. Every fortnight to three weeks, a man's facial hair (his beard, moustache, sideburns and 'whiskers') would typically be shaved.[21] Razors cost just 2*s* 6*d* a pair in nineteenth-century Britain, and were wholly reusable for they tended not to rust or dullen like razors today.[22] However, hair removal could also be achieved by depilatory creams, which would commonly be made from potash, lime and arsenic and caused horrific ulcers and burns.[23] Alternatively, both men and women could employ the use of waxing strips to aid them in removing body and facial hair; these were made from tar, pitch or honey left to harden on leather strips before being painfully ripped off.[24] Eyebrows and even eyelashes were regularly trimmed in the nineteenth century 'every six weeks', or as often as required.[25] On the whole, however, facial hair was preferably left to grow 'as nature has made it', and therefore varied in style from person to person.[26]

This belief even extended to the body hair of women, which was typically left alone unless personal preference dictated otherwise. Only recently becoming a topic of debate, female body hair was just an accepted part of life in Victorian England, with leg, underarm and pubic hair embraced because it indicated that a person was healthy. However, for those who did choose to remove their body hair, creams made from quicklime and wormwood could be purchased or made and left upon the skin to bubble and burn away hair follicles. It was painful, smelled horrible and had long-lasting effects such as causing rashes, burns and even the total dissolving of the skin.[27] After all, quicklime as a substance can be used to dissolve bone and stone; human skin was simply no match for it.

Cleaning the Home

Given the source evidence we have of life in the Victorian slums, is it a fair estimate to say that the poor did not keep their living spaces clean? On the one hand, contemporary testimonies to the disgusting conditions of the Victorian slums exist in such sources as Henry Mayhew's *London Labour and London Poor*, though on the other, records detailing the purchasing of cleaning products, written cleaning routines and the fact that such things as hanging laundry had been noted as occurring in the slums points otherwise. If we consider that many women who lived in the slums of Victorian London were themselves employed in domestic help as charwomen and performed the daily cleaning of the homes of others, why is it so hard to imagine that they did not keep their own dwellings clean?

Indeed, records exist which point toward even the poorest members of society purchasing products and supplies to keep their homes clean.[1] Books and guides such as Isabella Beeton's *Household Management* detailed at length the rigorous cleaning routines that were expected to be upheld within the home. This book in particular was akin to a Bible for housekeepers, maids and charwomen in the nineteenth century; even if they could not read the words themselves, they would have been accustomed to the practices written inside. In the book, Beeton writes that every housemaid should have in her repertoire a sturdy wooden box filled with hard- and soft-bristled brushes, sponges, scissors, leather scraps, cloths and lanterns.[2] A housemaid should be expected to own her own mop, broom and bucket, which she would carry from house to house in search of employment. Beeton even writes that some charwomen would use wheelbarrows to cart their cleaning supplies with them, and that such things as rakes and oil cans could even be found within.[3] Additionally, a domestic maid would have been expected to utilize such things as dust pans and cinder pails, as well as ironing boards and blankets (to prevent the board from charring), along with heavy irons that required heating upon the open flames of the fire.[4]

For those too poor to purchase their own supplies, domestic staff could easily make their own. Scrubbing brushes, for example, could be made from coarse boar or 'dead horse's tail' hair, then bound with leather and fixed atop a wooden handle with sticky paste.[5] Failing that, scrubbing tools could be made from somewhat bizarre items, such as feathers and even coconut husks.[6] Rags made from fabric offcuts were typically used to wipe, polish and shine surfaces, while chamois cloths were made from dried leather.

Furniture polish, a staple in any maid's cleaning caddy, would be made from linseed oil, turpentine, vinegar and alcohol spirits, while wax was made from a mixture of beeswax, white candle wax, soap, turpentine and boiling water.[7] Bicarbonate of soda would be scrubbed into stubborn stains and then dissolved with water or vinegar, while citrus peels and even tea leaves could be scattered throughout the home to alleviate bad smells.

The daily routine of a Victorian housewife was strenuous and seemingly never-ending. It would start with the making and tidying of the bed, then opening any available window (if their hovels were lucky to have any) to air out the room and let out condensation.[8] She would then sweep the floor and any carpets, dust down the furniture and ensure that the outfit for the day was free from dust and residual dirt. She would empty, clean and refill the washing basin and drinking jug, sweep and clean the fireplace and chimney breast to ensure that no cinder build-up remained, and then relight the fire if she could afford to do so. A woman was expected to do all of these tasks before the rest of her family had awoken (at around six in the morning), yet realistically this probably occurred infrequently. Expected to clean and prepare the home, as well as wrangle any small children and infants awoken by her movement in the room, the Victorian housewife's hard day of work had only just begun.

If she had children, a housewife would be expected to prepare their clothes for the day by airing, shaking and warming them, before dressing her children and ensuring that they were clean and fed. She would have to clean up any soiled cloth nappies by washing them in a pail of soapy water, as well as clearing any other mess her child might make around the home. She would also have to 'empty the slops', a job that even the most diligent of housewives detested.[9] Each morning, the woman of the house would take the communal bedpan or ceramic 'potty' (chamber pot) that would have been used by her family and other lodgers to relieve themselves throughout the night, and throw it away in a cesspit or river outside of the dwelling. Contrary to popular belief, throwing away the contents of a filled chamber pot upon the streets from open windows, and on to the heads of unsuspecting people who walked below, did not happen regularly. Instead, human waste would typically be dumped as far from places of inhabitation as possible to prevent effluvia and disease. Once emptied, the pot would be rinsed with scalding water and soap or turpentine, then rinsed again to ensure that no lingering bacteria remained.[10]

Yet more chores still needed to be done. Mantelpieces, chairs, window panes, mirrors and shelves were wiped down every day, as well as any ornaments or other special items a family might own.[11] Any curtains or coverings would be shaken, brushed and removed of any vermin, while candles would be replaced as needed and doorsteps swept. A housewife would be expected to scrub the floors and skirting boards on her hands and knees weekly, or more often if the need arose, with a mixture of yellow soap, water and bicarbonate of soda and a stiff scrubbing brush.[12] Though expensive in the Victorian era and far out of the reach of the poor of the slums, vacuum cleaners did exist. Much more primitive than our modern versions, a Victorian vacuum cleaner typically resembled a large box machine which would be wound with the turn of a crank. A long spout at the top of the machine would have a small brush attached to its end, which was used to suck up any dirt or dust upon the floor.[13] One particular vacuum cleaner marketed in the 1880s was the Bissell Carpet Sweeper, which worked 'noiselessly' and 'prevents dust rising', cleaning carpets with 'minimal labour'.[14] It would take another half a century for mod-cons ('modern conveniences' like electric vacuum cleaners) to be introduced to the market, finally bringing great relief to overworked and exhausted housewives and domestic cleaners.

Another chore that Victorians had to tackle without the luxury of a mod-con was laundry. Notoriously hard work, laundry could be a back-breaking, muscle-numbing experience. For this reason, many Victorians wore their clothes for as long as they possibly could before relinquishing them to the wash tub, with any grease spots or staining being spot-treated or brushed away to prevent the need for laundering. Wool and other heavy materials would be beaten to remove dust and residual dirt, while other fabrics would be brushed with soft-bristles or with a handkerchief. More delicate fabrics such as lace or silk would be brushed gently with a ball of soft felted wool.[15] Leather could be restored by rubbing fish oil into the material.[16]

To remove grease, Victorians could make an absorbent paste from soap, lemon juice, bull's blood and potter's clay, which would be applied to the clothing when dry and then rinsed out.[17] For fruit juice, wine or food stains, clothing would be soaked in cold, soapy water and then delicately dabbed with a paintbrush or feather that had been dipped into sodium chloride.[18] Paint would be removed in the same way. For the removal of blood, grass or soot stains, a mixture of half a pint of gin, half a pound of honey, half a pound of soft soap and half a pint water would be scrubbed into the clothing, then rinsed and left to dry.[19]

If clothing required more arduous scrubbing, then a large pail (often the same tub in which a family bathed) would be filled with hot or cold water. The articles would be left to soak momentarily, before soap flakes were added. Typically, laundry soap took the form of 'blonde toilet soap', white soap cakes which would be perfumed with various pleasant scents. Also added could be 'fig-blue', a type of bleach which would be used to whiten and brighten the clothes. Fig-blue was sold in small cubes and could be purchased from retailers, who made the surprisingly effective product from a mix of baking soda and ultramarine.[20] If fig-blue could not be afforded, poorer Victorians could simply dissolve cubes of sugar within their laundry basin or create their own bleaching products from half a pint of vinegar, an ounce of chicken dung and the juice of two large onions.[21] This would then be spread over the clothes as a paste and left to harden, before being washed twice to remove any excess.

Once the clothing had soaked, it was time for the heavy labour. 'Vowels', or large mangles set into washing basins, were the precursor of the modern-day washing machine, allowing the housewife to repeatedly scrub the laundry while a heavy rolling pin-like implement squeezed out any waste water. These vowels were heavy and required turning with a stiff crank, and sold for £3 15*s* in the mid-nineteenth century.[22] Alternatively, 'washing dollies' could be used to thrash about the clothing within the sudsy water. These dollies were long poles with a pronged base, which assisted housewives in stirring their laundry pots so that they did not have to manually scrub the clothes by hand. Washing clothes by hand could be exhausting, often resulting in housewives complaining of sore muscles, backs and hands, the latter of which would crack and break from the harshness of the laundry soap. Once her load was washed, a Victorian housewife would either employ a mangle (which clothes could be passed through to expel excess water) or squeeze the waterlogged laundry by hand. She would then hang it either from lines erected in the street or within the very room in which people lived.

Again, it would be a long while before the introduction of mod-cons to British housewives, with the modern-day washing machine not marketed for home use until well into the 1930s. However, some form of washing machine did exist in the Victorian period that required no human involvement whatsoever, though they were only found within large businesses and the most affluent of homes. The Bank of England in London had one such machine, which awed visitors with its sole reliance on machinery. On a visit to the city in 1853, Max Schlesinger wrote of clothes 'washed by wheels; then dragged into hot water and next into cold water, wrung out and hung up in a drying room. And all by steam – all by machinery!'[23] He went on to express that these machines should become more commonplace within the home, stating that it would result in 'no washing days … and no bust [tired] housewife'.[24]

Chapter 5

'Please Sir, I Want Some More': Food and Diet in the Slums

'It is our duty to bring every wholesome kind of cheap food to the notice of the poor, so that with a little exertion, they may live and live well.'
Alexis Soyer, *A Shilling Cookery for the People* (1854)

Everybody in the nineteenth century needed to eat. Whether it be through necessity or genuine enjoyment, the consumption of food and drink united every man, woman and child in Victorian Britain, regardless of their wealth or social standing. 'Dining is the privilege of civilisation', wrote Isabella Beeton in her *Book of Household Management* in 1861, stressing the importance of bringing together family over shared meals around the dinner table.[1] Beeton was one of the earliest 'celebrity' chefs of her time, frequently contributing to magazines and newspaper articles with recipes conjured from her own kitchen. Her *Book of Household Management* was a compilation of such recipes, with food and drink designed for the pleasure of every member of the family, from the weaning infant to the elderly and infirm. It covered all sorts of dishes, from the cheap and simple to the most impressive of dinner party banquets. Isabella Beeton helped spark a cultural revolution that launched the publication of cookery books and easy-to-follow recipes, many of which were favoured even by the poorest of working-class citizens. Recipe books such as Alexis Soyer's *Shilling Cookery for the People* (1854) assisted the poor in creating meals that could be made of even the cheapest ingredients, as did *A Plain Cookery Book for the Working Classes*, published by Queen Victoria's very own chef, Charles Elmé Francatelli, in 1852.

With the introduction of dedicated cookery books and recipe pamphlets, even the poorest of Victorian society could learn to employ a 'domestic economy' and tend to their own kitchens, no matter what they looked like.[2] If they were lucky enough to have dedicated kitchens in their homes, the poor most likely would have had access to such things as ovens, water basins and basic utensils like knives, spoons and forks. Even if their homes did not have any semblance of a kitchen, the poorest of slum-dwellers would probably have still owned rudimentary cookery tools such as trivets (tripods that allowed stewing pots to hang over open fires) and kettles, which could be bought cheaply from markets and trading stalls. While the poor were certainly more limited in their kitchens than the wealthier classes due to available space and lack of funds, they were by no means entirely lacking. Indeed, even vagrants were recorded with teaspoons and butterknives in their possession, which they would carry with them as they wandered in search of shelter, indicating that they may have been some of the most important items a person could own in the Victorian era and were essential to survival in the slums.[3]

Beeton's *Household Management* supplied readers with a list of every necessary item to equip a suitable kitchen. Although it is most likely that the very destitute of Victorian society would have not been able to have afforded such luxuries, it is plausible to suggest that the vast majority of homes did at least own a few of the items listed. Among these were teapots, sold for around 6*s*, frying pans (4*s*) and bellows to encourage the flames of the fire for just 2*s*.[4] If a family could afford them, other kitchen essentials came in the form of salt cellars and pepper pots, glass jars and earthenware vessels which would contain homemade preserves and condiments like jams and pickles. Dripping stands (which would collect the liquid fats that ran off freshly cooked meat), fish kettles (metal pots which were used solely to boil fish), jelly moulds and griddle irons may have also been found in the homes of working-class Victorians, as could biscuit tins, weighing scales and spice cannisters.

The Victorian kitchen resembled something much different to what we would recognize today. Instead of electrical refrigeration or gas stoves, the Victorians would have been accustomed to cold slabs of marble in butteries and larders to keep their produce fresh and coal-stoked ovens to cook their food. In the homes of the especially destitute, one of these ovens, or merely just a fireplace, might be all that constituted a 'kitchen' and would most likely be located in the same living areas where families communed, slept and bathed. In her memoirs of early Victorian society, C.S. Peel wrote that the poor would carry their wash ewers close to the coal ovens that simultaneously cooked their food, for it was the only source of heat within the entire dwelling.[5] Likewise, when Isabella Bird visited the slums of Edinburgh in 1869, she was alarmed to find that they were lacking entirely in water pipes and drainage systems, in sinks and water closets, and even in proper ventilation and receptacles to catch ash from the fire.[6] To have an oven in the Victorian period was to have a great responsibility. If fires were not properly maintained, cinders were not swept or smoke prevented from escaping through windows, dangers could arise. Not only could wayward sparks threaten to catch household items alight, but families in cramped rooms could suffer suffocation or carbon monoxide poisoning. Fires were dangerous, especially in close living quarters, hence why authors such as Isabella Beeton advocated for caution and sensibility when tending to them.

Another issue within the kitchens of the Victorian poor was cleanliness. Without adequate drainage, water-borne diseases such as cholera could thrive and threaten the health of the family and others who shared cramped tenement buildings. Additionally, without sophisticated refrigeration, rotting food and mouldering produce could cause a serious health risk to inhabitants. Not only would bacteria thus spread, but so too could vermin and insects be enticed into the home by the smell of decay. In an interview with a desperately poor pauper, Richard Rowe was repulsed to find the man chewing on the waste rind of a wheel of cheese. The cheese itself had been consumed and tossed away with the rest of the household waste, so that only the inedible rind remained. It was 'black with dirt', but the pauper seemed not to mind, treating it simply as 'a mere condiment' which only added additional flavour.[7]

It is unfair, however, to suggest that every poor Victorian dismissed food hygiene and safety. After all, these people were disgusted by dirt and rot, just as we are today, and understood that expired food (particularly dirt-coated cheese rinds) were greatly harmful to their health. Even in cases of extreme desperation, many a Victorian pauper would rather go without than consume food that had been slowly decomposing in open rubbish heaps or peppered with bacteria and disease. As such, it was imperative that kitchens should be kept as clean as they most possibly could.

Despite knowledge of germ theory still being in its infancy in the nineteenth century, the Victorians were nonetheless aware that raw meat and its juices could result in disastrous food poisoning if not properly cleaned, and that green mould spores could spread to other foodstuffs if not removed. To clean the kitchen was a task principally in the domain of the woman, though children were also frequently enlisted to help keep areas hygienic.[8] Despite household advice advocating the washing of dishes just twice a week, that is by no means evidence that the Victorians waived hygiene and cleanliness within the kitchen.[9] Most dishes and crockery in Victorian England were not washed, but scoured with emery sands or salt, and on a daily basis.[10] Copper and brass (materials typically used in the manufacture of cutlery, crockery and utensils such as saucepans in the nineteenth century) would be cleaned with 'rottenstone powder', a very fine abrasive that would be mixed with oil to make a paste-like solution.[11] Other types of metal such as pewter would be polished with a soft brush and plate powder, for example the non-mercurial type created by J. Goddard & Sons in Leicester throughout the nineteenth century and still sold today.[12] If the poor could not afford to purchase these powerful cleaning solutions, they could use rags soaked in methylated sprits or hartshorn, a gelatinous soapy substance produced from the antlers of a male deer, in order to loosen any baked-on food or stubborn staining.[13]

Until the introduction of the dish soap Fairy Liquid in 1898, which drastically improved the way Victorians washed their dishes, housewives could also rely on 'yellow' soap, commonly used on crockery for it left no unpleasant odour or lingering taste, unlike some of the other products used at the time.[14] Another favourite was Sapolia Scouring Soap, a paste which was sold in puck-shaped cakes and rubbed onto dishes with rags. Isabella Beeton encouraged the poor to simply submerge dishes and kitchen utensils in warm water after use, and to employ the use of a bristled brush or soaped-paper (cloth dipped in liquid soap and left to harden), which would dissolve any dried food.[15] Dishes would be shaken in the water, rather than wiped with a cloth or scrubbed with a sponge, and then rinsed in cold water and left to dry.[16]

The Victorians generally kept their eating and cooking areas well maintained and clean, as evidenced by contemporary sources which highlighted the importance of cleaning products and stressed high standards of sanitation. To maintain a clean kitchen was an impressive feat considering the general dilapidation of Victorian slum dwellings, particularly as its services would have been used at least three times throughout the day for the preparation of meals.

Meals

A typical day in Victorian Britain was dictated not by the number on the clockface, but by the times that people ate. As today, most working-class Victorians woke in the early morning, eating some form of a breakfast around 6.00 am or before work began at 8.00 am. For those members of society privileged enough to enjoy lie-ins every morning, breakfast would typically be served at around 9.00 or 10.00 am. This would be followed by lunch, or 'luncheon', at around midday, after which a mid-afternoon tea would be savoured before a final meal of dinner was enjoyed at around 7.00 or 8.00 pm.[1] Queen Victoria dined late in the evening; preferring dinners set at around 9.00 pm, while others, particularly those who had been hard at work all day, settled for evening suppers at 10.00 pm or just before they went to bed.[2] Snacks were occasional treats in the Victorian period, though frequent grazing was considered unbecoming in certain circles of society. For the poor, however, who were lucky to have even one meal a day, eating was not reserved for a specific time, but rather occurred whenever the opportunity arose and their stomachs grumbled.

Breakfast, as the name suggests, was the first meal of the day, intended to break the period of fasting throughout the night as people slept. Most commonly, breakfasts were served as cold dishes, with favourites being fresh fruits like strawberries, grapes and currants, as well as produce such as sliced cheese or collared meat and fish (which would be served still on the bone).[3] Other favourite breakfast dishes amongst the working class included cooked mackerel or kippers, pork sausage, bacon rashers, boiled eggs and toast served with either butter or jam.[4] The establishment of brands like Hovis in 1886, and Tiptree Jam even earlier in 1757, led to Britons firmly consolidating the humble slice of toast as a favourite breakfast delicacy.

For those preferring dishes with bite, cereals and other grain-based products were also marketed for consumption at breakfast time. Kellogg's introduced its famous Corn Flakes in 1895, enjoyed by many thousands of people across the country, while Quaker Oats sold inestimable amounts of porridge to customers from 1877 onwards. English muffins toasted upon an open fire, buttered crumpets and Jacob's Cream Crackers were also firm favourites of those who could afford them freshly baked, as was cold toasted bread served with a side of stewed eel.[5]

After breakfast had been savoured and a few hours of work carried out, thoughts turned to luncheon. Typically a small dish, lunch would either be eaten at home or in the workplace, and as such had to be both sustaining and portable. Favourite lunchtime dishes included much of what we would eat today, for example sandwiches filled with cheese and meats, as well as salads and hot pastries.[6] Sandwich fillings could be made more exciting with the inclusion of ingredients like mustard, pickled gherkins and even Marmite, which divided consumers at its launch in 1902 with its distinct malty taste. Other lunchtime treats included biscuits with cheese and stone fruit (such as plums), boiled, poached or fried eggs, and even sweet 'light pudding' that typically resembled steamed cakes.[7] If eating lunch at home, hot dishes of cauliflower cheese, stewed kidneys and omelettes slathered with cream cheese could be enjoyed for relatively little money.[8]

Luncheon would often be accompanied by sauces and condiments in some form, such as mayonnaise, salad dressing and even 'hot spice', the Victorian equivalent of modern-day hot sauce.[9] Other ways to elevate lunch came in the form of butter flavoured with chive or onion, or even sweetened with sugar, as well as vinegar and curry sauce, made popular by the influx of Indian immigrants who had settled in Britain and made their homes in the second half of Victoria's reign.[10] Ketchup was another favourite of Victorians, who either made their own using ripe tomatoes or mushrooms, or bought it pre-bottled from companies like Heinz, which was established in 1895.[11]

Condiments were cheap, versatile and offered flavours which not only elevated dishes but also served to disguise unpleasant flavours or signs of rot within the food. In cases of dire deprivation, when food was so scarce that people had to consume whatever they could find, rotting overripe fruits and mouldering stale bread were common sights. In an age before expiry dates, genetic-modification and modern refrigeration, food had a much shorter shelf life than it typically does today. As a result, many poor families bought food only when it was needed, so as not to generate unnecessary waste. 'Great care should be taken that nothing is thrown away, or suffered to be wasted in the kitchen,' wrote Mrs Beeton in her *Household Management*, who encouraged families to use up every possible scrap of food that they could. By offering recipes that used waste products as ingredients – such as bones, meat offcuts and softening fruits – Beeton helped revolutionize the way that families viewed leftovers. Vegetable peels and meat bones could be used to make a stock, she instructed, while fruit could be dried and eaten as confectionery or turned into preserves.[12] The poorest members of Victorian society certainly appeared to be the strongest advocates against food waste, and were aghast at the amount of surplus refuse generated by the wealthy on a daily basis. 'They'll throw away what a poor man would think a Lord Mayor's feast,' mourned one hungry pauper living exposed on a London street.[13]

However, if one sought to preserve the food that was bought, intending it to last for future meals, Beeton advised that 'much waste is always prevented by keeping every article in the place best suited to it[14]. For example, vegetables should be kept on cold stone floors, and meat in cool dry places like pantries or larders and wrapped in paper to stave off vermin.[15] Cool dry places were also suggested for salt, sugar, spices and even candles, with edible seeds, rice, grains and flour kept in closed tins to ward off weevils or 'destroyers' that would otherwise ravage them.[16] Meat should be hung to prevent spoiling, but 'as soon, therefore, as the slightest trace of putrescence is detected […] it should be dressed immediately' and eaten.[17] In warmer months, when larders (or single-roomed dwellings) were more difficult to keep cool, and meat kept fresh, Beeton instructed that 'it should, therefore, be well examined when it comes, and if flies have touched it, the part must be cut off, and the remainder well washed' and consumed. It appeared that even in the case of putrescence, Beeton stayed firm in her belief that absolutely nothing should ever go to waste.

The thought of consuming days-old, unrefrigerated meat would turn the stomach of modern consumers, but for many impoverished Victorians it was the only option they had if they wished to eat meat at all. 'Broxy' cuts of meat were sold cheaply due to disease within the animal when it had been slaughtered, and were particularly popular with the poor who could afford little else. By eating broxy meat, the poor were exposing themselves to diseases like tuberculosis and ringworm that particularly affected animals such as sheep and cows. To disguise the taste of this meat, the poor would be encouraged to mince, broil or pickle it, or turn it into sausage or a patty. Favourite recipes using broxy meat included marinaded broiled animal's heart and minced liver.[19] Pickled tongue in vinegar, stuffed offal, and animal brains mixed with suet were other ways to utilize the disease-riddled meat.[20]

If broxy meat was a stretch too far for desperate Victorians, they could instead settle for cheap cuts of meat that would otherwise be thrown away after butchery. These cuts included the neck, clod (shoulder), 'sticking pieces' (fatty nuggets of meat), bones, offal, blood and marrow of larger animals like pigs, cows and sheep. Poultry was also relatively cheap, meaning birds such as chicken, duck, pigeon and even goose were eaten regularly within the slums. Favourite meat dishes that could be made from cheap offcuts included black pudding, cooked discs of congealed animal blood that would most often be eaten cold, or broiled bones slathered in butter and cracked open to reveal the pinkish-white marrow within.[21] Meat was also boiled to such softness that it could be spread upon bread, and there was the slow stewing of animal ribs and the frying of giblets and other innards.[22] Kidneys could be bought for just 1*d* each, and were economical options for those craving meat.[23] Tripe, the digestive tracts of large animals like cattle, was equally economical, sold for just 7*d* per pound, which was a trifling price for such a large, generous quantity.[24] Even whole sheep's heads were available for just 8*d* each, and would be stewed over successive days and carved in such a way that every last morsel of available meat would be eaten.[25]

Cheap cuts of meat were not the only option of protein available to poor, hungry Victorians. Fish was another way in which people could fill their bellies for a small price, with haddock, herring, mackerel and sardines being the most popular amongst the poor. For just 1*d* per pound, a pauper could purchase sprats (small herring-like fish) or even four fresh oysters, which were considered to be the food of the lowly in nineteenth-century society.[26] Cod would be gutted and deboned and turned into pie, while flounder was typically cut into thin fillets. Cod's liver in particular was bought for its benefits to health, where it would be steamed and served in a gloopy mixture of milky tapioca.[27] Another favourite fish of the Victorian poor were eels, which were particularly sold along the banks of the River Thames, where they were caught on a daily basis. Boiled eels cost just 6*d* per pound, or they could be tossed in a butter sauce or with vinegar for a penny more.[28] They could also be dried and eaten as crunchy snacks, or jellied in aspic (a savoury gelatine), which earned them the reputation of being a traditional Cockney (a term for an East Londoner) dish.[29]

Other affordable dinner dishes included mashed, fried or jacketed potatoes, sweet corn cobs slathered in butter, and baked beans.[30] Fried mushrooms, boiled beetroot and stewed cucumbers were also popular side dishes eaten by poor Victorians at dinnertime.[31] So too was savoury vegetable aspic pudding, typically made to celebrate occasions. In a mould, boiled cabbage, sprouts, carrots, turnips, beetroot, parsnips, potatoes, leek, celery and onions would be layered, followed by a sprinkling of peas and white sugar to 'improve flavour'.[32] A salty liquid made from melted beef gelatine, as well as vegetable broth, would then be poured over the top and left to set until it could be turned out to resemble a rather impressive (though thoroughly unappetizing) dome.

Broths were popular dishes amongst the dwellers of Victorian slums, as they were cheap and simple to make and required very few ingredients. One vegetable broth recipe cost just a penny to make, and required only the scraps of root vegetables like carrot, turnip and parsnip.[33] Potato 'broth' was a watery dish of potatoes simmered until they were soft enough to mash, and was particularly popular with mothers, who fed it to their teething infants.[34] Bread broth, which cost just 4*d* per quart, was made by stewing loaves of bread in salted water.[35] Not every broth was thin and watery; some Victorians made soups thickened with meats and ingredients like rice and oats.[36] 'Meagre Soup', made from milk, salt, pepper, peas and flour, was a rather glutinous but surprisingly filling option, as was 'Clear Soup', which was made from veal knuckle, bacon and onion.[37] The latter soup in particular was designed to last in the larders of Victorians for long durations, with the creator of the recipe, Alexis Soyer, claiming that it could 'last for years' if kept correctly jarred.[38] Perhaps the most infamous of Victorian broths and soup-like dishes came in the form of a gloopy porridge made popular by Charles Dickens in his *Oliver Twist.* In the famous and beloved scene, young Oliver holds aloft an empty bowl as he quietly but confidently declares: 'Please Sir, I want some more.'[39] This dish was gruel.

Gruel, a staple meal in the Victorian slums, was regularly served in institutions like hospitals, schools and workhouses because it was incredibly cheap to make. Not particularly nutritious, gruel could be made either sweet or savoury, thick or thinned with liquids such as milk or salty broth. It did, however, keep rumbling stomachs full for relatively long durations of time, no doubt because it was calorie-dense and awfully stodgy, as the recipe below suggests.

A Recipe for Gruel
from *A Shilling Cookery for the People*
by Alexis Soyer[40]

Ingredients
1 Cup of oats or cornmeal
1 Cup of milk
1 Cup of water

Method
Pour the water and milk into a pot. Add your oats, and bring to the boil or leave to stew until thick.

For a savoury gruel, season with salt; for sweet, season with sugar, lemon juice or cinnamon.

Not every dish in the nineteenth century was as unappetizing as gruel or jellied broxy meat. Some cheap but delightful recipes were beloved by Victorians, as they still are today. Griddled chicken and beef patties served between bread with ketchup was one particular favourite, serving the purpose of using up any scraps of leftover meat.[41] Fragrant chicken curries served with rice, boiled meat sausages accompanied by sweet grilled onions, and even macaroni served in a thick cheese sauce were just among others.[42] Pasta, a foodstuff which seems so modern, was described as being 'plentiful and cheap', at just 5*d* per pound, making it a staple on the shelves of Victorians just as it is in our kitchens today.[43]

Sweet dishes were equally enjoyed by Victorians regardless of their wealth. Sugary biscuits and fluffy sponge cakes were frequently purchased from market stalls for mere pennies, and were enjoyed at home alongside hot cups of tea or coffee. Many cakes were made not from flour but from rice, or had fruit components.[44] Indeed, fruit was enjoyed in many ways in the nineteenth century, whether it be fresh, dried, candied or in jam form. The most common and popular fruits in the Victorian slums were stone-types like cherries, peaches and plums, as well as numerous varieties of apples, which kept juicy and fresh for long periods without needing to be kept cool or dry. After the 1840s, an influx of 'foreign' fruits hit the British market, with grapes, pineapples and citruses such as limes and grapefruit available from grocer's shops and accessible for the first time to poor consumers.[45] These fruits in particular could be made into syrups and used to flavour shaved ice, frozen cream or chilled rice puddings, which were especially popular during the summer.[46] If a poor Victorian could not afford to purchase these exotic foodstuffs, they could use their ingenuity to turn traditionally savoury ingredients into their own sweet treats. Omelettes, for example, could be made with sugar and currants or other dried fruits, while potatoes formed the basis of 'Potato Pudding'.[47] The latter dish consisted of mashed potatoes sweetened with sugar, lemon juice and milk, and baked until it formed a golden crust.[48]

Desserts were particularly popular with Victorians who hosted friends and family during festive periods. Even the poorest members of society celebrated special occasions through food, with contemporaries writing that Britons were so fond of dinner and eating, that 'if London were to be destroyed by an earthquake, the Londoners would meet at a public dinner to consider the subject'.[49] Hosting a dinner party in some form or another was a favourite way to catch up with family and friends in the nineteenth century, even if household funds were stretched or entirely lacking. A particularly impressive treat to serve at such a dinner party was the Victoria sponge cake, oozing with fresh cream and strawberry preserve sandwiched between two simple sponges. Victoria sponges could be purchased relatively cheaply from bakeries or market vendors, and numerous recipes exist from the period for Victorians to make their own at home. Contrary to popular belief, and despite its name, the Victoria sponge was not invented for Queen Victoria, but rather is believed to date from the fifteenth century. It is thought to have received its name due to the fact that it was a particular favourite of the portly queen, who insisted that it be served at her daily afternoon teas. Ever since, the Victoria sponge has been associated with the Royal Family, solidifying it as one of the most ubiquitously British of dishes.

Other sweet confectionery like bars of chocolate, sugary pastilles and boiled lozenges were available to be bought from market stalls and dedicated sweetshops that sold their eye-catching treats in large glass jars. Prior to the nineteenth century, many chocolatiers in Europe had exported their bars of silky, creamy chocolate into the country for a high price, making it a treat that only the wealthier classes could afford. However, with the establishment of Cadbury's in 1824 at Bournville, near Birmingham, the world of chocolate was revolutionized. Even the poorest of Victorians could now afford penny bars of the rich delicacy, which quickly took new forms, flavours and shapes as it rose in popularity, and was even sold in sharable boxes.

The establishment of Maynard Bassett's in 1842, Rowntree's in 1862 and Halls in 1893 also helped change the way candy was produced and sold in Britain. Until the construction of their factories – which led to the mass production of sweet treats like soft gummies, liquorice twists and boiled candy – sweets were typically made on a much smaller scale by individual vendors. This was a business where standards and regulations were not enforced, however, and authorities could not govern or review the ingredients that went into these candy products. It was a problem that would have dire consequences. On 13 November 1858, the *Dover Telegraph* reported on a tragic incident involving a 7-year-old girl, Elizabeth Mary Midgley, who came from a working-class background. Earlier in the day, Elizabeth's grandmother had bought her 2 ounces of sweet lozenges from a stall at Bradford Greenmarket in Yorkshire, before taking them home for the family to enjoy. Later, Elizabeth's siblings, parents and extended family all complained of mysterious stomach pains and shallow breathing, though by evening they had all appeared to make a full recovery. Little Elizabeth, however, was not so fortunate. She died that night, having consumed just two of the lozenges bought from the market. When an investigation into her death was conducted, it was found that instead of plaster of Paris (an already unsafe ingredient to ingest) used to bind the candy, powdered arsenic had been used instead. Had the inclusion of the powdered poison been a genuine accident, or had the confectioner who sold the lozenges intended to commit crimes that day? Whatever the case, fifteen other members of the public would later die from ingesting the lozenges, among them men, women and children alike.[50]

Children were the target for much of the marketed food in the nineteenth century, just as they are today. From sweets and chocolate to individual hand pies and delightful-shaped gingerbread pieces, vendors were aware that catching the eye of children would pressure parents into parting ways with their money. During the summer months, iced milk would be sold to children unwillingly dragged through busy markets by their parents, while warming beef tea and sweet jellies were reserved for winter months.[51] Drinks made of fizzy soda water and raspberry cordial were also sold primarily to children, as well as sugar-dusted fried dough (similar to funnel cakes or doughnuts), and even sausage rolls (sausages wrapped in buttery pastry).[52] The very youngest of society were catered for too, their diets typically consisting of soft foods that were easy to digest and swallow without requiring the use of teeth.[53] Victorian babies were typically fed milk either from the breasts of their mothers or deriving from animals, with cow, goat and even donkey milk sold at market. Weaning infants would be given mashed vegetables or unsweetened porridge, and some parenting manuals from the time even encouraged parents to give teething babies fatty bits of meat to chew and suck on.[54]

It was not just infants who found themselves requiring soft foods. The diets of the elderly, the infirm and the sick were surprisingly well provided for, even amongst the poorest echelons of society. In cases of sickness, plain foods like dry toast or soda crackers would be given in the hope of alleviating nausea, while a glass of raspberry-infused vinegar was given to those struggling to overcome the symptoms of influenza and the common cold.[55] For a more substantial meal, Isabella Beeton recommended giving the sick soft meats such as boiled chicken, rabbit and calf's feet, as well as flaky fish and light, unsweetened puddings made from rice.[56] 'Toast Sandwiches', which were quite literally two slices of bread filled with a slice of dry toast, would also be given to invalids, as would a drink of 'Toast and Water', which was made by leaving a slice of bread to dissolve in a cup of warm water throughout the day.[57]

Hospital food was not the most appetizing. Typical meals in medical facilities like psychiatric hospitals or on contagious wards were bland and unnourishing, and certainly did not benefit the patients, who had little choice but to eat them. Despite contemporaries stressing the importance of a healthy, balanced diet, and writing that 'to have a good brain the stomach must be cared for', hospital food did not reflect the same values.[58] In her groundbreaking investigative report *Ten Days in a Madhouse*, journalist Nellie Bly was sickened to record the provisions made for patients, all of which she was forced to consume first-hand. For one meal, Bly reported that the female patients of Blackwell's Insane Asylum were given a slice of cold, unrecognizable fatty boiled meat and a single potato, which was also stone cold, as well as wedge of thick, unbuttered bread that was 'nothing more than dried dough'.[59] Other meals consisted of watery beef or chicken broth, as well as plain beans, soda crackers and stodgy gruel. Occasional treats came in the form of a glass of milk, exactly five prunes or oatmeal with syrup, though this certainly was not the norm of daily routines. During Bly's undercover stay at the asylum, she reported that the tea was always pink and tasted 'like copper', that the boiled beef was spoiled and green, and that even her slice of bread at breakfast had been baked with a spider within it.[60] To be a patient in a hospital in the nineteenth century was to effectively wave goodbye to nutrition and to flavour, and instead endure unpalatable meals that barely passed as edible food.

Even the furriest of family members were catered for in the Victorian period, regardless of the social class from which that family came. Pets were kept and loved in the nineteenth century just as they are now, with dogs and cats being particularly favoured by the poorer classes. Elizabeth Prater, an eyewitness interviewed in the aftermath of the murder of Mary Jane Kelly in 1888, told policemen that she had been kept awake that night due to her young kitten Diddles climbing across her as she slept.[61] It was not uncommon for poor families in particular to take in or care for the stray animals which roamed the city streets, their hearts touched by the animals' poor plight. The establishment of Battersea Dog's Home (a charity that now provides also for the care of felines) in 1871 led to the rehoming of otherwise abandoned or unloved dogs. Some poor families also kept birds, rabbits or even typical farmyard animals like chickens within their households, though these cases tended to appear more within the upper classes of society.

Although there was a dedicated pet section at the luxury department store Harrods as early as the nineteenth century, it was unlikely that the dwellers of the slums would ever set foot across its threshold.[62] In order to purchase food and treats for their pets, the poor turned to butchers to purchase offcuts of meat or whatever else could be found. Animals would be fed the discarded ends of vegetables such as carrots or the bony remains of boiled fish, for example. Some animals even sustained themselves on a diet of vermin, such as mice and rats, and as such were particularly useful to keep within the home to free it from any infestations.

If, however, a pet owner wished to purchase food produced with the healthy diet of their beloved four-legged friend in mind, they could purchase tins or boxes of food marketed specifically toward animals. Typically, this food would be made up of meat offcuts that even the poorest of humans would not eat, such as animal eyes, bones, trotters or other viscera. Sometimes even the pelts, hides and skins of butchered animals made up this concoction. Market stalls catering for animal care would sell this food amongst other items marketed toward pets, such as beds, collars, leads and toys, including rubber balls. A Mrs Hardman and her 16-year-old son even sold 'cat meat' (food *for* cats, not made *from* cats) and other pet ephemera from the window of her shared tenement house to customers walking past.[63]

Pet care was taken very seriously in the nineteenth century, where even their drinking water was expected to be of the utmost quality to be beneficial to the animal's health. This water should never be cold, nor hard, and especially not stagnant or muddy, which could be 'positively injurious' to the animal, wrote Isabella Beeton.[64] She continued by encouraging pet owners to make regular trips to running streams and rivers, for this type of water was deemed to be the best for animals to consume.[65]

That their pets deserved the best of lives was a belief adopted by people then just as it is now. The extent that Victorian pet owners went in ensuring that their animals were well provided for highlights just how much they treasured and loved these additional members of their families, even going so far as perhaps offering them a better diet than they had themselves.

Beverages

As well as food, the Victorians understood the importance of hydration. Contrary to popular belief, water was one of the most popular drinks in the nineteenth century and could be gathered fresh from running taps, pumps or deep wells. Water was recognized as being vital to the human body and its function, with scientists writing that 'water is the only liquid which is necessary to the formation, development and support of [the human] frame'.[1] Indeed, the gathering of water was an activity that many a pauper was accustomed to carrying out daily, for unlike the houses of the wealthier members of society, who had running water taps installed within their homes; no such convenience was available to the poor. In her *Notes on Old Edinburgh*, Isabella Bird observed that 'children carrying buckets nearly as big as themselves are sometimes known to wait from one to five hours for the water which is to wash the faces, cook the food, and quench the thirst of the family'.[2] It was not uncommon, she continued, to see paupers standing in long lines to gather water from 6.00 am all the way through to midnight.[3] It was no wonder that the gathering of water could sometimes take the entirety of the day, particularly when whole rows of houses required the precious substance for purposes such as drinking, cooking, cleaning and bathing. As such, the gathering of water from communal water butts, taps, pumps or wells was a job frequently given to children too young to otherwise work for a living, so they could keep a space in long queues while their parents were away at work. It was little wonder that the overflowing heavy buckets dragged behind the skinny frames of slum children would be almost empty from spillage by the time they reached their destination.[4]

Although it was written that 'water is unquestionably the natural drink of adults, and meets the wants of the body more perfectly than any of the artificial liquids [like beer]', other drinks were available to all members of the Victorian social strata.[5] These 'artificial liquids' were treats that even the poorest could afford, and would be sold either from market stalls or vendors, or as mixtures taken back home for consumers to dilute in their own kitchens. One such example was Eiffel Tower Lemonade, which claimed to be made in France from Italian lemons, but actually originated in Maidstone, Kent. The extract from the lemons would be sold in concentrated pouches for buyers to mix into water at home. Drinkers could add sugar to the concoction if they so wished, in order to sweeten the taste of the otherwise intensely bitter and sour drink. The manufacturer even issued an assurance that, despite the bitter taste, it was 'a lemonade as refreshing, as pleasant to the most critical taste, and as harmless as it is possible to obtain'.[6] For those who soured at the thought of drinking straight citrus juice, their tastes were quickly changed when brands such as Schweppes in 1783 and R. Whites in 1845 began marketing ready-made sweetened glass bottles of still and sparkling lemonade that were far more palatable.

Lemonade was not the only drink sold in glass bottles and produced on a rapidly increasing scale. Established in 1892, one of the world's most enduring soft drink brands, Coca-Cola, quickly established itself as a firm favourite of drinkers all across the globe. Between the impressively long period of 1856–1959, Coca-Cola cost just 5 cents per bottle in the United States, and was sold for just mere pennies in the United Kingdom.[7] Marketed as 'brain tonic' and the 'intellectual's beverage', Coca-Cola was made from coca leaves, which produced small amounts of cocaine when distilled (approximately 9 milligrams per glass).[8] This miniscule figure, however, was enough to get Victorians hooked. Vendors were swamped with buyers seeking their daily fix, which sky-rocketed sales of the drink and led to a boom in its production. So too did promises that Coca-Cola served as a remedy for anything from headache to hysteria and melancholy, so much so that it was even recommended as a genuine treatment by doctors of the time.[9] This apparent miracle drink, however, raised concern in 1903 when drinkers found themselves worryingly shaking, twitching and intensely craving the drink if they had not had a sip of it for a period of time. When it was discovered that the drink was causing narcotic effects in consumers, manufacturers tweaked the recipe by including less coca leaf and replacing it with caffeine.[10] It was not until 1929, however, that the ingredient of cocaine was fully removed from the sugary soft drink.[11]

Another drink with addictive tendencies that was available to the Victorians was coffee, which lured consumers in with rich smells and promises of energy. Coffee was one of the principal drinks of the Victorian slums, being widely available to the people who lived in them. Like soft drinks, coffee could either be purchased ready-made and boiling from street vendors or dedicated coffee stalls and shops, or in bundles of ground or whole beans. Coffee available to take away in disposable cups was not something yet available to the Victorians; instead, it was common particularly in residential and communal areas for people to drink coffee in teacups provided by beverage carts as they conversed in parks, on benches or on garden walls with neighbours and friends. Coffee was drank only in the morning, after lunch, or during early evening dinner, but never at night, or else consumers would experience so-called 'murder sleep' due to the effects of the caffeine.[12]

The process of making a cup of coffee was not as instantaneous as it is today. Instead of granules being boiled, whole coffee beans would be roasted, then ground and left to soak in warm water for fifteen minutes. Once that time had elapsed, boiling water would be poured on top, along with milk or cream to lessen its bitterness.[13] Drinkers may also have added additional ingredients like sugar or cinnamon to disguise the strong taste; after all, it was recommended that coffee be made from a heaped dessertspoon of grounds per cup, a frankly enormous amount.[14] Such a large quantity of ground coffee per cup made it a drink too expensive for recurrent daily consumption by the poor, who substituted beans with roots from the chicory plant. To make coffee in this way was cheaper, non-caffeinated and much thicker than using beans; however, it also reportedly tasted unpleasantly like 'boiled crusts' of bread.[15]

For a sweeter treat, Victorians could enjoy cups of drinking chocolate, of which two distinct versions existed. The first, hot chocolate, more resembled what we would recognize today, and was made from melted bars of chocolate and steamed milk. It was a favourite of Victorians perusing winter market stalls and was the preferred hot drink of children. It was far more palatable than its alternative, hot cocoa, which had not the sweetness nor the viscosity of hot chocolate, and was far more bitter. Instead of using actual processed chocolate as an ingredient, hot cocoa was typically made from the cocoa bean itself, which would be roasted and sweetened with brown sugar. Hot cocoa was a cheaper alternative than the luxuriously thick treat of hot chocolate, and was therefore more typically drank within the Victorian slums.

Perhaps the favourite beverage of the Victorian era was the same drink enjoyed by millions on a daily basis in today's society. This beverage, which has endured in the hearts of Britons for centuries, became especially popular during the Stuart and Georgian period, and enjoyed further popularity under Victoria when she became Empress of India in 1876. This steaming drink, made by boiling fragrant leaves, has remained a constant of kitchens ever since: the humble cup of tea.

Tea was sold in Victorian Britain not in bags or pouches as it is today, but in its loose leaf form. Tea leaves were typically imported from countries such as India, Ceylon (modern-day Sri Lanka) and China, and made up a significant portion of perishable trade in the nineteenth century. It was a foodstuff that became its own commodity, and almost everyone – regardless of wealth or social standing – could enjoy a boiling cup from the comfort of their own home. This accessibility was furthered with the establishment of dedicated tea brands like Twining's in 1706, Tetley in 1837 and Lipton in 1880, which made the purchase of sacks, boxes and tins of tea leaves convenient and cheap. 'There is very little art in making good tea,' wrote Isabella Beeton. 'If the water is boiling, and there is no sparing of the fragrant leaf, the beverage will almost invariably be good.'[16] To make a cup of 'bumping' tea, Victorians were instructed to use a teaspoonful of leaves per person and leave it to steep in a metal kettle or porcelain teapot.[17] By using a metal or porcelain pot to brew the tea rather than an earthenware one, it was believed to taste considerably better and less like clay.[18] However, for many poorer members of society who could not afford such sophisticated means to boil their tea, they had to make do with cheaply produced pottery or metals that were prone to rusting, thus tingeing the liquid pink and skimming it with 'fur'.[19]

There exists much evidence to suggest that the poor were great lovers of tea. Though often associated with delicate afternoon teas and refined soirées of the Victorian era, even paupers were known to be fond of the fragrant beverage, which came in many forms. As well as breakfast tea, manufacturers began offering blends of Earl Grey (which was flavoured with the aromatic rind of bergamot), as well as sage, chamomile, ground ivy, hawthorn, sloe and blackcurrant variants. The Victorians even drank green tea, though it gained a reputation for being 'drunk by hypochondriacs' who wished to reap its health benefits.[20] Having a bracing cup of tea was a favourite treat at all levels of Victorian society, and even the poorest enjoyed the notion of engaging in 'afternoon tea'. Unlike the high teas enjoyed by wealthier families in the nineteenth century, where small morsels of pastries and baked goods were enjoyed during the period between lunch and dinner, the afternoon tea of a pauper (which consisted solely of a steaming cup and possibly a small treat like a biscuit or sandwich) was intended to bolster their energy and boost their stamina for the afternoon.[21] It was true, wrote a household manual of the time, that; 'a cup of tea is an excellent thing after any fatigue'.[22]

That tea was such a commodity in the nineteenth century is highlighted by the fact that the deprived and needy would carry their teapots, cups and leaves with them at all times, for it was often the only luxury which they owned.[23] Indeed, when her body was inspected following her murder in 1888, Catherine Eddowes was found to have been carrying with her tea, sugar and a stirring spoon.[24] There was even a black-market of sorts for the selling of tea in the nineteenth century, where so-called 'tea leafers' or 'recyclers' would take the already-used leaves of their colleagues or employers, dry them and then resell them to the needy.[25] Clearly, a cup of tea was a greatly valued thing in Victorian British society.

As well as tea, one of the most popular drinks amongst the adult population of the Victorian slums was alcohol. Although it is typically believed that children would be given small cups of this fermented beverage due to the dangers of drinking water, there is very little evidence to suggest that this was the norm. While there are certainly references to children enjoying half-pints of watered-down beer or 'small' ale, these sources tend to be outliers. Indeed, in cases where they do crop up, contemporaries scorn the parents or guardians who allowed their children to sample alcoholic drinks. Social journalist Henry Mayhew disdainfully commented on a 'regularly drunk ten-year-old' who would frequent cheap lodging houses, and it was recognized that providing children with alcohol was wholly illegal and certainly not beneficial to the child whatsoever.[26] Children under the age of 11 could not consume or sell alcohol, or even be within any premises that was licensed to sell 'intoxicating liquors', and any adult found to purchase alcohol on a child's behalf was heavily fined.[27]

Alcohol was an adult's drink. It was sold in a variety of ways in the nineteenth century, from whisky and wine to port, ale and brandy. A cup of alcohol was surprisingly cheap in Victorian Britain, principally due to many public house owners fermenting, brewing and distilling their own products rather than relying on expensive foreign imports. Beer cost just 3*d* per pint, and whisky just a penny more, a shockingly low price for something 'which makes life brighter for an hour'.[28] It was no wonder then that many adults in the Victorian slums relied upon alcohol to numb their senses and while away hours spent in dilapidated, inhabitable homes. Drunkenness and anti-social behaviour was a significant issue for Victorian law courts, which found their holding cells packed with intoxicated revellers on a daily basis. Despite their best efforts, there was very little that the police or local jurisdictions could do to govern drunkenness within the streets; after all, it was recognized even by contemporaries that 'limited water and unlimited whiskey, crowded dens and unwholesome air; we need nothing more to make a city full of drunkards'.[29] In an attempt to push the poor away from relying on a liquid diet of alcohol, efforts were put in place to encourage healthier eating and drinking, endorsed by scientists and doctors who assured that a balanced diet was more beneficial to the health than any other possible thing.

Diet

Advertisements and articles written in the newspapers of the time advocated for healthy eating, targeting not only the rich but the poor as well. Endorsed by doctors, celebrities and even the Royal Family, a lifestyle of measured eating and drinking was hoped to attract people desperate to better their health and wellbeing. A regular routine of exercise and fresh air was said to be so beneficial to one's health that it gave a countenance as if the 'veins were full of wine'.[1] Not only would you *feel* better for adopting this lifestyle change, but you would also *look* better. People, particularly young women, were encouraged to avoid a diet of frequent hot coffee and buttered bread, as well as greasy foods and alcohol, or else risk weight gain and yellowing, jaundiced skin.[2]

The vast majority of the poorest of Victorian citizens need not have worried about being overweight. Their typical meagre diets were so insufficient and lacking in calories and nutrition that their bodies had barely any fat upon them whatsoever. However, in cases where the destitute were self-conscious of their thickening waist lines, they could turn to fashionable fad diets which cycled through periods of popularity. One fad, which came from France, instructed people to drink a small glass of straight vinegar on an empty stomach each morning.[3] If that failed to work, a diet of other fermented or bitter liquids could be employed, such as lemon juice 'and other acids'.[4] Fad diets ranged from the harmless, if not slightly eccentric, to the downright dangerous. One health handbook from the nineteenth century encouraged people wishing to lose weight to create their own emetics and laxatives by mixing a drachm of Epsom salts within warm water.[5] It would be drunk at least four times a day, and was greatly harmful to one's health due to the effects of vomiting and diarrhoea it would produce.

If consuming liquids aimed at stimulating weight loss was not preferred, one could turn to even more drastic means. Believed to be popular mainly with the wealthier classes of the nineteenth century, it is wholly plausible to imagine that poorer people too became influenced by the consumption of cocaine, a stimulant known to result in excitability and constant movement. Cocaine could be purchased for relatively little money from chemists at the time – or even in liquid forms, like in Coca-Cola – and at the time had not been recognized as an addictive substance that we know it as today. By taking cocaine, muscles barely relaxed and users suffered constant unsettledness. It did work to some extent in removing excess body weight, but it also led to far greater problems such as addiction and serious withdrawal symptoms.

Yet another solution to dieting and losing weight came in the form of a disgusting treatment whereby people would swallow tiny capsules of tapeworm eggs. Once swallowed, these eggs would hatch within the digestive tract and grow to full size, causing discomfort and stomach complaints in people who chose this method of extreme weight loss. These tapeworms would absorb whatever food the person had ingested, depriving their human host of incredibly important calories and nutrients. Once the desired weight had been achieved, or the individual could no longer stand the squirming within their bellies, a drug sold from chemist shops could be swallowed to kill the worm, which would then be passed out of the body in stools. Other methods of removing the tapeworm came rather ineffectively in the form of a 'poultice of bread', which was believed to draw out the ravenous worm from beneath the skin. It was a method endorsed by Francis Pears of the Pears soap empire, who also stressed that a mixture of warm, sudsy water washed over the skin would be enough to kill the worm from within.[6]

One emerging diet trend in the nineteenth century was vegetarianism, which was particularly popular with 'intellectuals, Indian immigrants [and] radicals'.[7] It also became the chosen diet choice of hypochondriacs, who believed that a fruit and vegetable-based diet would stave off typhoid and other infectious diseases. Newspapers and magazines even advertised the health benefits of living as a vegetarian, with one declaring in 1858 that 'no vegetarian in this country has ever been attacked with cholera'.[8]

A vegetarian lifestyle was favoured amongst many of the Victorian poor, who could better afford organic grown produce than meat and fish. For this reason, vegetarianism earned a label as a poor-man's diet, with dishes being compared to food served in prisons, workhouses and hospitals.[9] It was believed by some stubborn contemporaries that a vegetarian diet did not provide consumers with the same strength, virility and stamina as omnivores, and that they would be prone to fevers, colds and chills.[10] It probably did not help that contemporaries referred to vegetables and fruit as 'safe only when used as an accompaniment to other food', and that they did not 'constitute a full meal at any time'.[11]

Despite this, records exist of cheap vegetarian-based dishes that the poorest members of Victorian society undoubtedly ate, as well as establishments dedicated to dining on meals made without meat or animal products. London in particular became a hotspot for solely vegetarian restaurants, which served savoury pies, bread and parsley fritters, shaped rice, blancmange and cheesecake.[12] The movement was particularly motivated by those choosing to adopt a healthier lifestyle or wishing to spend less on their weekly grocery shop. Some were motivated by religious and moral beliefs, with members of society opposing terrible farmyard conditions, forced breeding and the butchery and slaughter of animals in abattoirs.[13] Some Victorians, who we would perhaps now identify as 'vegans', opposed entirely any by-product of animal derivation, avoiding the wearing of furs, the consumption of such things as honey and butter, and even going as far as to campaign against butcher's shops which hung meat on hooks outside their doors by damaging the products.[14] The movement reached such a head that in September 1847, Victorian vegetarians established their own

Vegetarian Society, which aimed to convert as many meat-eaters as possible to their cause.

The vegetarians of the nineteenth century found that their efforts were far more challenging than initially expected, however. As today, many in Victorian times opposed the thought of a purely herbivore diet, and took to writing scathing reports of the activities of vegetarian social clubs in newspapers and magazines.[15] On 30 September 1848, satirical magazine *Punch* wrote that one such society 'devote[s] its entire energies to the eating of vegetables, and the members meet occasionally for the purpose of masticating mashed potatoes and munching cabbage leaves'.[16] Even George Orwell wrote that vegetarians had a tendency to enjoy nudism and sexual immorality, and wore open-toed sandals while they gathered to drink fruit juice.[17] On the whole, the vast majority of Victorian society, including its poorest members, preferred an omnivorous diet, consuming both vegetables and meat no matter what the cost.

Purchasing Food

The cost of living in the nineteenth century varied throughout Victoria's reign, with periods of financial inflation affecting the prices of food, drink and other consumables. Household budgets in Victorian Britain had not only to factor in weekly groceries, but also such things as candles, coal and oil, as well as medicine and healthcare.[1] Victorian families also had to account for clothing provisions and the education of their children, which for many was not without cost. Utilities and rent, taxes and insurance also cost money, leaving families with very little leftover cash to spend on even the most basic of necessities. One magazine from 1901 observed that the cost of living far greater affected the poorer members of society than the wealthier and middle classes, who could afford to spend their disposable income and need not worry about budgeting or saving their hard-earned wages.[2]

In the nineteenth century, a typical grocery list for the poor included only the most basic of necessities, and certainly did not stretch to include any treats unless a family had been particularly lucky in acquiring their wages that week. The *Cornhill Magazine* listed a typical grocery list to last an average-sized family for a week until new provisions could be bought at market. It included a pound of sugar sold in a loaf for 2*d*, eight eggs for 6*d* and a pound of bacon for 8*d*.[3] Also considered necessities was half a pound of butter and half a pound of cheese, coming to 6*d* and 3*d* respectively.[4] If a family could afford it, perhaps they could also stretch their budgets to include cuts of meat such as pork loin for 4*d*, oxtail for 2*d* and a pound of beef for 6*d*.[5] A quarter pound of loose-leaf tea came to 4*d*, a bagful of peas 3*d* and a pound of apples just 1*d*.[6]

Contemporary social observer Arthur Sherwell also drew up an example grocery list kept by paupers of the Victorian slums, which included things like oil for 3*d*, milk for 5*d* and soap for 1*s*.[7] Without stable work to bring in a regular income, however, the poorest members of society could only hope to purchase such vital foodstuffs and provisions. It was not uncommon for people to sell the 'door-knobs and fittings to raise pennies for food', for example.[8] Some paupers even sold metal and wood scraps found upon the street to raise enough money to buy even the most basic of meals.[9]

In an age before trading regulations and grocery chain stores, however, the lowest class of Victorian Britain could take advantage of the widely varying prices of products that differed from vendor to vendor. For example, paupers would typically be the first customers of the day of street vendors, who sold their stale food leftover from trading the previous day for fractionally less than if it had been sold fresh. Some engaged in trades, offering items such as cloth or candles in exchange for bread and cheese. Some poor Victorians even relied on foraged foods to supplement their diet, with herbs, roots and berries particularly popular.[10] It was not until the establishment of chains of grocery shops across Britain – such as The Co-op in 1844, Sainsbury's in 1869 and Marks & Spencer's in 1884 – that there was any standardization and fixing of food prices across the country.

As well as being open to offers of trade and haggling, Victorian market stalls also had the advantage of selling homecooked, fresh fast food, whereas grocers did not. Hot or cold jellied eels, fried fish and pickled whelks were all popular along the banks of the Thames, as were roasted sheep's trotters, bowls of steaming buttered green peas and simple ham sandwiches.[11] 'Penny pies', meat puddings small enough to fit in the palm of a hand and baked potatoes were other savoury dishes on offer.[12] At Leadenhall Market, boiled rabbit was a favourite.[13] Sweet options included muffins and cakes, sticky sweet buns, chocolates, sweets and cough drops.[14] Some foods could even be delivered to the home, from fresh produce and fish to warm baked goods or bottled soft drinks.[15]

Wheeled coffee carts on street corners provided options for those who sought hot and cold beverages. Henry Mayhew reckoned that there were around 200 of these coffee stalls in the markets of London alone (as well as 500 that principally sold watercress!).[16] Coffee carts with covered buckets full of hot drinks like tea, coffee, cocoa and even mulled wine attracted customers, who could buy it by the cup. Once empty, these cups would be reused by the next customer, and were scarcely ever rinsed out. Mayhew goes on to write in his description of London market scenes that men, women and children alike would swarm around these carts, which also supplied ginger beer, lemonade, curds and whey, and water.[17] In warmer months, wheeled carts sold iced-creams and fruit juices, and it was not uncommon to see men leading cows around so that customers could purchase a cup of milk as fresh as could be possible straight from the udder.[18]

Convenience foods that could be purchased and taken away were popular in the nineteenth century just as they are today, particularly in urban areas where people rushed to hectic jobs. Convenience foods were also favoured by families who sought to feed their children cheaply while out on excursions. Records from the Great Exhibition in London mention that many working-class families brought their own picnics to eat within the grounds, which were described as being littered with 'greasy sandwich wrappers' upon their departure.[19] Other families purchased hot drinks and sweet buns for their children to share. If families preferred to dine at one of the refreshment rooms at the Great Exhibition, they could enjoy cold sandwiches and beer for just 9*d*. Wealthier patrons could purchase 'unlimited veal and ham pie, roast and boiled beef, salad, bread and cheese' for just 18*d*, as well as pigeon, chicken or tongue pies, and a dessert of sweet jelly or creamy pudding for 6*d* extra.[20] If the poor could not afford those treats, they could settle for 'meal deals' of bread, cheese and a pint of port for just 1*s*.[21] Many stalls also sold confectionery such as sweets, chocolate and biscuits for peckish patrons who had worked up an appetite while exploring the Exhibition.

The Great Exhibition thrilled visitors even further by regularly changing and recycling its menus. When he visited in 1851, George Augustus Sala had 'pillaf and kibabs' as well as 'thick grouty Mocha coffee' as part of a package promoting the opening of a new Middle Eastern exhibit.[22] On occasion, the Exhibition also hosted children's days, providing young visitors with sweet treats and delicious beverages. Sala wrote in his review:

> 'To behold the youngsters at tea was likewise a joy. The quantities of bread and butter they put away; the cups of tea and cocoa and milk and water they consumed; the numbers of buns and slices of plum-cake they contrived to dispose of filled me not only with delight, but with bewilderment.'[23]

Food had the gift of bringing great enjoyment to people who otherwise had very little else in the nineteenth century. But not only did eating and cooking revolutionize the kitchen and the living space around it, it also had wide-reaching effects on society as a whole.

The Consumer Revolution of the nineteenth century was a period in which consumerism dramatically shifted. The Industrial Revolution had not only led to a boom in population as workers moved to urban areas in search of new labouring jobs, but also an uptick in commerce and trade. In just 100 years, the population of London grew from nine million to thirty-six million, putting great strain on the existing commerce of the city. Provisions were stretched and food began to be sparse as more and more families settled into their new lives in the city. In an attempt to combat this, factories, mills and farms began hiring cheap labour on a grand scale in order to produce enough supply to meet demand.

As more and more working-class members of society finally began earning wages of their own, families could begin to save their money for the very first time instead of living hand-to-mouth. Although their wealth was by no means considerable, it was nonetheless enough to better the lives of the desperately needy who relied on their pittances to raise them from the deprivation of the slums where they lived. As families slowly began to be able to save their money, poor Victorians experienced for the first time something that had otherwise eluded them: disposable income. With money now in their pockets to spend as they chose, even the poorest members of society started treating themselves to purchases outside of necessities. A wider variety of food, more expensive household items and even trips away from home could now be afforded by the working class, whose general quality of life had begun to change for the better.

With people spending more money in their stores, the newly established brick-and-mortar grocer's shops could begin to invest in more stock and imports, leading to the introduction of 'exotic' foods and items from overseas that had otherwise been unavailable to people in Britain. Soon, however, when it became clear that these shops were simply not large enough to sell their widening catalogue of goods, dedicated stores offering more streamlined and niche products began cropping up across the country, in both urban and rural areas. Marketing had truly changed. No longer did housewives have to rely on weekly market stalls to purchase their groceries; they could now shop for their goods whenever they felt like it. Shopping had become an enjoyable pastime instead of a necessity, and even children could spend their penny allowances on the growing market of treats and toys.

This increase in wages also resulted in the division of work and leisure, for people no longer had to work long hours or throughout the whole week just to be able to afford basic necessities to survive. With more time to enjoy leisurely pursuits, the weekend became established as a period for relaxation and recreation, which was furthered by the growth of social clubs and spectator sports, as well as steam railway networks that allowed for travel both domestically and abroad.

Something so simple as food and the way that it was sold had made a vast difference to the lives of nineteenth-century Britons as a whole, but none reaped its benefits more than the poorest members who dwelled in its dark and dingy slums.

Chapter 6

Fun and Games: Entertainment in the Slums

'His leisure is devoted to the beer-shop, the dancing-room, or the theatre.'

Henry Mayhew, *London Labour and the London Poor* (1851)

The Consumer Revolution of the nineteenth century had made great strides in the way that leisure and entertainment was enjoyed in wealthy and poorer communities alike. No longer was work and wages the sole drive of Victorian paupers; now, they could devote their new-found free time to leisure and fun.

The importance of recreation was keenly felt by Victorians, who considered it 'to the mind as whetting is to the scythe, to sharpen the edge of it, which would otherwise grow dull and blunt'.[1] There is a common misconception that the working classes of Victorian Britain had no time for relaxation, that their lives were dominated by long hours of toil and labour. Though to some extent this is true, with working hours being vastly longer than ours legally are today, even the poorest members of society could enjoy downtime and much-earned rest. This was helped in part by the Factory Act of 1850, which required all work to stop on Saturdays at 2.00 pm sharp, leaving the rest of the afternoon and evening for recreation.

Although Henry Mayhew wrote that 'home has few attractions to a man whose life is street life', many working-class paupers did indeed enjoy pastimes from the comfort of their own homes.[2] Popular games that could be played at home, particularly by adults, included card games of numerous varieties, as well as betting and gambling, either with real money or just for fun.[3] Children were particularly fond of skittles, a game played similarly to ten-pin bowling, in which the aim was to topple as many standing pegs as possible to earn points. Skittles could be played with a proper set of pins and balls, though resourceful children often made their own from whatever objects they could find around the home, in the streets or even poking out from rubbish heaps.

Board games such as chess and draughts were also popular, and could be played by numerous people at once. Quizzes, dominoes and even games of lotto have been recorded as frequently played by poor Victorians, who would gather in communal areas to play with family, friends, neighbours or even curious onlookers who wandered by.[4] Children played with dolls and tin soldiers, either bought from shops or handmade by their parents or other talented relations.[5] Wooden miniature carts with wheels that actually turned, soft stuffed creatures and even 'chemical volcanoes' (a mixture of bicarbonate of soda and vinegar which would cause a flurry of effervescence for clay 'volcanoes') were other cheap ways to keep children quiet and entertained, and bring their parents much-needed peace.

For the more mischievous of working-class youths, painted rubber snakes and clockwork spiders that moved through a sophisticated network of cogs could thrill and delight, and were used by children to spook their families and passers-by on the street.[6] One gift box stuffed full with toys was Dugwell and Son's Guinea Box of Everlasting Amusements, which achieved precisely what it had set out to do.[7] This box, full of magic tricks and whimsical delights, even included incantations said to attract fairies and imps, as well as cards that promised genuine magical spells.[8]

Sometimes, the games of children and youths in the Victorian slums bordered on the dangerous or the illegal. One activity enjoyed by particularly unruly children was the baiting of policemen while they were out on their beat. The children would lead them down dead ends or send them on false quests to capture purely fictional criminals they had supposedly seen walking past. The game became competitive, particularly in urban areas that had high numbers of on-duty police officers, with the champion being he (or she) who had 'muzzle[d] half a dozen bobbies before breakfast'.[9] Children got in trouble with the local law courts when they were caught betting on who could steal the most objects from street vendors and market stalls, as well as for 'fighting with cheap theatrical swords' in public places and disturbing those around them. They also became a nuisance by climbing up the drainpipes of their neighbour's houses and onto the roofs of buildings to slide off into bales of hay that cushioned their falls below.[10]

Many children were fond of playing with 'pop' guns, little wooden guns that were stoppered with cork and released with pulleys, resulting in a 'pop!' that kept them entertained for hours. With toys like these, along with tiny rickety perambulators and stuffed or ceramic baby dolls, children could emulate their elders and engage in imaginative play that resembled the world around them.[11] Children have roleplayed as adults in their games throughout history, perhaps in preparation for their own adult lives.[12] Others may have been imagining a lifestyle far different to their own, a future to which they could only hope but aspire.[13] Whatever the case, the games of the young within the Victorian slums were hopeful releases that distracted them from the reality of the deprivation and hopelessness that surrounded them. For just a moment, those children could be somewhere else.

Henry Mayhew wrote that young men were particularly fond of violent activities, noting in his survey *London Labour and London Poor* that the youths took great pleasure in bare-knuckled boxing, pigeon shooting, rat killing and dog fighting[14]. Dog fighting, a dangerous sport not just for the animals but also for their handlers, was an especially violent pastime and was banned in many towns and cities for the danger it would cause. Breeds of dogs known for their reactive tempers and lust for blood – such as bull terriers, rottweilers and mastiffs – would be bred and kept in inhumane captivity, starved almost to death and taunted with cruelty to increase their viciousness. Breeders knew that their work was highly unethical and unjust, and could land them hefty fines or prison sentences if caught. As such, handlers of vicious dogs would employ seekers to keep watch for any policemen who wandered uncomfortably close to their fighting rings and breeding dens. Dog fighting was an upsetting sport, one in which owners could expect to lose their animals; even if injured or maimed, many dog breeders of the time believed it to be more humane to put the poor creature out of its misery by shooting it than forcing it to live disabled within the dark and dingy streets.

Betting on fights, whether it be dog or human, was a favourite hobby of males in the nineteenth century. From the very richest to the very poorest, betting on wrestling matches and fist fights could be an easy way to earn (or lose) a few extra pennies for practically no effort at all. The Victorian era was a time in which sport was increasingly popular as a spectator hobby, becoming far more accessible to larger groups of people than ever before. As a result, a wave of betting hysteria gripped the nation whenever sporting clubs got together to duel on pitches and courts, spurred on by their adoring and fanatical supporters.

Football was one of the most popular sports in Victorian England, and was played by wealthy schoolboys, fitness fanatics and working-class men alike. Even women played matches on both a casual and competitive level, with the *Glasgow Herald* reporting in 1881 on a ladies' international match between Scotland and England.[15] It was a 'curious' game, wrote male commentators, who took issue with the match on account of the players' sex, as well as the fact that they wore baggy pantaloons instead of long skirts, a rather unbecoming, masculine garb.[16] For the most part, football was a male game; played by men and watched by men. Women rarely – if ever – watched matches between teams, standing along boundary lines on freezing cold pitches or tightly packed into seated stands. Comfortable football stadiums had not yet been built in Britain, and many matches were played without any semblance of shelter at all. Even where clubs had amassed large followings, the majority of matches were played outside on often uneven grass pitches, no matter the weather. At the Great Exhibition (also known as the Crystal Palace) at Sydenham, casual football matches attracted such crowds of spectators that a dedicated pitch had to be built to stop young men from churning up the surrounding fields with their boots. The newly built football ground at Crystal Palace now had the capacity to seat 60,000 spectators, most of whom hailed from the poorer social classes of London.[17]

Some of the oldest and largest football teams still in existence in Britain today had their origins rooted in the nineteenth century. Notts County Football Club was established in 1862, followed by its sister team, Nottingham Forest, a few years later in 1865. Stoke, known then as the Stoke Ramblers, was established in 1863, and Sheffield Wednesday in 1867. These were by no means the earliest football teams in Britain, however. Many of the first clubs established in the nineteenth century are no longer extant, such as the Surrey Football Club which was formed by working-class men in 1849. One of the earliest English football teams was even made up of players who also competed in weekly summer cricket matches, hence naming itself the Great Leicestershire Cricket and Football Club, established in 1840.

Cricket was a particular favourite with Victorians, and the sport quickly gained the reputation of being the chosen sport of the gentile in nineteenth and twentieth-century Britain, along with golf and croquet. In reality, cricket was played by a cross-section of society, rich and poor alike, with teams often finding themselves face-to-face with wealthier or poorer opposing sides. If a man wished to reap the benefits of exercise and team spirit, but did not enjoy ball games, he could join clubs offering other types of sports like boat-racing, acrobatics and gymnastics, cross-country running and boxing, all of which were popular amongst working-class men. Some men even found these team sports lucrative, with a lucky few going on to establish careers in sport and becoming early celebrities of their time. This was furthered by the sale of memorabilia and merchandise that could be purchased from vendors at matches, popularizing ball games and team sports within every community of Victorian Britain. Children also played sports in teams of their own, though not at league level or as serious competitors. They could also sign up to gymnastic clubs regardless of their age or sex, though it was emphasized by the government that lithe acrobatic children must strictly *not* join the circus.[18]

Other immensely popular sports in nineteenth-century Britain were racquet-based, such as badminton, squash and tennis. Played by both males and females, many poorer families constructed (sometimes rather shoddily) their own racquets from sanded wooden frames and tightly-pulled strings. The poor could even make their own tennis balls, shuttlecocks and cricket balls, or buy bouncy rubber versions relatively cheaply from dedicated sporting shops and stalls. Racquet sports enjoyed a surge in popularity in the latter part of the nineteenth century, following the first ever Grand Slam Tournament played at Wimbledon in 1877. That very first year, only male tennis players battled for the title of champion, on courts on the flat expanse of Wimbledon Common. Until the Victorian era, tennis had been split into two categories: 'lawn' tennis, played on perfectly manicured green lawns, and 'real' tennis, played within closed courts on hard surfaces. Real tennis was particularly popular with the wealthy aristocracy, who had favoured the privacy of indoor courts, just as King Henry VIII (who had been a great fan and helped popularize the sport in England) had in the sixteenth century.[19] For the majority of people, who could not afford to rent out special tennis halls to play their matches or did not have access to perfectly curated flat garden courts, they had to make do with mere lengths of string as makeshift tennis nets pulled taut across cobblestone pavements, or even utilize the fences that separated their houses from others. Unlike football, poor Victorians could not hope to make much of a career out of playing tennis unless it was at a county level, for the vast majority of players at Wimbledon and other major tennis matches in the nineteenth century hailed from the wealthier classes and had received years of dedicated training and practice. They could, however, hope to purchase tickets to watch such tennis tournaments. At Wimbledon in 1877, the ticket price was just one shilling, or around £3 in today's money, a miniscule price.[20] Some 200 people crowded to watch the first Wimbledon final, among them members of the working class.

Excursions

Days out to attend sporting matches were not the only chance for working-class families to leave their hovels for a short while and have fun. Holidays, both domestically and abroad, were annual events for members of the wealthier classes, with hotspots like the coastal towns of Britain particularly favoured. These excursions, however, were expensive, out of the reach of the vast majority of working-class people and paupers in Victorian society. Unless they had been especially fortunate, the poor could not afford to travel with their entire families purely for fun and recreation. If they ever did leave the areas in which they had been born and raised, it would most likely be for reasons of work or relocation. For example, Catherine Eddowes, the fourth victim of Jack the Ripper, went on yearly trips to the English countryside to participate in working the harvest, travelling by foot and staying in lodging houses along the way.[1] Most poor Londoners enjoyed days out closer to home, where there was much to keep them occupied for mere pennies or entirely without cost.

Every Sunday there was an expectation that most people would attend religious services in churches and chapels. Attending church not only allowed for religious and spiritual devotion, but also gave Victorians a chance to catch up with friends and share gossip and stories gathered during the week. The most popular denomination of Christianity in Victorian London was the Church of England, followed by Roman Catholicism, Methodism and Anglicanism. Regardless of one's spiritual beliefs, attending church gave people the opportunity to make new friends and forge connections, to partake in collective events and express their opinions at community meetings, as well as giving weary workers a change of scenery from their places of employment to which they had been shackled throughout the week. Attending church was an expected way of life in the nineteenth century, but attendance numbers slowly dwindled and less emphasis was placed on its spiritual importance as the decades rolled by. This was nowhere more keenly felt that in slum populations, who were the first to cease attending church services on a weekly basis. In her interview of slum tenants in 1869, Isabella Bird reported that out of thirty-two families, only two women had regularly attended church.[2] She went on to interview a further forty people, with only one, a mother, admitting to attending services every Sunday.[3]

It appears that less emphasis was placed on devotion and prayer in the Victorian era than in any previous century, particularly amongst members of the working classes. That does not mean to say that the Victorians did not visit churches, chapels and other places of religious interest for other reasons. If not particularly spiritual, a poor Victorian could still tour the old and beautiful churches of their parishes and beyond. Indeed, 'church-crawling' seemed to be a particular interest of people in the nineteenth century. Excursions to medieval churches to gaze at beautiful panels of stained glass, or wander around graveyards to seek out names of the famous buried there, were popular. On a grander scale, many Victorians – rich and poor alike – enjoyed visits to imposing cathedrals and abbeys located in their area, regardless of whether they were ruined or still standing. None was more popular than the impressive Westminster Abbey, a place where praying parishioners and curious tourists alike milled through double doors to explore the cavernous areas within.

Admission to Westminster Abbey was entirely free, and many Victorians took advantage to visit with their friends and families. Rich and poor mingled amongst the pews and the statues, and bonded over their shared awe of the ancient monument. Tourists particularly enjoyed visiting the graves of its famous dead, from William Shakespeare to Geoffrey Chaucer, and the musical genius that was Handel. In years to come, Charles Dickens would find himself nestled amongst other literary greats at Poet's Corner, which attracted hundreds of thousands of visitors annually who paid their respects to the distinguished and beloved author.[4] If visitors to the abbey wished to venture further into its alcoves, they could pay just 6*d* for admission to the Henry VII Chapel, where legendary Tudor kings and queens had been buried. According to Charles Dickens Jr, the son of the author, the Victorians had been particularly enthralled by the gold-plated effigy of Queen Elizabeth I, as well as those of her grandparents, King Henry VII and Elizabeth of York.[5] They were also attracted by St Edward's Chair (used in the coronation of monarchs since Henry IV), which, despite its relative simplicity, exuded a sense of magnificence and grandeur. Young Victorians were so attracted to the throne (which they could sit on for a fee) that they etched their names and initials into the softening 600-year-old oak.

Victorians in London in the nineteenth century had arguably a closer relationship to the monarchy and the Royal Family than in any previous generation. Queen Victoria and her family had been more accessible to the masses than ever before, in part thanks to the central location of their main residences. With the rise in popularity of print newspapers and magazines in the eighteenth and nineteenth centuries, subjects could come to know much more about their monarchs and their families. The Royal Family had become more relevant and relatable; court circulars which informed the public of the daily routines of the Queen and her family were featured in all national newspapers, as were drawings of the royals and later monochrome printed photographs. It was not uncommon for households across Britain to hang pictures of the Queen in their own homes, no matter their social standing, a tradition that lasted well into the reigns of Victoria's successors, Edward VII and George V.

Despite this new-found relevancy, the chasm between subject and ruler remained as great as ever. In spite of this, Victoria's subjects living in London could at least hope to catch a glimpse of the monarch as her magnificent gilt carriages regularly rattled down the cobblestones of The Mall and surrounding areas. Victoria's main residence, Buckingham Palace, had been renovated at the beginning of her reign, bringing the monarchy into the heart of the communities of her subjects. On one end of The Mall stood the imposing and magnificent Buckingham Palace, St James's Palace and Clarence House, while at the other, busy thoroughfares of working-class citizens thrummed with the sound of pedlars, street vendors and costermongers. That the Londoners could consider the Queen herself as their neighbour was a turning point in changing the way that subjects felt about their monarch. Tourists in the nineteenth century itched to get a glimpse of these palaces and grand homes, just as many still do today. No longer was the monarch a distant and unreachable figure; now, Victorians felt as though they had some connection to their Queen. Despite Queen Victoria herself complaining that Buckingham Palace had 'insufficient accommodation', and commentators considering it 'a more total failure [...] I would not live in it rent-free [for] the absence of pure taste', the vast majority of working-class Victorians found it an astonishing sight to behold.[6]

Visiting The Mall was a must in Victorian Britain, no matter your social standing. Flanked on both sides by St James's Park and Green Park, The Mall could be considered as one of the atriums of the beating heart of Victorian London. At one end of the great stretch was Buckingham Palace, the principal residence of the Royal Family, while Trafalgar Square was at the other. From there, Londoners could visit Horse Guards Parade or journey on to Westminster and pass the Houses of Parliament. Heading north would take them to the busy shopping districts of London – Oxford Street and Covent Garden – while ambles beyond Buckingham Palace would take them in the direction of upmarket Chelsea and Kensington.

Kensington, one of the more affluent areas of Victorian London, was by no means inaccessible to the poor and the needy. As a child, Queen Victoria had been raised within the gorgeous Georgian brick walls of Kensington Palace, a place she had considered to be akin to a prison. The gardens which surrounded the palace were a particular hotspot for Victorians, rich and poor alike, who crowded to its expanse of rolling fields and wild meadows at the first sign of bright sun and warm weather. Kensington Gardens led on to the equally impressive Hyde Park, which stretched for miles and was accessed by crossing a bridge across the Serpentine Lake. Both parks were much greener than they are today, and regularly hosted picnics or had wandering vendors selling drinks and treats to visitors who passed by. The gardens were also a favourite stomping ground of various animals, with exotic birds such as pelicans and parakeets perching in its trees, as well as sheep and cows which could regularly be found grazing there. The Round Pond, located just outside Kensington Palace, was home for many a Victorian duck, goose and swan, and was used for model-boat sailing in warmer months and ice-skating in the winter.[7]

Meandering through the gardens, poor Victorians could enjoy free entry to the South Kensington Museum, which contained special collections on a grand scale. Initially located at Marlborough House on The Mall, the South Kensington Museum was visited by curious tourists awed by arts and culture. The museum's halls were filled with collections of ornamental art and a gallery of animal products, as well as a food museum and a library of fine artworks. The museum was also home to educational collections, a gallery of sculptures, a library, numerous refreshment rooms and even training schools for aspiring artists.[8] In 1899, it was rebranded and extended, and became what is known today as the Victoria and Albert Museum.

To visit a museum in the nineteenth century was to broaden your horizons. Museums in London, which were mostly free to enter, could allow even the poorest of society to experience culture on a scale they may have never before seen. Historical artefacts, art and sculpture could all be admired for no fee whatsoever, and the poor could learn about geography, science and other fascinating subjects to which they would have otherwise had little access. One of the most eminent museums then, as it still is now, was the British Museum, which held artefacts dating from ancient times, up to more recent years, and was again entirely free to all visitors. Crowds of Victorians ascended its steps and flooded into its halls, gazing in awe at the exhibits inside. Egyptian mummies and Roman jewels, indigenous masks and medieval manuscripts were just some of the treasures awaiting those who visited.[9]

The Bethnal Green Museum was another that admitted visitors free of charge. Not only could people peruse anthropological and historical artefact collections, but also chemistry and scientific displays and even food competitions. It also contained in one gallery a national collection of portraits which were on loan from the gallery at St Martin's Place in Trafalgar Square, now known as the National Portrait Gallery.[10]

But perhaps the grandest and most interesting of London museums in the nineteenth century was the Great Exhibition, also known as the Crystal Palace due to its walls being made from glistening cut-glass, located in Hyde Park. Built in 1851 under the watchful supervision of Albert, the Prince Consort, the Great Exhibition was expected to attract 400,000 visitors in its first year, a number it easily achieved.[11] Within just 114 days of it opening, more than six million visitors had passed through its vast halls.[12] Neither did its popularity dwindle as time went on, despite its relocation to Sydenham in 1854. Indeed, the Great Exhibition remained a firm favourite with Londoners and those who had travelled across the globe to see it until 1936, when a stray spark caused a fire which burned it to the ground.

Upon entering into its crystal halls, visitors wandered through linked 'courts', which took them on journeys through the past. These courts were set up to resemble rooms as they had been in long-lost eras. Visitors began at the Pompeiian room, before traipsing through Ancient Egypt and Greece, the Byzantine Empire, the Palatial Alhambra, the Middle Ages, the Elizabethan Court and the European Renaissance.[13] Once they had absorbed the history within each room, and had thoroughly inspected genuine artefacts from each period, visitors could move to the modern section of the Great Exhibition. Here, great halls dedicated to science and manufacturing, art and music were to be found, as well as 'a miniature of the actual world which Trade and Commerce, Enterprise and Invention, brighten and enrich'.[14] This miniature diorama of Britain was particularly popular with visiting children, who crowded around to watch toy trains rattle on their rails, puffs of cotton-wool 'steam' fixed to their chimneys, as well as clockwork people that actually moved to the tinkle of a music-box amidst 'mountains' made from painted cork and 'waterfalls' made from glass.[15]

As well as rooms dedicated to history and scientific discovery, the Great Exhibition housed an aquarium with live fish and marine oddities, along with a library for study and quiet reading, a greenhouse, a letter-writing room and a long gallery filled with the busts, effigies and statuettes of famous people including Queen Elizabeth I, Mary, Queen of Scots, William Shakespeare and Richard the Lionheart.[16] If visitors still wished for more to entertain them, then they could visit the adjoining Industrial Museum, showcasing the history of steam and naval travel, as well as a room filled with genuine dinosaur fossils and even a hall lined with a collection of stuffed animals.[17]

Outside the Great Exhibition was an ice-skating rink, an area for bird-watching, a racecourse for horses and a swimming pool.[18] There were also boats to hire for use on the nearby lake, which was particularly favoured by lovers and sweethearts.[19] Every Thursday, fireworks would be lit in the grounds of the Crystal Palace, while children's music concerts and gymnastic competitions took place on a monthly basis.[20]

With so many activities and so much to see, it was no wonder that the Great Exhibition was so popular with the London masses. In his visit to the exhibition in 1851, tourist George Augustus Sala wrote mirthfully of the swarms of children who escaped the clutches of their parents and rushed about the gallery. 'It was enrapturing to listen to their rippling laughter and chatter', he observed, as children from every level of the social strata mingled regardless of their birth. It was simply, he concluded, the 'finest playground for children in the whole kingdom'.[21] Indeed, the Great Exhibition allowed Victorians to experience something which they had previously had little access to: associations with members of opposing social classes.

That the rich and the wealthy would mingle with the poor and the destitute was otherwise uncommon in Victorian Britain, and never would the learned and academic dream of gazing upon the same artefacts as the illiterate and those who had never once received even a day of schooling in their lives. Yet here at the Great Exhibition, any sense of class seemed to cease; rich and poor gossiped as they sat around indoor fountains, or ate on tables adjacent to each other in the host of dining rooms available. Before the Great Exhibition opened its doors in 1851, there existed an initial unease amongst the wealthier classes, who worried about the behaviour of the poor people they would soon come into contact with. On the streets, the middling and richer classes could avoid the slums of the city and those who lived there, but in such close quarters as the Great Exhibition they would be forced to come face-to-face. This unease rose to such a head that *Punch Magazine* published a satirical piece on the Great Exhibition in 1851, entitled 'The Pound and the Shilling', which served as an analogy of the rich meeting the poor for the very first time.[22] Henry Mayhew, the infamous social commentator, also wrote about the nervousness of the rich at the thought of mixing with the poor:

> 'For many days before the "shilling people" were admitted to the building, the great topic of conversation was the probable behaviour of the people. Would they come sober? Will they destroy things?

> Will they want to cut their initials, or scratch their names on the panes of the glass[?]'[23]

However, it turned out that the dread and unease had been for naught. '[T]hey have surpassed in decorum the hopes of their well-wishers,' continued Mayhew, '[and] the fact is, the Great Exhibition is to them more of a school than a show.'[24]

As the nineteenth century slowly melted into the twentieth, relations between the rich and the poor of London began to blend. Gone were the days of segregation and prejudice. The classes were now more tolerant of each other, helped in part by the fact that they could visit and enjoy the same areas of cultural interest. London's green spaces – Hyde Park and Kensington Gardens, Battersea, Greenwich and St James's – were now areas where families could relax and lounge regardless of their backgrounds and wealth. Boat trips along the Serpentine and down the Thames were enjoyed not only by the wealthy, but also by the poor, who found enjoyment in renting cheap paddle boats. Monuments in London such as the Duke of York's Column, the Duke of Wellington's Clock Tower and the Monument – which memorialized the 1666 Great Fire of London – were now meeting spots for newly made friends about to embark on adventures around the great city. Other places of enjoyment and entertainment that were accessible to every echelon of society included the exhilarating theatres of Drury Lane and the West End, and even the shopping districts of Covent Garden and Leadenhall Market. London Zoo opened in 1828, to the delight of rich and poor men, women and children alike, followed by the establishment of Madame Tussaud's waxwork museum in 1835, which both awed and spooked visitors as they stared into the waxen faces of beheaded hardened criminals. Even graveyards had become places of leisure; the so-called 'Magnificent Seven' of great cemeteries in London (Kensal Green, Highgate, West Norwood, Abney Park, Tower Hamlets, Nunhead and Brompton) allowed for peaceful and private contemplative walks and a chance to reflect, away from the chaos of the city.

Another location that attracted the more contemplative of Victorians was the Tower of London, the impressive Norman-built stronghold that had existed on the banks of the Thames since 1097. 'Could the stones of this gate speak, what grim stories they would tell of those who passed through to life-long imprisonment or death,' the pamphlet *The Queen's London* stated in 1896.[25] Truly, 'there was no sadder spot on earth'.[26] The Victorians, always fond of tales of violence and the macabre, crowded the Tower of London and its surroundings, seeking out hidden areas like the Traitor's Gate and watching the red-cloaked Beefeaters as they completed their rounds guarding the Tower with their golden staffs in hand. Ghost tours at the Tower of London, as well as other nearby areas, were firm favourites of Victorians, who loved to be spooked, popularized in part by whispers of ghostly apparitions seen floating around the Tower's walls. The supernatural and the bizarre were particular draws to the Victorians, many of whom whiled away long dark nights engaged in séances or listening to public readings of the latest horror story that had been printed in the 'Penny Dreadfuls'.

Disembodied voices and eery apparitions aside, the Victorians craved stories of bloodlust, gore and shocking crime, just as many still do today. Unsolved riddles of mysterious murders and grisly tales appealed to Victorian audiences, who sought to hear more through whatever means possible. The poor, wrote Henry Mayhew in *London Labour and London Poor*, 'enjoy theatre shows with a good murder in them', and that the more ghoulish the story, the better.[27] Indeed, theatre shows were one way in which the illiterate especially could engage with stories like never before. In an age before cinema and television, Victorians could enjoy retellings of their favourite stories by watching them come to life upon the stage, something that had been immensely popular within London especially since the time of William Shakespeare and the Globe Theatre.

In 1871, the Royal Albert Hall opened to theatre-goers, just outside Kensington Gardens and adjacent to the dazzlingly beautiful Prince Albert Memorial that was erected on the orders of Queen Victoria the following year. Though principally drawing in crowds of the wealthier classes, poorer members of the community could also purchase tickets to orchestral concerts and operatic serenades that had typically been deemed more 'high-brow' than suitable for the working classes. Despite this, when poorer theatregoers did attend shows either at the Albert Hall or within the warrens of the West End's theatre district, they ensured that they 'always stay[ed] to the last, because we've paid for it all'.[28] To attend such a brilliant and expensive event was often the highlight of many a poor Victorian's life, and no hard-earned half-penny would be wasted or spent in vain. To memorialize this entertaining excursion, some members of the poorer communities in the city sought physical reminders that they could keep and treasure for the rest of their lives. If merchandise had been too expensive for purchase at theatre shows or museum exhibitions, the poor could hope instead for something for a lot less money, but a lot more sentiment: photographs.

Early in the nineteenth century, a revolution changed the way people perceived their memories. No longer did people have to rely solely on their recollections of their lived past, which often fell victim to the haze of age; now, they had permanent reminders of the lives that they had led. Invented in 1826 and further established in subsequent years, photography gave Victorians what humans had long sought: a way to stop time and remain immortal. Thanks to the ingenuity of inventors such as Nicéphore Niépce and Louis Daguerre, photography became an accessible and beloved form of art that even the poor could collect and hang in their otherwise bare-walled hovels. The photograph – monochromatic and prone to fading in sunlight – gave Victorians the chance to remember the faces of their loved ones and commemorate the days and occasions on which they had been taken. It was no wonder that Victorians were enticed by advertisements stating 'no more bad portraits' that offered to freeze time and bring joy to the sitters, who could remember forever the memories that they had forged. Photographic studios began cropping up across major cities and towns, and, for just a small fee, would take the portraits of whoever walked through their doors. Sitting in wedding dresses, holding tiny infants or standing statue-like behind their wrinkled elders, photography became a way in which Victorians could convey their love for their kin. Many professionally shot photographs of the time, such as those by esteemed London photographer C. Timms of Newington Causeway, were most likely taken on a day of great excitement to remember occasions such as an excursion which had brought the poor so much joy.[29]

Special Occasions

Just because a man was poor in the nineteenth century did not mean that he and his family could not enjoy celebrating a special occasion. In Victorian Britain, celebrating alongside extended families, friends and even close neighbours was a favourite way of giving thanks to the community and those networks who had made life in the dark and dingy slums just that little bit easier. Just as today, the Victorians loved any excuse for a celebration, whether it be a night of socializing and dancing or a simple drink in the local public house, and no occasion was more special than an individual's birthday.

We are often led to believe that our ancestors did not celebrate their birthdays, and that it is a tradition made popular only in more recent times. Of course, for many in poorer communities throughout history who may not have known precisely the date of their birth, celebrating each birthday milestone would have been rather challenging. However, evidence suggests that even in cases where children did not know the dates of their births, efforts were still made to celebrate the rites of passage an individual would be expected to achieve in life. For example, a child may not have been aware of the specific day of its birth but would have still had some rough estimate as to its age, which would be marked by milestones such as its first steps, losing its milk teeth or the onset of puberty. As Professor Nicholas Orme, an eminent childhood historian, writes, without knowing one's age, an individual would find such things as entering into employment very difficult. It could also cause problems with the law in terms of the legality of marriage due to one party potentially being underage, or how to enforce the appropriate punishment doled out in cases of crime.[1] Additionally, children and adults without any sense of their age would have found it difficult to engage with their peers, as well as crossing the bridge from childhood into adulthood.[2]

Concern about knowing when one's birthdate had been, however, was on the whole a lessening issue in the nineteenth century, thanks to the introduction of parish records, which included birth and baptismal records from the later Middle Ages onwards.[3] Even if the exact date itself had not been recorded, most children by the Victorian era had some sense of the year in which they had been born, assisted perhaps by remembering other key dates – such as the Queen's Coronation, for example – or monthly events like Easter, and using it as a measure of their age. On the whole, birthdays had been celebrated, or at least remembered by loved ones, from the Early Modern era onwards in Britain, and it is certainly not the modern invention that we are led to believe.[4] Isabella Beeton confirms this in her *Household Management*, which offers advice on the hosting of birthday parties for a member of the family. No matter whose birthday it was, Beeton wrote, whether adult or child, or even alive, 'long dead and buried [...] or otherwise esteemed', it would be cause for celebration.[5] Records exist of wealthier members of Victorian society receiving gifts of wrapped toys or other valuable ephemera in the nineteenth century, though for the poor, birthday gifts were markedly less expensive. A child may have received a toy hand-made by a relative or bought at market, and an adult perhaps practical items such as a new lace handkerchief or pair of socks. Treats like gingerbread, fresh fruit, warm buttery pancakes and even sponge cakes (such as the layered Victoria sponge) were also known to have been enjoyed by the poor on their birthdays.[6] It may not have been much, especially compared to their wealthier peers, but these efforts to celebrate the births of their loved ones showed that above all, Victorian paupers stressed the importance of kinship and family.

Families also came together to celebrate occasions like christenings, engagements and weddings. Close-knit communities would congregate to make these special days even more memorable for those involved, and there are heartwarming accounts of neighbours and friends pitching in to afford such things as baby blankets for newly christened infants, and even collectively baking 'Bride' cakes, simple and dense fruit-laden sponges which were cut by the bride and groom once they had been married.[7] The importance of community was never more evident than during the observation of religious holidays such as Good Friday and Easter Sunday, celebrated by both the more devotional of slum dwellers and those simply yearning for a cause to celebrate. The 1833 Factory Act had entitled all British workers to two days of religious observance a year, one of them being Good Friday and the other Christmas Day.[8] As such, Victorians made sure to celebrate with vigour, even if their funds called for frugality. At Easter, for example, Victorians would relish fresh eggs during their single day of religious observation, the shells of which were often then cautiously and delicately coloured by children with whatever they had available to them (such as fruit juices).[9] Confectionery was also on sale during this time, particularly in the form of charming modelled-sugar rabbits and flower petals.[10] The Victorian era created an Easter tradition still beloved today: the chocolate egg. Made in the nineteenth century by moulding chocolate dough into solid ovular shapes, or purchased ready-made from confectioner's shops, the chocolate egg would endure in the hearts of children and adults alike during Easter time.[11]

Perhaps the most eagerly anticipated and popular of holidays in the Victorian calendar was the one that footnoted the year and brought it to a close: Christmas. In his delightful recollection of London at Christmas, Henry Mayhew writes that, just as today, railways and roads into and out of the city were bustling with travellers eager to get home to their families to celebrate the festive period.[12] He notes that green sprigs of holly would be hung from whatever space was available, left there not by the local authorities but by merry revellers seeking to spread their festive joy. During this festive period, weddings occurred across the country, for during Advent the 'parish would marry poor couples without a fee'.[13] Churches bedecked in beautiful swathes of laurel, pine and mistletoe greeted celebrators and lined the paths of newlyweds as they made their way to their new home as husband and wife. Shops would close on 25 December, but were open in the lead up to Christmas

Day for customers to purchase last-minute gifts and food to celebrate the holiday. Despite the closure of shops, streets bustled with the hum of London life on Christmas Day as extended families spilled into the road singing carols, attending pantomimes and theatre shows, and showing their neighbours the cherished gifts that they had received that morning.[14]

In 1843, just one week before Christmas Day, Charles Dickens published one of his most famous works: *A Christmas Carol*. It was sold for just five shillings, a number set purposely by Dickens who wished for even the poorest members of society to read the tale of the miserly Ebeneezer Scrooge and the struggling Cratchit family, whose lives on the bread-line was a reality mirrored by many in Britain at the time.[15] Though already the most popular of holidays, *A Christmas Carol* had further established Christmas as a period of thanksgiving and graciousness, marking the importance of family and of compassion, values which Dickens hoped his readers would take away after reading the tale. To some extent, the book had a more far-reaching impact than even Dickens had hoped, as items such as Christmas cards (which had been introduced to Britain in the mainstream that same year) had flooded local post offices as long-lost relatives picked up pens to write to their distant loved ones.[16] These cards would be sent and delivered by postmen of the Royal Mail, with 'penny black' stamps featuring the bust of the monarch, Queen Victoria, firmly upon them.

Queen Victoria had famously loved Christmas, celebrating it in domestic bliss with her beloved Albert and their nine children, principally at their Scottish home in Balmoral. Victoria and Albert influenced in many ways how their subjects celebrated the holiday. Christmas trees, for example, were popularized when an illustration of the Royal Family appeared in the *Illustrated London News* in 1848, depicting them cheerfully decorating one of their own.[17] So too did Victoria and Albert influence eating habits at Christmas time, their lavish dinners of dressed poultry and succulent, seasoned trimmings enticing their subjects to celebrate in the same way at home. For those who could afford a large bird, such as a traditional turkey or a goose, it would be boiled (not roasted) in advance on Christmas Eve until it was soft enough to fall apart and eat the next day. If such a large treat could not be afforded, then cookery books of the time encouraged poor Victorians to substitute with whatever they had available to them, whether it be bacon or poultry giblets, tripe or chitterlings (pig's intestines).[18] Alongside the meat would be a stuffing made from onions, flour, milk and butter, and used either to stuff the bird's hollow orifices or spooned alongside it. Unlike in today's traditional Christmas dinner, however, poor Victorians did not tend to serve their meat and stuffing with rich gravy or roasted vegetables. Instead, they would cook cheap foodstuffs such as rice and vermicelli noodles, or a single baked potato if they were lucky, to be served alongside the meat and stuffing.[19] Dinner was typically followed by a steamed plum pudding, as stories of ghosts and ghouls were shared beside the fireplace while children played with their simple gifts upon the floor.[20]

Modern appetites seem to swell to unimaginable proportions on Christmas Day, and the Victorians were no different. Even the poor would ration their food so that by the time Christmas arrived they could lavish in 'feasts' of both fresh and dried candied fruits, nuts and sweet confectionery. Invented in 1848 by British confectioner Thomas Smith, Christmas crackers would be purchased and pulled by celebrating family members, who feasted on the chocolates and small hard candies that would be contained inside.[21] Paupers could even hope to enjoy drinks of mulled wine and egg nogg, or hot chocolate, tea and coffee, which they had saved up for this most special of occasions.[22]

The day after Christmas Day, 26 December, got its name from a tradition partaken by poor Victorians. Boxing Day was named after so-called 'Christmas Boxes', with tiny sums of money given to servants and employees, children and friends on the day following Christmas Day. Anyone could ask anybody for their 'Christmas Box', and there are examples of paupers amassing quite a stash of coins from particularly charitable strangers they had walked past in the street.[23] There are even records of postmen on their rounds knocking on each door of a street row of houses, earning a considerable pocketful of pennies in response.[24]

Once Christmas had ended and people trudged back to their routines at work, friends shared stories of their holidays with co-workers and peers. These stories brought together communities and strengthened bonds, so much so that Henry Mayhew writes that the tales told in break rooms and communal areas were anticipated with glee.[25] Piling into common rooms, men would tell stories of theatre shows that they had visited or curiosities that they had seen at exhibitions. They read aloud from newspapers that listed the scores of football matches and sports games, and delightfully passed around drawings and photographs to illiterate friends who otherwise could not read any of these stories for themselves.[26]

In the early nineteenth century, illiteracy rates were at an all-time high, no doubt in part due to the rapidly increasing birth rate of already crowded cities. As such, it was an impossible task for children to find places in schools and gain an education, instead being ushered into employment at an early age to help keep their families afloat. It was estimated that only one in ten poor men could read in the time of Henry Mayhew, who wrote that merchants and vendors were much more capable of reading than labourers and menial traders.[27] However, as the century ticked by and standards of education slowly began to improve across Britain, reading became a hobby enjoyed by ever-growing audiences of men, women and children. In 1848, W.H. Smith opened his first book stall in London, selling books, newspapers, pamphlets and magazines to inquisitive customers. Here, children could purchase 'penny' books, which – as the name suggests – cost just one penny and were highly collectible due to the serialized stories that would be told within. Reading for leisure was no longer the pastime of the genteel; now, even paupers were filing into public libraries and tracing their fingers over lengthy words. Ladies blushed as they paged through romantic novellas, while men tentatively read ghost stories, cautiously looking over their shoulders and into the dancing shadows of candlelight. Children craved to read the tales of swashbuckling heroes, who they emulated in games played with their friends barefoot in cobblestone back alleys and on manure-flecked busy roads. Thanks to improved literacy rates, the chasm between rich and poor was lessening, and now they could enjoy similar interests at the same level of enjoyment.

Indeed, the nineteenth century was a period where leisure activities previously ascribed to wealthier classes could now be enjoyed by the poor. Carpentry, painting and other physical hobbies enjoyed by men could be utilized as a method to make money and supplement their family income. For women, selling crochet or lace, homemade Christmas, Valentine's and Easter cards, or beautifully framed pressed flowers could do the same. In the 1880s, women in particular could enjoy hobbies such as colouring-in black and white photographs and bringing life to the sitter's features, or they could develop personal interests in art by taking still-life or landscape drawing classes. There are also references to women partaking in pottery and stained-glass painting.[28] Poor Victorians could take up gardening if space allowed it, growing their own produce to eat or just for fun. They could (and did) keep bees, play instruments or take up whittling in order to make wooden toys for their children.[29] Dancing, singing and even 'nocturnal hair brushing' have all been recorded as hobbies enjoyed by the poor of Victorian society, indicating that even the lowliest of slum dwellers knew how to have fun.[30]

Chapter 7

Growing Up in Victorian Britain: The Children of the Slums

'It is said that the children of the very poor are not
brought up, but dragged up.'
Charles Dickens, *Bleak House* (1852)

In his book *London by Day and Night*, published in 1852, D.W. Bartlett wrote that 'a true English home is intelligent, educated, and full of love'.[1] It was an ideal aspired to by many of the upper classes of the nineteenth century, who could afford the luxury of domestic bliss. For the poor, however, who could scarcely afford to feed themselves and keep a roof above their heads, were such things so important?

Families have always existed in human history, and children have always formed part of the household. However, myths perpetuating the claim that children were little cared for or little loved in the past continue to influence historical thought even today, skewing our understanding of childhood in history. No matter what the time period, historiography treats childhood as a mere stage of one's life, with little else to admire about it, and studies of the nineteenth century are no different. We are led to believe that, because poor parents could not afford to clothe, feed, entertain or educate their children in the Victorian slums, they did not care for them. We are presented with sorrowful images of orphans, foundlings and street urchins in contemporary literature, which lead us into believing that this was the norm for poor children in Victorian Britain. Oliver Twist, Tiny Tim and the Little Matchstick Girl are all faces of Victorian children that we have come to recognize; faces which we affix to real life children who were born, lived and died in the nineteenth century. But how truly do these figures reflect the lives of children in the Victorian era, and are they a fair representation of childhood in nineteenth-century Britain?

Every story starts with a beginning.

Pregnancy in Victorian Britain was as divisive then as it is now. Some women were thrilled to discover that deep within their wombs a child stirred, while others awaited the arrival of their child with dread and anxiety. Victorian women were by no means naïve to the process of falling pregnant, and each knew the risks of conception every time they engaged in sexual intercourse. Birth control did exist, but in a very primitive form, with couples adopting the use of vinegar-soaked sponges or discs inserted deep into the vagina to prevent sperm from entering the uterus. John Stuart Mill, a Liberal Member of Parliament, was among the early campaigners for the introduction of safe and accessible birth control in the nineteenth century, the movement having come about in response to an ever-increasing birth rate.[1] Mill's advocation for the choice to conceive was viewed as radical at the time, particularly due to the fact that Mill was a man. In the later Victorian and Edwardian eras, the advocation of birth control methods would eventually fall under the political umbrella of the suffragists, who principally consisted of women desperate for a degree of control over their own bodies.

To be pregnant, or 'in the family way', could be dangerous in the nineteenth century. Complications either during or after birth could be fatal, and the mortality rates of both mothers and their babies continued to be at an all-time high. Despite this, care for poor pregnant women as we know it today did not exist, with even expectant mothers who endured high-risk pregnancies expected to work 'down to the day of their confinement' and labour.[2] There was no maternity leave in the nineteenth century, and no government provisions available to those awaiting the imminent arrivals of their child. All an expectant mother could do in the Victorian slums was rely on other women around her to assist in her pregnancy and labour, and to answer any queries or reassure any anxieties she may have had about her body.

If a woman suspected that she was with child in Victorian Britain, she would seek out an elder, presumably one who had experienced many pregnancies and labours, to determine if she was indeed pregnant or not. In an age before modern pregnancy tests, Victorian women would scrutinize their bodies for any changes, such as the engorging of breasts and the cessation of her monthly menstruation. Other women may have also pressed upon her stomach to attempt to feel around for a baby within, or enquired about any nausea and vomiting, hair growth or hair fall, and changes to the skin that she may have experienced. Indeed, so common was the practice of other women determining the pregnancy of expectant mothers in the Victorian slums that it was written that they would often learn of the pregnancy before even the mother did.[3]

Once a pregnancy had been determined, a woman had to make a choice. In the nineteenth century, particularly within the poorer districts of urban dwellings where there were higher rates of prostitution and underage sex, abortions provided an opportunity to women who chose to remain childless. Surprisingly more commonplace than is typically believed, abortion was even considered as a form of extreme birth control in the nineteenth century, with campaigners such as Marie Stopes encouraging the practice to prevent 'inferior or low-class women from having children'.[4] It was a belief adopted even by some of the most radical of Victorian paupers, who preferred to abort their babies than bring them into the world. Of course, a Victorian woman would have had varying reasons why she chose to terminate her pregnancy, such as lack of money or fear of medical complications, though there also exist numerous shocking and distressing records of some women choosing to abort simply because they did not 'want to be bothered with any more brats'.[5] One woman was even recorded as wanting 'to get rid of a baby because her husband was going to Europe in the spring, and she wanted to go with him and couldn't be bothered by a young one'.[6]

Contrary to popular belief, abortion was not considered wholly unethical and immoral in the nineteenth century, and there was much understanding as to why a woman may choose to abort. If the father of the child had abandoned the mother, for example, then the wishes of the 'poor, deluded girl – seduced, betrayed, abandoned' would be respected by the community around her.[6] If a woman fell pregnant with the illegitimate child (known in the nineteenth century as 'chance children') of an already-married man, then it would be he who would be held to blame; 'the married shirk, who disregards her' would be treated with disdain and contempt.[7] Some women were forced into aborting their babies by the fathers of their children or by their families, particularly in cases where the mother was especially young herself. Others knew that with an additional mouth to feed, their already stretched household would reach breaking point. One unfortunate woman even confessed upon her deathbed to having twenty-one abortions in her lifetime.[8]

To acquire an abortion, women would go 'to visit family' or travel away in order to 'recuperate from illness', usually hiding away from society in nondescript locations and staying until the abortion had been carried out and the mother had recovered. Back-alley surgeries in chemist shops, dedicated clinics which operated behind disguises, common tenement buildings and even the houses of the wealthy all offered abortions to both rich and poor, married or unmarried women.[9] One clinic probably visited by poor Victorian mothers in London was located at No 10 Norfolk Street on Tottenham Court Road, where a Dr Currie would carry out the procedure using stolen implements for £10.[10]

The procedure was drawn-out and painful, and most required women to drink grey 'bitter powders' dissolved in warm water to stimulate menses.[11] The woman would then be instructed to lie upon a table, sofa or bed while a sharp instrument was inserted into the vagina that was twisted 'round like a worm or a corkscrew' for thirty minutes, a process which would be carried out numerous times per day until the abortion had been achieved.[12] Once the foetus had been expelled from the body, it would be wrapped in paper and buried in hidden locations to evade discovery.

Another alternative to remaining child-free in the nineteenth century was to leave new-born babes in the care of orphanages, work houses or foundling hospitals. Even if both parents were still alive, a baby could be left upon the doorstep of an orphanage with claims that it had no relatives left to care for it. Indeed, 'abandoning' an infant was apparently such common practice in nineteenth-century London that authors like Charles Dickens chose to include in their books emotional scenes of mothers relinquishing their children to the care of others, aware that the audiences reading the stories would be somewhat familiar with them. No Victorian orphan was more well-known (and beloved) than little Oliver Twist, 'a parish child, the orphan of a workhouse – the humble, half-starved drudge – to be cuffed and buffeted through the world – despised by all and pitied by none'.[13] Though Oliver Twist's story is a tale of fiction, contemporary reports of abandoned children at the time describe lifestyles which Oliver himself experiences in the book. One set of abandoned children, wrote Isabella Bird in 1869, had been 'locked out into the cold or wet, scantily clad, meanly fed, kicked about in the morning, kicked about at night, cursed instead of kissed, utterly neglected in body and soul', and raised 'without attaching no meaning whatever to the words love and home'.[14]

Yet to say that this was the norm for abandoned children in Victorian London is certainly not a fair estimation. Rather, it appears that Bird chose to write about these particular children for their circumstances were notably unfortunate, her attention drawn to their particularly pitiable situation. These children – just as Oliver Twist had been – were outliers, and arguably did not represent the standard of 'unwanted' children in nineteenth-century Britain as a whole. Instead, despite their negative depiction in literature and in popular belief, homes for children in Victorian London and further afield provided considerably for their charges, and certainly presented a more favourable alternative than a life on the streets of the dark and dingy slums.

The efforts of two particularly influential men changed the lives of thousands of children who were otherwise without homes and families in Victorian Britain. Captain Thomas Coram, a sea captain who lived in the mid-eighteenth century, had been distraught to find so many children lying exposed upon the streets, often left by their mothers in the hope that particularly charitable strangers would find it within their hearts to adopt the babes as their own. It sparked a life-long philanthropic passion for the care of abandoned children, which Coram would later come to describe as his 'darling project'.[15] As early as 1739, Thomas Coram had received a charter from King George II that would enable him to establish what would later become known as the Foundling Hospital, which first began admitting children in areas surrounding Hatton Garden two years later. Aware that his task would be one on a scale far larger than he had initially anticipated, Coram relocated the hospital to Bloomsbury, where it still stands today, a large manorial-like home which provided bed, board and an education to the children it cared for. It also provided medical care and spiritual salvation to children, who prayed in an adjoining chapel visited by public congregations. Frequent visitors included the artist William Hogarth, the composer George Frideric Handel and Charles Dickens, who quietly observed the children from his pew, later using them as inspiration for the children in *Oliver Twist*.

Children could be admitted to the Foundling Hospital as young as newly born, and many stayed until they reached early adolescence. As well as provisions for their education, the hospital also encouraged children to write to their families (if they had them) on the outside, and receive regular visits from their loved ones. The Foundling Hospital even assured anxious parents that the handing over of their babies did not have to be a permanent solution, explaining that the children were free to go home to their families whenever they chose. As such, Coram's Foundling Hospital came to be considered more as a boarding house for children whose parents struggled to afford their care, rather than the cruel institutions that Victorian children's homes came to be known as.

Another significant figure in the history of children and childhood was Thomas Barnardo, a philanthropist who, like Coram, had been touched by the hardships of poor youths in Victorian England. Initially training to become a medical doctor, Thomas Barnardo was struck to find tiny children sleeping naked in gutters, drains and even upon roofs, huddled together to keep out the worst of the cold and owning nothing to their names.[16] So deeply affected by what he saw was he that Barnardo quickly abandoned his dream of entering medical school to instead campaign and care for these poor children. Funded by generous donations, Barnardo opened his Home for Boys in 1870, where youths were taught carpentry, metalwork and shoemaking, all practical skills which would benefit them when seeking employment and apprenticeships. Initially there had been a limit on how many boys would be admitted to the Home for Boys, yet when Barnardo saw a ragged 11-year-old boy who had sought shelter dead just two days later, he vowed never to turn another child away.

In 1873, Thomas Barnardo established a Home for Girls with his wife, Syrie Louise, which was set upon a 60-acre site in Barking, East London. Syrie Louise was especially keen to take in sexually abused and prostituted girls who had been mistreated; so many were accepted into the Home for Girls that sixty-five separate cottages of girls residing in 'family' groups, along with a matron, had to be established within the site.[17] When he died in 1905, Thomas Barnardo had established ninety-six homes for children across Britain, and in just twenty years had provided for more than 4,000 children who were either 'fostered out' or permanently adopted by families.

Giving birth in the slums of Victorian London was perilous. Labouring mothers typically relied upon the assistance of other women around them as they began the process of childbirth, many of whose only experience with birth had been in situations of their own. Typically performed at home and without the involvement of doctors, in their stead family members, friends and even neighbours acted as makeshift surgeons and birthing partners. Fathers would not be permitted into the birthing room unless in the most dire of circumstances, where it was clear that his partner and their child might die. In fact, men were not permitted into the birthing room until well into the late 1900s, and even in some societies today, labour is a wholly female-attended event.

Labouring mothers would typically lie upon a bed or a couch, if one was available, or would rest upon a chair, gravity assisting with the natural movement of the baby. Some women required caesareans, yet those too poor to afford one, even if they required it in an emergency, would be left to suffer without. In many cases, having no access to an emergency caesarean would prove fatal to both mother and child, with records of complications in pregnancy from the time numbering well into the thousands. Medicines which aimed to alleviate the pain of childbirth were not widely available to the poor, who instead resorted to dangerous means such as opiates and heavy alcohol intake to numb their senses. For the most part, poor women had to make do with pain-relieving methods such as hot compresses and soothing words of encouragement to help them in their labour. After Dr John Snow (the medic who had helped quell the spread of cholera in London) assisted Queen Victoria during two of her labours, he admitted to using anaesthetics upon the monarch to ease her pain.[18]

Once a baby was born, it would be wrapped within a covering of some kind. For most mothers, clean towels would be available to clothe the baby, though there are references to new-borns being wrapped in unwashed fabric scraps and even curtains, carpets and rugs.[19] The infant would be handed to the mother, whose placenta would be cut away, and encouraged to feed upon her breast. Henry Mayhew writes that breastfeeding was a common sight in the streets of the London slums, and that if a mother could not naturally express milk of her own, then friends, family and neighbours who had recently had babies of their own would generously offer their assistance.[20] These very same people would likely form quasi-familial networks around the child, caring for them in close-knit relationships as if they had been born their own.[21]

Infancy and Childhood

Due to these quasi-familial networks which ran deep within the veins of the Victorian slums, many children were left to their own devices upon streets or within dwellings while their parents were away at work. Although compared to modern standards this practice appears neglectful, leaving a child at home was often the safest alternative. At home, children would be watched over by diligent neighbours as they played in the streets, or by other relatives such as grandparents, aunts and uncles.[1] In many ways, leaving poor children to play with others under the watchful eye of adult supervision was no different to wealthier parents leaving their children with matrons or nannies. By leaving their children at home while they themselves were away, Victorian parents also gave their offspring the chance to 'learn to take care of themselves' at an early age and to develop important life skills such as resilience and self-reliance.[2]

There existed amongst the wealthier of society a school of thought that poor children were more likely to 'be educated into hardened criminality', as well as falling 'naturally into a life of shame [or be] sentenced to reformatories'.[3] Likewise, some social commentaries of the era present the children of the poor as ill-behaved, ill-mannered and ill-tempered as a result of their ignorance 'of love [as well as] of cleanliness, decency and happiness'.[4] 'These children have never known cleanliness or decency,' wrote Isabella Bird, with a degree of partiality, in 1896; 'hideous blasphemies all around came from infant lips' as a result of their 'stinted, joyless, loveless misused childhood'.[5]

Of course, while some particularly undignified children undoubtedly existed in Victorian Britain, it is an unfair claim to suggest that every child in the slums of the nineteenth century was the same. Many sources from the time depict poor children as polite, carefree and joyous, even if their physical appearance was lacking.[6] Indeed, despite her earlier prejudices, Isabella Bird went on to write that 'dirty little children' with 'haggard, wrinkled, vicious faces' were busy in play, or occupied themselves with tasks inside the home.[7] Some rolled about with mirth 'in the gutter', their imaginations forging whimsical games, while others observed strangers from the kerb-stone as they passed.[8] Some, despite their lack of shoes and sore feet, still engaged in play, and sat in communal stairwells to continue their games when interrupted by rain or snow.[9]

Many of the games that children played in the Victorian era would be recognized today. Favourites included hopscotch, skipping, tag and 'house', where they would imitate the roles of adults in imaginary mock homes of their own. Children would recite nursery rhymes and be enraptured by every word of fairy-tales their parents would tell them at bed-time to ease them into sleep. When they were old enough to be trusted without constant supervision, slum children would wander to green spaces and parks, ponds and secluded back alleys, as well as into the houses of their friends.[10] Children of both genders would play with models and figures, particularly of soldiers or animals. Evidence also shows that even the poorest of children would play with toys such as dolls, horses or wheeled carts, which were often substituted by simple items such as spoons and brought to life using their imaginations.[11] One form of doll played with by children of all ages was 'decorative scraps', small paper dolls which would be cut out from magazines and 'dressed'. These scraps, which resembled models wearing the latest fashions or famous figures such as book characters or the Royal Family, could be played with as dolls or pasted within scrapbooks, and were cheap, readily accessible and entertaining. As a child grew and matured, they would have accompanied their parents on outings to places such as the market or excursions to areas of cultural interest like museums, picture houses and the theatre. Indeed, children would gain entry into these places for half the price of adults.[12]

As they continued to grow, the children of the slums turned into young adults. No longer concerned with imaginary play, and chafing to escape the suffocation of their parents and younger siblings, adolescents were instead believed to be troubled only by thoughts of 'their girls, their eating and their gambling'.[13] After years of abiding by the rules of their elders, adolescents in Victorian Britain began to experience a sense of independence. Some teenage Victorians channelled their rebelliousness through their appearance, much as modern adolescents do today. Wearing 'dandy' clothing and styling their hair long or 'done in "figure-six" curls', youths exercised their own autonomy in an otherwise oppressive world. Teenagers would also attend raffles, dance halls and go to the public house for the first time to purchase their very own half-pints.[15] Some left home to pursue careers as apprentices, while others engaged in sexual relationships, much to the chagrin of their parents.

Henry Mayhew wrote that 'it is not uncommon for a lad of fifteen to be living with a girl of the same age, as man and wife' in the Victorian slums, and that 'many live with their girls until they have grown to be men'.[16] Indeed, Mayhew stated that it was not uncommon for youths 'from ten and twelve years [to be] sleeping together' in the London slums, such was their passion, desire and virility.[17] Records certainly exist of teenage boys which detail their 'desire for sexual intercourse', which was most keenly felt 'by the male on attaining puberty' and often led to promiscuity and underage pregnancy. Teenage sex could also result in other, more dire consequences. In her adulthood, one woman admitted that as a child of just 11 she had entered into a 'marriage' with a 15-year-old boy.[18] Their passionate union had lasted just three months, until she was forced to seek medical treatment when she had been 'made ill through him' with a sexually transmitted disease. The girl, so desperate to secure medical aid, resorted to breaking the windows of a local chapel so that she would be transported to prison, where she could be treated.

Although adolescent waywardness would never truly be controlled throughout the Victorian period, it was at least suppressed by institutions which educated young people about the consequences of underage sex and other hazards that they may encounter in their early lives. One such institution was the Field Lane School, which gave lessons to poor pupils about conception, pregnancy and infant care.[19] Field Lane was a so-called 'ragged school', institutions provided by charitable donations that offered free education to poor children.[20] In an age where many pauper children had 'never been inside a school or church', education could be hard to come by.[21] When conducting a study into the extent of literacy and learning of sixty-two children in one particular slum, it was determined that only twenty had ever set foot within a school, with just one attending it on a regular (but not daily) basis.[22] Henry Mayhew furthered this study, estimating that only one in every hundred working-class children went to school regularly, for they were more likely to go to work with their parents.[23]

With so few children attending schools and receiving an education in Victorian Britain, social reformers knew it was time for change. If the masses could not read or write, they asked, how would they survive in society? Significant social campaigners like John Stuart Mill (who had advocated for birth control) pressed the government into incentivizing young people to get off the streets and instead enrol in compulsory schooling. Other influential figures included Charles Booth, who not only sought to improve the living conditions of the working classes, but also the education of their children. His survey of poverty in London contributed directly to the compulsory education of children when it was discovered that 25,000 children in Liverpool alone had received no semblance of an education, could not read or write, and were wholly lacking in skills important in sustaining themselves.[24] The efforts of Booth and Mill resulted in great strides being made towards achieving free and accessible education for even the poorest of society's children, helping pave the way for the Education Act of 1870, which gave the right to secular schooling to every child regardless of their social standing.[25]

Ragged schools furthered the accessibility of schooling to poor children in nineteenth-century Britain. Prior to the Education Act, only the wealthiest or most talented of children would attend school on a regular basis, and even fewer could hope to further their prospects by receiving secondary education in colleges and universities. In a report for the *Daily News* in 1846, Charles Dickens wrote sympathetically that the children of the poor were 'too ragged, wretched, filthy, and forlorn, to enter any other place', and must instead settle for attending these subsidised public schools.[26] Although providing children and young adults with an education ranging from reading and writing to counting and study of the Bible, as well as basic lessons in geography, history and science, some contemporaries still complained about the quality of ragged schools. In the report by Dickens, for example, he described one ragged school as consisting of 'two or three miserable rooms, upstairs in a miserable house', with pitiful children 'huddled together on a bench' and taught orally, for they could not be 'trusted with books'.[27] Nevertheless, by the late 1800s it was estimated that almost half of the slums' child population had utilized these ragged schools, while one report published in 1857 established that half a million children in London alone were now receiving a regular education due to the efforts of the ragged schools.[28]

Even Queen Victoria wrote favourably of ragged schools and the services they provided to young children. In one diary entry, the monarch wrote:

> 'We drove past the statue of Achilles, right on the grass, in the middle of the Park where 30,000 poor children, boys & girls with their schoolmasters & mistresses, were assembled. Tents had been pitched for them to dine in & all sorts of amusements had been provided for them. Each received an earthenware pot with my portrait on it.'[29]

It appears that ragged schools had been a shining success.

Indeed, thanks to the educational reforms of the nineteenth century, schooling in Britain would change forever. Further reforms would make educational compulsory for children from the ages of at least 5 to 16, and encouraged children to pursue post-education activities such as apprenticeships and schooling in tactile trades. Furthermore, the educational reforms of Victorian Britain led to the establishment of dedicated school regulating institutions, which employed school inspectors nationwide to scrutinize parish schools in their curricula and ensure that standards were being met.

'The education of these children is such only as the streets afford; and the streets teach them,' wrote Henry Mayhew in 1851.[30] Yet change was on the horizon, and nineteenth-century children could finally pursue opportunities to which they had never before been privy.

Chapter 8

Crime, Punishment and the Victorian Justice System

'So used are the inhabitants there to drunken brawls and cries of "Murder!", that they took no notice of it.'
The East London Observer (1 September 1888)

When picturing the slums of Victorian London, images of Dickens-esque criminals often come to mind. Characters like *Oliver Twist*'s beloved pickpocket, The Artful Dodger, or the wickedly charming 'receiver of stolen goods', Fagin, helped stereotype the working classes of Victorian London as rogues, swindlers and scallywags. The image of Victorian London as a hotbed of crime and corruption was also perpetuated by brutal murders committed within the warrens of the city, the most infamous of all occurring in Whitechapel in 1888 by the hands of the elusive and legendary 'Jack the Ripper'. But is it fair to suggest that the paupers of the Victorian slums relied upon a life of crime to support themselves, and to what extent had these criminals been pressured into a life of sin through necessity? Were the dark and dingy slums of Victorian London truly as dangerous as we are led to believe?

In the nineteenth century, there existed a belief that the poorest classes had a 'love of cruelty' and that they were particularly pugnacious people who had been motivated in their life of violence by the emergence of heavy industry which threatened their jobs.[1] Indeed, it is fair to say that the vast majority of crimes committed in Victorian London had been carried out by members of the poorest classes, and often took the form of acts of retribution and revenge. The so-called 'Scuttlers' of Manchester, a group of young men who would attack the wealthy with belt buckles and knives, were believed to be motivated in their hate crime by the chasm which existed between the two social groups.[2] Likewise, a similar gang named the 'Hooligans', who ravaged South London in the nineteenth century, had been motivated by joblessness and unemployment, their desperate situations culminating in a particularly violent riot that took place over the August Bank Holiday of 1898.[3] Perhaps the most infamous of street gangs, the 'Peaky Blinders' of Birmingham, had come about due to a shared lack of adequate wages, resulting in men turning to black-market trades such as gambling and theft.

Found all across the country, gangs like these threatened the upper and middle classes of Victorian society, but were otherwise harmless to the members of their own class and creed. Indeed, crimes such as theft were reportedly uncommon betwixt the poorest members of society, who instead shared what little they had with each other. Victorian thieves (known as 'cross chaps') tended to work on a larger scale, targeting the homes of the wealthier members of society and threatening them in the streets.[5] Even children would be employed as cross chaps, their litheness and agility allowing them to easily be passed through open windows and doors and speed around houses in search of treasures without making too much of a noise.[6] Once an item had been acquired by a thief, he or she could sell it at a 'Flash House', a place where criminals congregated to fence their stolen goods.[7] These Flash Houses were not specifically brick-and-mortar dwellings, but rather simple shacks that could be dismantled and moved about so to avoid detection by the police and punishment by the law. One particular Flash House that stood at Field Lane in London seemed to be especially popular with thieves, and in one week alone recorded the acquisition of no less than 5,000 silken handkerchiefs.[8]

Scams were another favoured way in which street criminals operated in Victorian London. Just like today, methods included distraction, whereby an apparently innocent person would enquire about the time or directions as his accomplice rifled through coat pockets or dipped into shopping bags. Another scam came in the form of beggary, with men, women and even children sitting mournfully on street corners, claiming ailment or fatal disease. Upon receiving a handful of pennies from kind-hearted and empathetic passers-by, the beggar would then stand and walk away effortlessly, their ailment having suddenly disappeared. Other scams were more creative. One man in Oakley Terrace, London, kept a live brown bear in the basement of his house. Claiming that the bear would be slaughtered if not enough funds were raised for its release back into the wild, the man would admit curious visitors into his cellar for a fee.[9] Weeks passed by, and the bear disappeared. Fearing the worst, passers-by mourned the loss of the bear; that was, until it was rediscovered held captive in a different cellar but by the same man who pleaded the exact same story.[10]

Other street crimes in Victorian London came in the form of 'upskirting', a particularly distressing method of sexual harassment in which the skirts of women would be cruelly lifted by reprobates, exposing their underwear or bare legs beneath.[11] It occurred with such frequency in London that Parliament was motivated into passing the Criminal Law Amendment Act of 1903, which improved the rights of women who had been subject to humiliating attacks such as upskirting, as well as falling victim to rape and other sexual crimes. Some particularly horrid criminals would also target the elderly, the infirm or the young. 'Garroting', whereby a criminal would slink a rope around their victim's neck, or hold them tightly while an accomplice stole from the poor soul, was a particularly cruel offence that earned criminals lengthy prison sentences.

Going to prison in nineteenth-century Britain was a fate many, even the most hardened of criminals, avoided if they could. Established in 1842, Pentonville Prison in London was just one of the institutions built to house dangerous criminals and crooks. Here, punishments of the incarcerated included daily verbal and physical abuse from policemen and prison guards, as well as beatings, incredibly hard manual labour, isolation in cramped, dark cells and even 'lavage', the force-feeding of criminals who refused to eat.[13] Prisons were cold, unhygienic and full of dangerous people, and proved to be a serious threat to life. Even innocent people who found themselves temporarily imprisoned for wrongdoings, or for crimes such as failing to repay debts, emerged from prison as entirely different people.[14] Subjected to frequent whippings, lashings and other painful tortures, criminals in nineteenth-century Britain were damaged not just in spirit but in body too. Women in particular would be subject to humiliating punishments, including being chained together in groups of three so that even eating and toileting would be difficult and entirely public.[15] Social reformists of the time, such as the Quaker, Elizabeth Fry, were so appalled by the treatment of prisoners that they appealed for penal reform. Such reform was slow in coming and required much overhaul, yet early advancements would come about in the late nineteenth century which provided social, spiritual and health aid to the incarcerated.

As these reforms slowly began to be introduced to Victorian prisons, a peculiar phenomenon appeared to occur. William Crooks, a journalist of the time, discovered that inmates of the Poplar Workhouse would specifically be violent and cause damage to machines and to others in order to be transferred to prison, such was the extent of the horrors of the workhouse. Indeed, despite the terrors of prisons at the time, they were arguably much better than an alternative of life spent in a workhouse or upon the cold, miserable streets of the city. Henry Mayhew even records that youths would smash church windows, deface buildings or commit lesser crimes so that they could be confined to prisons for a short while, a welcome reprieve from life in the dark and dingy slums.[16] One 19-year-old boy had even been sentenced upward of fourteen times in order to escape the realities of street life in Victorian London.[17]

If they were lucky, however, British criminals in the nineteenth century could avoid imprisonment altogether if courts instead chose to send them to penal colonies. These colonies, located halfway across the world in Australia, were communities consisting of criminals and offenders who were punished with years of hard labour. One of the most infamous pick-pockets of nineteenth-century London, Ilkey Solomon, was shipped out from the city's docks on the *Zetland*, a prison-hulk (a ship used specifically for penal transport) bound for Tasmania. Initially supposed to serve a sentence of just four years, Solomon eventually gained freedom due to his improved behaviour, later going on to establish a family and a home of his own, and living until he died of old age in apparent happiness and comfort.[18] It was estimated that around 5,000 British prisoners were transported each year to penal colonies in Australia between the 1830s and the 1850s, but such sentences became less popular and were eventually abolished in 1857.[19]

Pick-pockets like Ilkey Solomon have come to characterize nineteenth-century London. Typically children or adolescents, pick-pockets would, as the name suggests, pick the pockets of wealthier people as they walked the streets of the city. Between 1830 and 1860, it was estimated that more than half of pick-pocketing crimes in the city had been performed by people under the age of 20.[20] These children (both boys and girls) would be trained under the watchful eye of so-called 'lads men' or 'kids men', who ran rings of pick-pockets and shared any funds acquired from their theft among them. One of the most infamous 'lads men' of Victorian London was 'Fingers Freddy', an Italian-American immigrant who targeted prostitutes and crowds of people as his boys distracted them from the crime that was being committed. Freddy, who was at one point suspected to have been Jack the Ripper, made a fortune from his crimes.[21] He followed in the stead of Ilkey Solomon, who is widely believed to have been the inspiration behind the character of Fagin in Charles Dickens's most famous work, *Oliver Twist*.

Just like adults, juveniles too could be sentenced and punished in Victorian Britain. Indeed, prison records of children as young as 7 exist, sentenced for such things as telling lies and stealing apples.[22] Three out of four petty crimes in London were believed to have been carried out by youths, an alarmingly high number. In 1800, it had been declared that children aged between 7 and 14 found guilty of committing criminal offences could be punished by imprisonment, transportation to penal colonies and even execution. Between 1801 and 1836, 103 child criminals in London alone were sentenced to death by hanging. Many of these executions were prevented, however, when the public threatened to boycott local law courts. Already disturbed by 'the screams of the boys' as they were whipped and beaten in jail, outraged Londoners lobbied Parliamentarians to reconsider the minimum age for the death penalty.[23]Their efforts succeeded: almost all of the boys who had been sentenced to death were pardoned and 'recommended to mercy on account of their youth'.[24] One of the only boys who was actually hung for his crimes was 14-year-old John Bell, of Maidstone in Kent, who was sentenced for murdering a 12-year-old. Bell's death in 1831 marked the last execution of a child in Great Britain, followed thirty-seven years later by the final public execution of an adult criminal outside the grounds of Newgate Prison.[25]

That executions were no longer public did not mean that they had entirely ceased, however. Capital punishment continued in England until 1964, although it occurred entirely behind closed doors. It remained a punishment doled out for the most serious, heinous and disturbing of crimes, such as serial murder, and was reserved for only a select few truly evil Victorians who killed indiscriminately and without remorse.

Cold-Blooded Killers

On 24 March 1873, Mary Ann Cotton ascended the steps of the scaffold. Her crimes had been numerous and horrific, so much so that she is often considered to be the first – and worst – female serial killer in British history. Known as 'the Black Widow', Mary is known to have killed at least one victim, and was suspected of scores more, with criminologists typically agreeing that she murdered around twenty people during her killing sprees.[1] Active between 1857 and 1872, Mary Ann

Cotton typically targeted children and other powerless people, among them eight of her own children, seven step-children, three of her husbands, her lover, her friend and even her own mother.

Mary Ann Cotton's murderous story began in the 1850s with the tragic deaths of four of her five children in quick succession. Three more children would be born, though they too followed their siblings to the grave. Initially, the local authorities thought little of the deaths of the children, despite their frequency, instead simply blaming the tragedies on the high infant death rates of the time. The authorities also failed to investigate the death of Mary's husband, William Mowbray, who died from a sudden and mysterious illness in January 1865.

What authorities did not know, however, was that Mary Ann Cotton had hatched a deadly plan. Armed with quantities of arsenic, Mary would poison members of her own family until they succumbed to their symptoms, whereupon she would cash in their life insurance policies and live off the amassed wealth. Mary knew that this was a lucrative loophole. If she disguised the deaths of her family as natural and unsuspicious, then she would avoid the scrutiny of the law and the authorities. She therefore painted herself as a tragic figure, keeping up appearances in public in faux mourning garb and in a state of distress. The ploy worked; sympathetic neighbours were assured that someone as unfortunate as Mary Ann Cotton could never commit such a crime.

Following the death of her first husband, Mary moved to County Durham with her sole surviving child, Isabella. There, she took up a job in an infirmary and cared for sick and injured patients, primarily suffering from diseases such as cholera and typhoid. While on her rounds, Mary formed a relationship with a patient, George Ward, whom she would later marry in August 1865. Just mere months later, however, Ward succumbed to a mysterious illness in which he had complained of intense stomach pains and digestive problems. Again, the local authorities believed Ward's death to be innocent, writing on his death certificate that he had died of complications from 'English cholera'.[2]

Deciding it best to cover her tracks to avoid arousing suspicion, Mary moved to Sunderland, having sent her daughter to live with her mother. In Sunderland, Mary took up a job as a housemaid within the home of James Robinson, a recently widowed mariner who had been left to raise three children alone. The youngest of these children, John, who was just a baby, died of 'gastric complications', leaving Robinson bereft. Finding comfort in Mary, she soon found herself pregnant with Robinson's child, and the pair married in 1867. Two children would be borne from this relationship: a son, George, and a daughter, Margaret, who would die less than a year following her birth.

Tragedy appeared to follow Mary Ann Cotton wherever she went, yet still the community viewed her with kindness and condolence. Her string of apparent misfortunes only worsened that same year when her mother, her eldest daughter, Isabella, and the remaining two children of James Robinson from his previous marriage died in quick succession. In the midst of his heartbreak, Robinson began to grow suspicious when his wife often asked him to take out life insurance. These suspicions furthered when he discovered that Mary had been amassing huge debts,

1. Typical slum dwellings often had very little furniture. Most families gathered around hearths or open fires in order to stay warm in their dilapidated, freezing and damp homes.

2. Backstreets and alleys were the meeting places and playgrounds of the poor. In her *Notes on Old Edinburgh* (1869), Isabella Bird noted the 'dirty little children' who were 'rolling in the gutter or sitting stolidly on the kerb-stone'.

3. Famous photojournalist John Thomson captured scenes of Victorian slum life along his travels. This striking photograph of a mother and her infant became one of his most well-known and endured in the hearts of Victorian reformists.

Right: 4. Terraced slum dwellings often backed onto dingy narrow alleyways. These dark labyrinthian warrens were vital in maintaining the camaraderie of slum communities, where neighbours were considered akin to family.

Below: 5. Gustave Doré's haunting illustrations of Victorian London offer a contemporary glimpse into life in the city. *Over London by Rail* depicts the cramped conditions of slum dwellings that were overlooked by other residences.

Above: 6. Penny sit-ups, two-penny hang-overs and four-penny coffins were introduced in the early 1800s in an attempt to combat street-dwelling and vagrancy. For just pennies, the poor could hire a spot for the night in communal sleeping halls in a last-ditch attempt at achieving a night's rest.

Left: 7. In this depiction of a poor family living in Harrow Alley, Aldgate, children and their parents tirelessly hawk their wares in the hope of a meagre earning. This was a reality for a vast majority of poor Victorians.

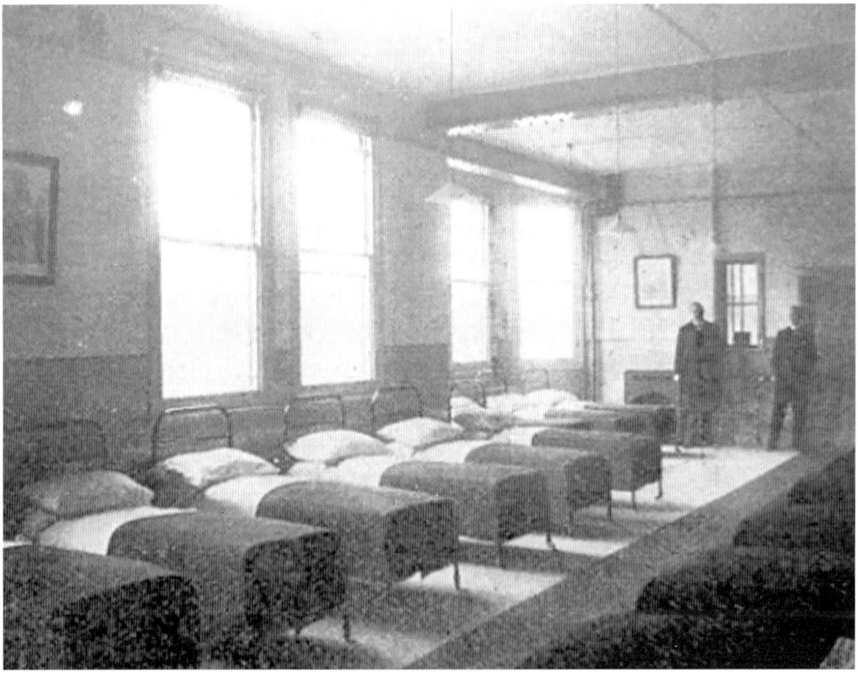

8. Established in 1730, the Workhouse of St Marylebone served as accommodation for the poor and an infirmary for the sick. By 1843, around 1,750 inmates resided in its dormitories – just three years later, this figure rose to almost 2,500.

9. Children were employed in cotton mills and factories because they were nimble and small enough to reach into crannies that adults could not. It led to countless accidents, including children getting crushed or caught in the machinery, and even to death.

Left: 10. Following an outbreak of typhus in 1838, radical reformer Edwin Chadwick's *Report on the Sanitary Condition of the Labouring Population* directly led to the first Public Health Act to be passed in 1848. Thanks to Chadwick, the medical and hygiene standards for the poorest of Victorian society vastly improved.

Below: 11. Introduced in 1845, Mrs Winslow's Soothing Syrup claimed to relieve teething and growing pains as well as assist in soothing babies to sleep. It quickly became a favourite of Victorian mothers, who were unaware that the syrup's main ingredient was morphine.

12. The Incurable Ward at Bethlem Hospital was first established in 1730, and was reserved for patients considered so severely unwell that they could not be discharged. Most patients, however, stayed at Bethlem for just twelve months before their discharge.

13. Cookery was an every-day part of life, irrespective of one's social position. The 1800s saw the popularization of dedicated cookery books, including Isabella Beeton's *Household Management* and Alexis Soyer's *A Shilling Cookery for the People*.

THE COSTER-GIRL.

"Apples! An 'aypenny a lot, Apples!"

[*From a Daguerreotype by* BEARD.]

14. Coster girls were common sights in Victorian marketplaces. Loaded with heavy baskets and trays, they would sell their wares of fruit, flowers and miscellanies to market-goers.

THE LONDON COFFEE-STALL.

[*From a Daguerreotype by* BEARD.]

15. Wheeled coffee stalls were popular with Victorians who crowded around carts in search of steaming cups of tea, coffee and cocoa. Henry Mayhew reckoned there were around 200 of these carts in London's busiest market at Billingsgate.

Above: 16. With the establishment of dedicated bricks-and-mortar stores such as W.H. Smith's Booksellers and Stationers in the early 1800s, entertainment in all forms was more accessible than ever. It led to a boom in consumer spending habits that even the poorest of society contributed to.

Right: 17. A favourite form of entertainment was 'decorative scraps', paper dolls that could be cut out from newspapers and magazines and played with or pasted into scrapbooks. Rich and poor, young and old alike were fond of these scraps, which resembled famous figures or wore the latest fashions.

Above: 18. The Victorians loved a feel-good Christmas story. One favourite was *A Christmas Transformation*, in which two poor girls begin their story in squalor and end as magical fairy ballerinas.

Left: 19. Established by Thomas Coram in the mid-eighteenth century, London's Foundling Hospital provided a safe, clean home for 'abandoned' and 'deserted' children, where they could receive an education, medical care and regular set meals.

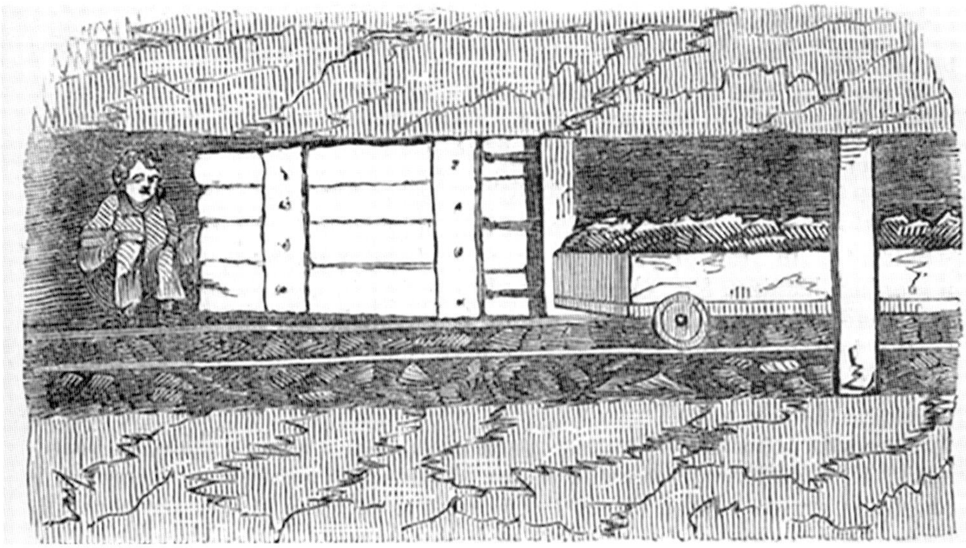

Above: 20. The 1842 Report of Children's Employment Commission shed light on the working conditions of children employed in mines. It went on to inspire anti-child exploitation literature, notably in the works of Charles Dickens.

Right: 21. As one of Dickens's most charming and endearing characters, Tiny Tim came to be seen as a symbol of childish innocence and good, and helped change the way people viewed disability in Victorian Britain.

Above: 22. The body of Mary Ann 'Polly' Nichols was found in Buck's Row, Whitechapel, on 1 September 1888. The macabre discovery would be the first in a long string of horrific events linked with infamous murderer Jack the Ripper.

Left: 23. Mary Ann Cotton, said to be Britain's first serial killer, is believed to have poisoned twenty-one people using arsenic, including her mother, three husbands and eleven of her own children.

Right: 24. Pickpocketing was a favourite pastime of casual criminals. Relatively lucrative, and easier to carry out than household theft, even children – like *Oliver Twist*'s The Artful Dodger – pickpocketed in the hopes of making a few pennies.

Below: 25. Bunhill Fields Cemetery in London came under criticism in 1856 for its dangerous overcrowding and use as a dumping ground for slum waste. The Metropolitan Public Gardens Association restored the cemetery as a peaceful green space for mourners in the 1880s.

Above: 26. Photography was a luxury in the Victorian era; if the poor could afford it, they would employ the use of a photographer to capture the likeness of their deceased relatives in the increasingly popular trend of mortuary photography. Even Queen Victoria sought to immortalize her beloved Albert in this way.

Left: 27. Body-snatching was a real worry for mourners in the early 1800s. 'Resurrection Men' would venture into cemeteries to ransack graves in order to supply surgeons and medical professionals with fresh corpses for their studies.

28. One small but significant introduction to educational reform was the Queen Victoria Medal, which incentivized poor children to attend school and receive an education.

29. In response to child poverty, Thomas Barnardo established 'ragged schools' in 1867, giving poor children the opportunity of an education. Barnardo went on to establish ninety-six children's homes before his death, and particularly focused on caring for the poor, the exploited and the disabled.

30. One of the most significant reforms of the twentieth century was the right to women's suffrage. Although women did not achieve the same voting rights as men until 1928, the Suffragette movement of the early 1900s made great strides in improving the franchise of women.

which she had attempted to pay off by selling items within the home. Outraged, Robinson threw Mary out, but made sure to keep in his custody their sole surviving child, George.

Finding herself on the streets, Mary resided for a while with a friend named Margaret, who introduced her to her unmarried brother, Frederick. Like James Robinson, Frederick had recently been widowed and had two children in tow, who Mary quickly took beneath her wing. Again, she soon found herself to be pregnant (for the twelfth time), and the couple married in 1870 before the birth of their son, Richard, in early 1871. Around this time, Mary's friend, Margaret, died of a sudden and unexpected illness, shortly followed by her brother, Frederick, in December of that year. Yet still Mary Ann Cotton evaded suspicion.

With no husband, no home and three children in her care (two from Frederick's previous marriage, as well as their son, Richard), Mary soon found herself lodging with another man, a Joseph Nattrass. Following a pattern which would soon become her trademark, Mary Ann Cotton would find herself bereaved yet again when her lover passed away in 1872. Just weeks later, however, she had already met another man, a Richard Quick-Manning (or Quick-Mann), and had found herself to be pregnant with his child. Mary pressed Richard into marriage, but before doing so ensured that her stepson, Frederick Jr., as well as her son, Richard, were well out of the picture. With just one child left in her custody, and one infant in her womb, Mary Ann Cotton's plan had apparently worked. Still, she kept up appearances within the community, acting as a kind and charitable neighbour to those around her. When nursing a sick parishioner out of the apparent kindness of her heart, Mary Ann Cotton was overheard complaining about her young stepson, Charles Edward, whom she had pushed to be institutionalized within the workhouse. Her attempt was rebuffed by one parish official, Thomas Riley, who told her that on account of his young age, Mary would have had to accompany him. Mary scoffed. 'I won't be troubled long,' she said chillingly. 'He'll go like all the rest of the Cottons.'[3]

She was right. Just five days later, Mary told Thomas Riley that young Charles Edward had died of a gastric fever. Unconvinced, Riley rushed to the coroner's office and begged them to carry out an intensive investigation upon the child's body. When arsenic was found within the child's lungs and stomach, further investigations took place upon the bodies of Mary Ann Cotton's other children, who had to be exhumed from their graves for the purpose. Arsenic was also found in their systems.

Mary Ann Cotton was arrested in late 1872, and following her trial was sentenced to death by hanging. While in prison awaiting her trial, Mary gave birth to her thirteenth and final child, a daughter whom she named Margaret Edith. Margaret Edith was one of just two of the children of Mary Ann Cotton to survive their childhoods, and was adopted after the execution of her mother on 24 March 1873. Mary's hanging was a botched affair, the noose having been hung intentionally too long for Mary's body, meaning she suffered a long, drawn-out death by strangulation. Once all signs of life had gone from her body, Mary Ann Cotton was cut down and her head was studied by the West Hartlepool Phrenological Society (who wished to determine if Mary had suffered from a mental ailment which had caused her to commit her crimes). She was then buried in an unmarked grave in the grounds of Durham prison.

Mary Ann Cotton is widely believed to have been the first female serial killer in Britain, though she was closely followed by another equally wicked woman who also targeted helpless and innocent children.

Amelia Dyer, known as the 'Ogress of Reading', was just 24 when she turned to 'baby-farming', a heinous crime in which newly born infants would be either sold or killed in exchange for cash. Originally trained as a midwifery nurse, Amelia had found that illicit baby farming was far more lucrative, fetching greater sums of money than attending to mothers and their infants in hospitals and infirmaries. Having had two children of her own, Amelia initially set out fostering unwanted (and often illegitimate) babies for a fee, providing them with care until they were old enough to be formally adopted by new families. However, as time passed, Amelia found the cost of caring for these babies expensive and pointless. After taking them in, Amelia would leave the infants to starve or freeze to death, or employed poisons or violence to hasten the process. Once deceased, she, like Mary Ann Cotton, would cash-in their life insurance and receive hefty sums. It was a routine which Amelia Dyer would follow for months until 1879, when one coroner grew suspicious about the number of death certificates he had had to write up for the Dyer residence. Amelia was arrested and charged with neglect, and was sentenced to six months of hard labour in prison.

Upon her release, Amelia Dyer was frequently admitted to numerous psychiatric hospitals on account of mental instability, these stays conveniently coinciding with times that Amelia knew that the police were keeping an especially watchful eye upon her activities. At some point in her career, Amelia had temporarily cared for the illegitimate child of a school governess; when the governess later returned to retrieve her baby, she was met with one that looked entirely different. The mother grew suspicious and stripped the baby, knowing that her own child had been born with numerous birthmarks upon its skin. When she found that this baby had no such marks, the governess threatened Amelia with legal action. In response, Amelia feigned a breakdown so that she would be admitted back into the psychiatric hospital to avoid penalty.

Amelia Dyer knew that the hypothetical noose was tightening. With the police keeping a watchful eye upon her, Amelia had to find other ways by which to dispose of the children, yet still receive their insurance money. Instead of presenting the bodies of the deceased infants to funeral directors to bury them, Amelia Dyer wrapped the corpses tightly in sacking bags and dumped them in the River Thames. To avoid detection, she would relocate often, regularly moving up and down the river so that her activities would not be noticed. However, on 30 March 1896, a bargeman travelling along the Thames found a brown paper package floating on the surface of the water. When the package was opened, the tiny corpse of a new-born baby girl was found inside. The package was taken to the local police station, where it was discovered that not only was a name written on the package, but so too was an address. It appeared that Amelia Dyer had overlooked one small detail which would ultimately cause her own downfall.

The police went to the address, employing the assistance of a young female who served as a decoy to dupe Dyer. Upon opening her door and expecting the woman, Amelia was instead shocked to find a hoard of police detectives in front of her. As they pushed into her home, they were met with the sickly-sweet cloying smell of death and decay. They also found stashes of insurance receipts, adoption paperwork and bundles of white lace which was used to strangle the infants. When asked about these items, Dyer responded: 'I used to like them with the tape around their neck, it was soon all over with them. She thus appeared to not only confess to the murders of the babies, but also her disdain at how quickly the method of death would take her victims.[4]

In May 1896, Dyer appeared at the Old Bailey, where her defence plea of insanity fell flat. Instead, the jury took just four minutes to decide their verdict: guilty. She was duly sentenced to death by hanging. Amelia Dyer admitted to just one murder at her trial, yet it had been enough to condemn her. After her execution at Newgate Prison on 10 June 1896, the true number of her victims was estimated to be in the hundreds. Indeed, some historians believe Dyer to have committed anywhere between 300 and 400 murders of babies and infants, with at least twenty-six which she can confidently be held accountable for. In the aftermath of Dyer's execution, numerous bereft mothers and heartbroken parents came forward to testify against her, detailing the dates of the adoption of their children as well as giving information about clothing, toys and other possessions they had left with them. With this knowledge, police conducted further investigations into Dyer and the areas in which she had operated. Two years after her execution, they found, bundled between the parcels of a mail coach, a mewling three-week-old baby girl. Dyer's grip on baby farming in Victorian England had still not loosened, as it was believed that the woman who had placed this helpless baby upon the mail coach had been Dyer's very own daughter, Polly.

Insurance payments also appear to have been one of the major motives for the most infamous of murderers in Victorian Britain. Between 1842 and 1845, the elderly Jonathan Balls began committing a string of poisonings upon members of his own family.[5] Purchasing a large quantity of arsenic in 1842 to tackle a supposed rat infestation, Balls first instead laced the food of his 24-year-old daughter, Maria, who succumbed to the horrifying symptoms. Just months later, Balls killed a 13-month-old infant on Christmas Day, followed by his granddaughter, Ann, and a 3-year-old boy, William Green. Still more victims followed, including 4-month-old Samuel Green (Balls's grandson) in 1845, his granddaughter, Elizabeth Anne, in 1846, and even his own bed-ridden wife, Elizabeth. Just three days later, apparently satisfied with his spree, Jonathan Balls committed suicide by ingesting the very same poison he had used to kill his victims. His motivation had been the same as Mary Ann Cotton and Amelia Dyer: money.

But for every murder motivated by money in Victorian Britain, there were also those committed without rhyme or reason. On 24 October 1884, a skull barely covered in a thin layer of decomposing flesh was found along Tottenham Court Road in London.[6] It had been found alongside a disembodied human thigh, as well as a tattooed forearm that had been neatly bundled into a wrapped package. In a time before sophisticated forensic analysis, the police were forced to simply note the bare details of what they had found, as well as their potential conclusions, which pointed to the mutilated body having belonged to a female. Dubbed the 'Tottenham Court Road Mystery', matters would only grow more curious when, five days later, a female torso was found on the doorstep of 33 Fitzroy Square. Again, the police were left fumbling over scant evidence. With so little to go on, no suspect could be identified or investigated, and the victim could get no retribution. Instead, the case was shelved and has remained unsolved ever since.

Unsolved mysterious murders were unfortunately common enough occurrences in Victorian Britain that the number of cold cases grew by the day. In the 1882 Parliamentary Returns, it was stated that no less than 544 corpses had been found in the Thames that year, with at least half of them resulting in open verdicts.[7] Such was the case in 1887, when a string of distressing discoveries disturbed Londoners up and down the Thames. Dubbed 'the Thames Torso Murders', the 'Thames Mysteries' and the 'Embankment Murders', these were by far the most gruesome murders Victorian Londoners had endured to date. Sparking mass hysteria and panic within the local population, women and children were escorted when walking at night, doors were double and triple-locked, and suspicious figures were reported to the police. However, the distressing discoveries continued to be made. With corpses washing up along the banks of the Thames, or disembodied limbs found hidden in backyard allies, anxiety in the city was at an all-time high. Nowhere were these sickening murders more prevalent than in one of the poorest districts of Victorian London, an area in which depravity and ruin reigned supreme: Whitechapel.

Jack the Ripper

No chapter about Victorian crime would be complete without telling the tale of one of the most bone-chilling murder investigations of all time. The legend of Jack the Ripper has endured in the memories of criminologists since the late nineteenth century, perpetuated by its mysterious appeal and lack of concrete conclusions. In the 136 years since the first mention of 'Jack' was recorded, numerous attempts have been made by casual and professional detectives alike to unveil the identity of history's most infamous serial killer. Although the list of suspects numbers well into double figures (and may even continue to grow), no one has ever been able to put a name to the (albeit anonymous) face of the Ripper.

What evidence has survived, however, is a prolific and detailed record of the Ripper's victims. Known as the 'Canonical Five', the women found murdered in the streets of Whitechapel between August and November of 1888 are conclusively accepted by Ripperologists and historians as sharing the same killer. Yet the brutal murders of a number of other Whitechapel women continue to mystify those unravelling the Ripper's web of butchery, leading them to believe that the reach of the Ripper went further than initially thought.

On the night of 3 April 1888, Emma Elizabeth Smith, a prostitute residing in Whitechapel, was in search of her next client. Emma was 45 and relied on prostitution as a means to pay rent to the landlord of her housing tenement. As a prostitute, Emma would have been no stranger to wandering alone in the darkest of nights, accustomed to the seedy underground of the city. Yet on this particular night, Emma had been approached by a gang of four youths in search of more than just a few moments of pleasure.

The gang each took turns in raping and beating Emma, before finishing their attack by jabbing a blunt object into her vagina.[1] Emma, weak from her attack and desperately losing blood, attempted to staunch its flow by wedging scraps of fabric between her legs. She managed to flag down bystanders, who rushed her to the London Hospital on Whitechapel Road, where it was discovered that Emma's perineum had been torn almost completely through. Despite attempts at suturing the wound, Emma slipped into unconsciousness and fell into a coma, succumbing to her injuries four days later.

Had Emma been the first victim of Jack the Ripper? Although some Ripperologists discredit Emma's murder as being carried out by the Ripper, others have postulated that the gang may have been headed by Jack, or that it had consisted of his cronies, carrying out his lust for blood-curdling violence.[2] Others still have attributed the brutal attack to the so-called 'high rip' gangs of London, who stalked the city at night and threatened local prostitutes with rape unless they paid the gang extortionate protection fees.[3] The identity of Emma Elizabeth Smith's killers are still to this day unknown, yet history remembers her as a woman unfairly targeted for her employ and standing in the Victorian world.

Martha Tabram was another alleged victim of the Ripper. Like Emma, Martha had turned to prostitution in the Whitechapel area in order to earn what little money she could to pay for her lodging in nearby Spitalfields. Martha's life had been a difficult one. She developed a habit for alcohol abuse, regularly spending the money intended for her rent in public houses. Drinking away her earnings, Martha lodged with a London hawker named Henry Turner, who made his money principally through the trading of cheap trinkets, pins, needles and menthol cones designed for the alleviation of influenza and common colds.[4] Martha's relationship with Henry has been disputed by historians as to whether it was romantic or not – either way, it did not dissuade Martha from heading out into the night of 6 August 1888 in search of a customer seeking entertainment of the sordid type.

Martha had been spotted by numerous eyewitnesses around midnight on 6 August, including a set of soldiers with whom she had apparently engaged. Yet just two hours after last being sighted, her corpse was quite literally stumbled upon by waterside labourer John Reeves, who had been heading from his apartment to work.[5] It was now around four o'clock in the morning, and Reeves could just make out a dark pool of blood beneath what he believed to be the body of a sleeping woman. Rushing to find a policeman, the pair attempted to rouse Tabram, but it proved in vain. A local medic, Dr Timothy Killeen, later pronounced Martha as deceased, offering the supposition that she had been brutally murdered by 'some long, strong instrument [perhaps] a sword, bayonet or dagger'.[6] Upon examination in the nearby mortuary, it was recorded that Tabram had suffered thirty-nine stab wounds, running from her throat to her abdomen, which had been caused by more than one blade.[7]

Had Martha Tabram been murdered by more than one hand, as in the case of Emma Elizabeth Smith, or had her killer simply utilized more than one weapon? Again, debate surrounds as to whether she was indeed a victim of Jack the Ripper, though startlingly, many contemporary investigators of the crime did attribute it to him. One detective who worked on the case, Inspector Walter Dew, even explicitly stated that the death of Tabram 'was the handiwork of the dread Ripper'.[8]

Still more victims of brutal murders carried out in London in 1888 continue to puzzle criminologists over their perpetrators. On 9 October, for example, the body of a woman was spotted floating in the Thames beneath Waterloo Bridge.[9] Disembodied arms were also found in the Thames, the female owner of which had later been found headless and limbless in a cellar at New Scotland Yard.[10] Yet another possible victim transpired in the case of 24-year-old Elizabeth Jackson, whose severed body parts were discovered when police boats observing activity on the Thames bumped into floating burlap sacks which contained them.[11] Further parcels containing her organs and remains were found hidden in Battersea, Fulham, Vauxhall and even in the gardens of Percy Shelley's home in Chelsea.[12] Further still, a foetus of around five months gestation had been found floating in a jar near Whitehall, leading investigators to believe that Elizabeth Jackson had been the victim of a botched abortion gone hideously wrong.

Indeed, contemporary theories regarding the identity of the Ripper pointed to a female abortionist, with even Sherlock Holmes author Arthur Conan Doyle suggesting that the reason the Ripper had never been identified was due to her unsuspiciousness as a female.[13] As we shall discover in the cases of the 'Canonical Five', many of the Ripper's victims had sustained injuries to their genitalia and sexual organs, suggesting that the murderer had anatomical knowledge of the female reproductive system. Some of the victims even had their uterus removed during their attack, potentially furthering the theory of the Ripper as a midwife-turned-abortionist.

Although this theory is unpopular amongst Ripperologists, one name in particular has been put forward as the potential identity of the Ripper. In October 1890, a woman named Mary Pearcey stabbed and slashed the throats of the wife and child of her lover, before dumping their bodies in a secluded street in the hope of evading detection.[14] Pearcey was later apprehended and sentenced to death by hanging, but not before sending a bizarre cryptic message to be printed in a Madrid newspaper, reading:

> 'M. E. C. P. last wish of M. E. W. Have not been betrayed.'[15]

Pearcey was hanged on 23 December 1890, with her cryptic message remaining uninterpreted. Had perhaps the Ripper fled to Madrid, and was he continuing his work through associates in London? Had Mary herself been the Ripper, successfully managing to evade detection until 1890? Whether Mary Pearcey had been the Ripper or not, the theory that 'Jack' may have actually been a 'Jill' still lingers as a possibility for Ripperologists today.[16]

As mentioned, at least three of the 'Canonical Five' victims of Jack the Ripper had sustained some sort of injury to their sexual organs, with Annie Chapman, Catherine Eddowes and Mary Jane Kelly each having their uterus entirely removed or eviscerated. Each of the victims had been mutilated in ways similar to the others, suggesting that their murders may have been conducted by the same person. Additionally, the relatively short time window in which they had been killed (between late August and early November 1888), as well as the close proximity in which their bodies had been found, bolsters the idea that they had a shared killer. It is most widely accepted that this killer began the string of murders in the late August of 1888, although, as we have seen in the cases of Emma Elizabeth Smith and Martha Tabram, it may have begun even earlier.

The first day of September 1888 marks an important date in the calendars of Ripperologists. It was during the early hours of that morning that two labourers, Charles Cross and Robert Paul, noticed a strange figure lying askew upon the pavement of Buck's Row, Whitechapel.[17] 'Come and look over here,' said Cross, cautiously approaching the figure and trying to distinguish its details in the darkness of the night, 'there's a woman!'[18] The two men, anxious not to be implicated as suspects of assault – and worried that they would be late for work – rushed at once in search for a policeman to assist what they believed was just an unconscious, probably drunk, woman.

Moments later, three policemen arrived at Buck's Row, their presence pronounced by the dim orange glow of their swaying hand-held lanterns. This was the only source of light around them, save for a single gas lamp located at the far end of the street.[19] As they approached the figure, the lanterns illuminated more clearly what Cross had correctly identified as a woman, but one whose throat had been cut.

The woman's body was promptly covered with a white sheet and transported to the nearby Whitechapel Mortuary, known colloquially as the 'Dead-House'.[20] There, the corpse was washed, stripped of its clothing and inspected in closer detail. 'Five teeth were missing,' wrote the coroner in the inquest testimony, 'and there was a slight laceration of the tongue.'[21] He added that there were 'several incisions running across the abdomen', and a 'circular incision' beneath the right jaw.[22] The fatal wound, however, had been the gash upon her throat, which had run so deep that it had severed the vessels and tissue in the neck entirely, and had exposed the vertebrae.[23]

'The poor woman was attacked by a maniac!' penned one horrified journalist in the *London Evening Standard*.[24] Indeed, as rumours of the bone-chilling attack spread throughout the twisted streets of Whitechapel, public interest in the case grew. Journalists were admitted into the Dead-House to view the body with the intention that their articles would help point detectives in the right direction to identify the poor woman's killer. However, news of such barbaric butchery sparked hysteria amongst Whitechapel residents, who were all too aware that not much time had passed since the murders of Emma Elizabeth Smith and Martha Tabram had come to light. This hysteria was not helped by creative-minded journalists who saw the murder as an opportunity to add emphatic flourishes to their articles. 'As the corpse lies in the mortuary it presents a ghastly sight,' even wrote one journalist.[25]

But who was this woman who lay, throat-gashed, upon the cold steel embalming table? Immediate efforts were launched to identify the poor soul. 'She appears to be in extreme poverty', wrote one journalist who viewed the body, with another adding that she looked to be 'of the class known as "unfortunate"'.[26] Indeed, scrutiny of the women's apparel and personal belongings seemed to indicate that she had not come from a wealthy standing, or any sort of standing at all. Aside from her threadbare linsey-woolsey dress, patterned ulster coat and worn pair of stockings, the woman had not much else in her possession when she was killed. Closer inspection of the woman's underclothes had yielded that her drawers had been made from flannel, as had her chest cloth, and that the two petticoats that she had worn had once been the property of Lambeth Workhouse.[27]

Whoever this woman was had not lived a comfortable life. Her pockets were filled with just three items, presumed to be her most valuable and prized possessions: a broken comb, a shattered shard of mirror and a handkerchief.[28] Many vagrants who stalked the Victorian slums – such as this woman had appeared to be – lived transitory lives, never settling in one area and establishing homes of their own. As such, they carried around minimal comforts, things that could be small enough to fit into pockets or sacks. Such meagre belongings were not unusual, but were useful to coroners in determining the social class from which their owners hailed.

Eventually, witnesses offering their testimonies of the morning of 1 September led detectives to arrive at the victim's identity; her name was Mary Ann Nichols. Also known by the name 'Polly', Nichols was a frequenter of workhouses, dosshouses and public houses. Described as 'clean' but a 'drunkard', Polly may have turned to prostitution in order to support herself financially. Certain historians, including Hallie Rubenhold, have discredited this theory, stating that, as a literate and therefore educated woman, Polly would have more likely earned her stingy wages from domestic employment than sex work.[29] It is likely, however, that Polly may have indeed been a prostitute, or had at least supplemented her income by this means – after all, she had resided for a time at the White House dosshouse, where men and women shared beds.[30] She was also known to be fond of gin, which, according to Ripperologist S.P. Ryder, was the typical going-rate for prostitution in the East London area.[31]

Whether Polly had been a prostitute or not, prejudice had been laid aside as the public came to the agreement that her murder had been a horrific, unprovoked attack. 'It is terrible to reflect that at the end of the nineteenth century,' wrote one journalist in the *Evening Standard*, 'after all our efforts, religious, educational, and philanthropic, such revolting and sickening barbarity should still be found in the heart of this great city.'[32] What the public did not know, however, was that this 'revolting and sickening barbarity' had only just begun.

John Davis, an elderly carman (delivery driver) at Leadenhall Market, awoke at his usual time of 5.45 am and made himself a cup of tea.[33] Careful so as not to disturb his wife and three sons, who were all still asleep in their shared one-room lodging, Davis quietly stepped out of the door and tiptoed to the communal outhouse in the shared courtyard. Seventeen people lived in this one tenement building at 29 Hanbury Street in the East End of London – at least, those whom we can identify concretely.[34] Among them was a Mr Thompson, his wife and their adopted little girl, and two spinster sisters who often left their door unlocked, fully trusting of their neighbours.[35]

Finishing his business in the outhouse, a bleary-eyed Davis stepped back into the courtyard. The early-morning sun had just begun to break through the autumn cloud, casting long shadows across the paving slabs. It was these shadows that caught Davis's eye. Huddled in a pile in the far-corner of the courtyard was a black mass, its details masked by the darkness. It was not uncommon for items, objects and even people to be slumped in the courtyard at Hanbury Street, which regularly found itself used as a makeshift shelter for the homeless and aimless drunks on their way home from the local public houses. Yet as Davis approached, he was met with a grotesque sight. This was no lolling drunk. There, lying stiffly upon her back, with her knees bent upright, was a middle-aged woman. Her eyes were partially open, and her swollen tongue protruded through a set of broken and bloody teeth. Her limbs were unnaturally stiff, particularly the blood-soaked arms that lay curled upon her breast, and her head was turned at an awkward angle.[36] This woman, Davis deduced, was certainly not sleeping.

Immediately, Davis set off in a desperate search for aid, his heart pounding and his stomach nauseated. No longer worried about waking the sleeping residents of Hanbury Street, he bounded through the house and called for help. Three men groggily answered, urging him to the nearby police station on Commercial Street once they had learned of the gravity of his discovery. The men were sure that this woman was dead, and had probably met her tragic end in a manner most horrific. It appeared that the Whitechapel murderer had struck again.

Within moments, a swarm of policemen had muscled their way through the growing throng of curious bystanders that had gathered at the scene of the crime. Although told to bring reinforcements to stave off spectators, the police were unable to herd away the crowd, which had grown to several hundred people in a matter of minutes.[37] By the time the Divisional Police Surgeon, Dr George Bagster Phillips, had arrived at Hanbury Street, the crowd had grown even larger, giving Police Inspector Joseph Chandler no other choice but to conceal the woman's body with a scrap of burlap sacking.[38]

Confirming what John Davis and the other men had suspected earlier that morning, Dr Phillips officially 'pronoun[ced] life extinct' within the woman.[39] He estimated that she had died at around 5.00 am that morning, and had, like Mary Ann Nichols, been killed by a fatal incision that had cut deep into the throat.[40] It was later discovered during the post-mortem inquest that the woman's womb had also been extracted from her body via deftly made cuts, as had her intestines and stomach, which had been placed upon her left shoulder.[41] That the woman's throat had been so deeply severed was enough for detectives to believe that the Hanbury Street corpse was linked to the murder of Mary Ann Nichols. But unlike Nichols, this unfortunate victim had appeared to be of relatively good social standing, as evidenced by her attire and personal possessions. Though still ragged and worn in her appearance, the Hanbury Street woman had the luxury of owning a number of brass rings, a hair comb and even a piece of soap.[42] She had also been wearing a neckerchief at the time of her murder, as well as brightly coloured striped stockings and a skirt with attachable pockets.[43]

The corpse was taken away from Hanbury Street in a wooden coffin and escorted to the shed-like Whitechapel Mortuary via police ambulance.[44] There, a closer examination of the corpse commenced, with Dr Phillips concluding that the perpetrator must have had a degree of anatomical knowledge due to the precision and intentional placement of the wounds. It was discovered that, along with the uterus, small intestine and part of the stomach, the woman's bladder had also been removed.[45] When each of the organs had been washed and examined, it was found that the woman had exhibited 'signs of great deprivation' on account of the little food within the stomach, and that she had been in the early stages of tuberculosis, chronic brain disease and possibly syphilis.[46] Though the woman's outward appearance had initially led detectives to believe that she had hailed from a higher rung of the social ladder, she was by no means wealthy or fortunate. Indeed, when Timothy Donovan, owner of a local lodging house in Spitalfields, identified the body, it was discovered that, following a fall from grace, the woman had slunk into a life of starvation, alcoholism and immense deprivation.

Annie Chapman is widely regarded as the second victim of Jack the Ripper. Hailing from a relatively comfortable family, Chapman had fallen into a life of alcohol abuse that had threatened her stability. She had married her distant cousin, John Chapman, in 1869, eventually producing three children: Emily Ruth, Annie Georgina and the sickly John Alfred, who was sent to live in a medical institution in the Windsor countryside.[47] Although Chapman had promised to live soberly for the benefit of her children, even going so far as to order her husband to hide bottles of medicine in their home so that she could not drink them, she was arrested on numerous occasions on account of public intoxication.[48] Annie, shunned by society, relocated alone to London, where she bounced between workhouses and lodging houses, supported by meagre earnings that she made by selling flowers and crocheted antimacassars (chair protectors).[49] She was known to frequent workhouse infirmaries, where she picked up bottles of medicine (presumably for her developing symptoms of tuberculosis) and borrowed slithers of soap in the hope of keeping clean.[50]

Annie's life in London was difficult. One eyewitness, interviewed by detectives in the aftermath of her murder, stated that she had 'never know[n] her to have a settled home'.[51] Indeed, Annie frequented many of the lodging houses in the East End of London, choosing her preferred accommodation by how cheap the daily rent was. She seemed to favour Crossingham's Lodging House in Spitalfields, which doled out beds for its 300 residents on a first-come, first-served basis.[51] Each resident would be given a number to correspond to their bed, which they had to seek out amongst the tightly packed rows of the communal dormitories. On many occasions, Annie had complained to the landlord of Crossingham's, Timothy Donovan, that the standard of her lodging was not worth the price of the rent, forcing her to go days without eating so that she could instead save up her pennies to make up what she owed him.[52] Donovan was not convinced, chastising Annie that 'you can find money for your beer and you can't find money for your bed!'.[53] Annie's plight was shared with hundreds, if not thousands of others in nineteenth-century London. 'The glimpses of life in these dens … is sufficient to make us feel that there is much in the nineteenth century civilisation of which we have small reason to be proud,' wrote the coroner who oversaw Annie's murder inquest; 'hear the sad tale of starvation, or semi-starvation, of misery, immorality, and wickedness…[this is] what life in a Spitalfields lodging-house means'.[54]

Elizabeth Stride emigrated to London from Gothenburg, Sweden, in 1866. Originally named Elisabeth Gustafsdotter, she had spent her childhood assisting on the family farm and later employed herself in domestic service.[55] During this time, Elizabeth had supplemented her income with casual prostitution, which had caused her to be arrested in 1865 as well as treated for venereal diseases in hospital on more than one occasion.[56] She had also fallen pregnant, and on 21 April 1865 gave birth to a stillborn daughter.

Choosing to leave behind the pain of her loss and difficult situation, Elizabeth sailed to London in search of a new life. She told fellow passengers conflicting reasons for her intention to travel, at times that she was due to be employed in the household of a wealthy gentleman, and at others that she would be reconnecting with long-lost family members. Whatever her true reason for relocating, those who met Elizabeth were impressed by her intelligence and gentle, generous nature. Kindly extending genuine friendship to her new London neighbours, she soon settled into life in the East End and married John Thomas Stride in 1869. The couple lived in a degree of comfort for the first few years of their marriage, owning a successful coffeehouse in Poplar that regularly drew in regular customers. However, just a few years later the Strides were forced to close the business due to financial ruin, leading to a chasm in their relationship that they would never get over.

Elizabeth is recorded as having frequented workhouses in the years succeeding her separation from John, suggesting that she had fallen on such desperate hardships that she could not even manage a meagre earning to rent out a bed in a lodging house.[57] Sometime in the late 1870s, Stride began lodging with a dock labourer named Michael Kidney, who took advantage of her desolate situation by abusing his power over her. After numerous physical beatings and an attempt by Kidney to padlock Elizabeth inside a cramped room, she sought help from the police and filed a formal assault charge against him.[58] This emancipation brought Elizabeth her safety, but also meant that she had to face the darkest and dangerous of London slums completely alone. There was no greater threat to life for women in the nineteenth century than a life on the streets. Danger lurked at every corner, ready to pounce on its unsuspecting victims. Such was the case with Elizabeth Stride, whose dreadful fate would forever link her with Mary Ann Nichols and Annie Chapman.

On 26 September 1888, a desolate and drunk Elizabeth was witnessed by none other than Dr Thomas Barnardo at a lodging house in Flower and Dean Street, Spitalfields.[59] Barnardo had been preaching in the nearby slum, an area known for its particularly degenerate violence and criminal trade, and later recounted that the purpose of his preaching was to save local children 'from the contamination of the common lodging houses and the street'.[60] Clearly, the area was not a particularly pleasant place to find yourself. Elizabeth busied herself in domestic work, distracting herself from the evils around her by acting as a hired charwoman for the wealthier residents of the locale.

Once her long day of heavy domestic duties had ended each evening, Elizabeth would amble around the public houses in the area, possibly in search of a male customer to warm her bed and line her pockets with loose pennies. She had been sighted doing just that on 30 September by dockworker James Brown, who was passing through the area, and PC William Smith, who observed her being backed against a wall by a stout man wearing a long black cloak. Elizabeth could apparently be overheard saying doggedly, 'No, not tonight. Some other night', suggesting that she was being pressured or elicited into sexual gratification by the unknown male.[61] Still, PC Smith believed Stride's situation to be of no concern, and left the woman in the arms of her presser before meandering through Whitechapel to finish his beat.

If PC Smith had approached the man who had been provoking Elizabeth Stride, perhaps history would have turned out very differently. Historians and Ripperologists now believe that the man in the long black cloak may have been the Ripper himself, and that, had Smith intervened, it would have prevented the deaths not only of Stride, but of two more of his victims. Indeed, just minutes after Smith had turned around the corner of Berner Street, a horse's whinny cried out.

Louis Diemschutz had been returning home on the evening of 30 September, and had driven his horse and cart down the lane where Elizabeth Stride, PC Smith and James Brown had been standing just twenty minutes prior. The horse had jolted at something in the road, though Diemschutz knew not what. Believing the horse to have been spooked by a 'dark object' on the ground, Diemschutz was horrified to discover that the body of a woman was blockading his path.[62] Just as in the cases of Mary Ann Nichols and Annie Chapman, the police and Divisional Surgeon Dr George Bagster had been called to attend the incident. Almost immediately, there was an understanding between the men that this case had been no accident, but rather that it had all the characteristics of the brutal butcheries that had taken place in the area just days beforehand. It was believed this woman had most likely been a victim of the same person to have murdered Nichols and Chapman.

In the post-mortem of Elizabeth Stride, it was revealed that rigor mortis had only recently began to set in, and that areas of her body had still been warm to the touch at the time of Diemschutz's discovery, prompting Bagster to believe that she had been murdered just minutes before his arrival on the street.[63] Like in the cases of Nichols and Chapman, Stride's throat had been deeply cut, the gash elongating from the neck to the jawbone. Her viscera had remained within her body, however, leading Bagster to believe that whoever committed the murder had not had enough time to perfect his butchery, as he had done with the bodies of his previous victims.

To an extent, Bagster was correct. More than one murder attributed to Jack the Ripper appears to have been committed on the night of 30 September 1888, which is widely known by Ripperologists as the 'Double Event'. Whoever had committed the murders had been deft and nimble – detectives reckoned that only around forty minutes or so separated the murders, leading them to firmly believe that the actions of the perpetrator had not been calculated. Rather, they believed that he preferred to kill on sight, completely unprovoked by his victims, in a desperate attempt to quench his bloodthirsty appetite. Indeed, the apparent trend with how the Ripper struck, targeting desolate women, probably prostitutes, led police to believe that the murderer had a particular detestation of women and even perhaps of sex.[64] One school of thought adopted by modern criminologists is that, by murdering prostitutes, the Ripper believed he was ridding the city of its evils in a twisted sense of anarchism.[65] Others have postulated that the Ripper may have been carrying out crimes of passion, and that he might have viewed killing his victims as a justifiable way to heal from lovelornness.[66] Some more revisionist historians have even believed that the Ripper's motivations stemmed from an unstable relationship with women, developed particularly in childhood. Whatever the Ripper's true intentions had been, there was no denying that in the 'Double Event', which saw the murders of Elizabeth Stride and Catherine Eddowes, there was no apparent premediated reason for attack.

Catherine Eddowes was found murdered at around 1.44 am on 31 September by PC Edward Watkins. She had been placed on her back and was severely mutilated, her intestines having been removed from the body cavity and placed upon her shoulder.[67] Her corpse had been smeared with faecal matter, and her face appeared to have been intentionally disfigured, with her nose having been cut almost entirely away from her face and the lobes of her ears cleanly cut through. Photographs of Eddowes taken in the Whitechapel Mortuary reveal the extent of her injuries – of all the other victims of the Ripper, Catherine appears to have received the worst wounds. However, the characteristic mark of the Ripper was still visible on the corpse, linking Eddowes with the other three victims. It appeared that the Ripper was leaving the police a message through the injuries he inflicted upon his victims.

Again, as in the case of Annie Chapman, it was believed by a number of doctors who worked on the cadaver that the murderer had some degree of anatomical knowledge, for Eddowes's kidneys were noted to have been carefully removed through a cut to the peritoneum.[68] Others believed that the perpetrator was 'in the habit of cutting up animals', such was the extent of his knowledge of butchery.[69] It had been a grotesque murder ypof a e never before seen by the detectives of the Whitechapel Police District. They prayed that the double murders that had occurred within the area would be the last, especially since the attacks seemed to grow in brutality each time. Yet the reprieve so desperately prayed for by the terrified residents of Whitechapel did not last as long as was hoped. Just when it seemed that the Ripper had finished his sadistic rounds of the district's slums, another murder took place, this time far more brutal than the others.

On 9 November 1888, exactly forty days after the double murders of Elizabeth Stride and Catherine Eddowes, the body of the last victim of Jack the Ripper was found at 13 Miller's Court on Dorset Street, Spitalfields.

It had been raining hard as Thomas Bowyer leapt over the murky puddles that had gathered in the drains of the street. A worker at McCarthy's Rents, Bowyer had been sent on a mission to collect the long-overdue payment from one of Mr McCarthy's usually fastidious customers.[70] As he approached the small tenement apartment, nothing out of the ordinary caught his attention. Dorset Street, though it had never been a particularly attractive place, was quiet and relatively clean, the slurry of the slum having been swirled down the drains by the rain. Bowyer knocked on the wooden door of Number 13. No reply came. He knocked again. When there was still no response, Bowyer swept aside the curtain of the open window and took in a sharp breath.

A ghastly sight met his eyes as they adjusted to the darkness of the room. There was little by way of furniture inside, save for a table, a washbasin and two chairs, as well as a large bed placed diagonally in the room as though purposely pushed away from the walls.[71] Upon the bed was a sight most foul; there, in the centre of the blood-soaked mattress and amongst putrid-smelling pieces of flesh, was the mutilated corpse of Mary Jane Kelly.

Mary had been a popular young woman. Known for her beauty and kindness, she possessed scholarly intelligence and worldly knowledge far beyond her age of 25, which was impressive considering the social class from which she had come. Fond of music, always of clean habits and fluent in Welsh, Mary had made a positive impression on her neighbours at Miller's Court, who described her as a 'good, quiet, pleasant girl [who had been] well liked by all of us'.[72] It meant that friendly faces had always been on the lookout for Mary as she returned home each night with mysterious men, hoping for an evening of entertainment and pleasure. One neighbour was keen to stress to snobbish police that Mary's plight for survival in the slums was borne of desperation, telling them: 'I do not believe she would have gone out as she did if she had not been obliged to do so to keep herself from starvation.' That none of the neighbours had seen anything unusual on the night of 9 November was therefore particularly unusual.

Bowyer had alerted the local police inspector, Walter Beck, to the gruesome sight. Using an axe to break through the locked door, Inspector Beck and his team of policemen were forced to cover their noses with handkerchiefs, such was the stench of the rapidly decomposing corpse. One member of the party, Dr Thomas Bond, was given permission by the Superintendent to approach the body, careful not to disturb any of the mounds of viscera piled up around the room that might be used as evidence. Bond's examination of the body would prove to be difficult, for very little of it remained intact. Starting from the head and working downward, Bond noted that the corpse's face had been mutilated beyond recognition, that its arms had been almost entirely abducted from their sockets and that the breasts had both been sliced off.[73] The abdominal cavity had been fully removed of all its internal organs, which had been placed in no apparent pattern around it; the uterus and kidneys lay beneath the head, the liver between the twisted legs, and the intestines placed to its right side.[74] The thighs had been placed upon the nearby table, as had the nose, eyebrows and ears; the chest cavity had been butchered so deeply that the intercostal muscles between the visible ribs had been torn, and the sexual organs had been cut away in a gash that stretched from the lower abdomen to the buttock.[75] Most chillingly of all, the corpse's throat had been hacked away to such a degree that the larynx, vertebrae and trachea had been damaged.[76] There was no denying that this, the signature that had become so ubiquitous with the murders in Whitechapel, had been the work of Jack the Ripper.

Mary Jane Kelly was buried on 19 November in a public grave at St Patrick's Roman Catholic Cemetery in the London borough of Waltham Forest. No family member of Kelly could be traced, so her simple funeral had been paid for through public subscription. Today, a simple marker heads her resting place, as do similar monuments dedicated to Mary Ann Nichols and Catherine Eddowes (who had been buried just metres apart). A plain white stone marks the grave of Elizabeth Stride in the East London Cemetery at Plaistow. The grave of Annie Chapman, however, remained unmarked until 2008, when cemetery authorities at Manor Park, London, erected a plaque to approximately mark the site of the public grave in which she had been buried. The memory of the canonical five victims of Jack the Ripper, it seems, would never be forgotten.

Something that continues to elude public knowledge, however, is the true identity of 'Jack'. Although a list of potential suspects has grown – and continues to do so – since the murders of 1888, no definitive perpetrator has ever been solidly agreed upon by criminologists and Ripper detectives. The closest anyone has come to revealing the true face of the Ripper came in 2014, when a shawl allegedly worn by Catherine Eddowes at the time of her murder underwent forensic examination. The shawl, which had been bought by author and Ripperologist Russell Edwards, was believed to have been speckled with splashes of Eddowes's blood and the Ripper's semen.[77] Biochemists at Liverpool John Moores and Leeds universities genetically tested the shawl against collected DNA samples believed to belong to descendants of Eddowes, as well as the Ripper, whom Russell Edwards adamantly claimed to be Aaron Kosminski.

Kosminski had been a key suspect of the Ripper murders as early as 1888. Born in 1865, he had emigrated from Poland to Whitechapel in the early 1880s, taking up employment as a hairdresser within the borough. He had suffered from mental ill health, including hallucinations and paranoia, and was recorded as an inmate at the lunatic asylum of Colney Hatch in London.[78] Kosminski became implicated with the case of Jack the Ripper in 1914, when the Assistant Chief Constable of the Metropolitan Police, Sir Melville Macnaghten, wrote a memoir of his experiences working through the active years of the Whitechapel murders. However, Macnaghten wrote the name of the suspect simply as 'Kosminski', so whether he had meant Aaron, or perhaps some other with the same surname, will never be known.[79]

Ultimately, the mitochondrial analysis of Catherine Eddowes's shawl yielded an unsatisfactory result; it could not be accurately determined if the semen and other residual DNA found on the shawl had belonged to Kosminski. Although lead biochemist Jari Louhelainen was firm in his convictions that the DNA on the shawl matched with Kosminski's, there remained too many outliers to conclusively name him as the perpetrator. For a start, Kosminski had died childless, so DNA had to be extracted from a distant descendent of his sister, Matilda.[80] Further problems presented in the likely muddying of the DNA due to the handling of the shawl by potentially scores of people since it had apparently been retrieved from the crime scene. Furthermore, the shadowy provenance of the shawl caused many to doubt the claims made by Louhelainen. How could it be determined that this shawl was indeed the same one owned by Catherine Eddowes? After all, no shawl had ever been recorded as being in her possession at the time of the in-depth medical report conducted on her corpse by the coroners.[81]

With Aaron Kosminski remaining a tenuous suspect in the lineup of potential Rippers, detectives turned to other men who may better fit the descriptions outlined by eyewitnesses in their testimonies of the murders. Suspects ranged from the peculiar, such as Lewis Carroll, the world-famous author of *Alice in Wonderland*, to the downright bizarre, like Prince Albert Victor, the grandson of Queen Victoria. Anti-monarchists had deliberately targeted Albert Victor to mar the face of the Royal Family. Believing that he had used the sexual services of the victims, before committing murder to stop them spreading rumours of his virility, some theorists had clearly overlooked the fact that at the time of all five of the murders, Albert Victor had been on the other side of the country.[82]

Still more suspects were named. Walter Sickert, the famous artist, was included on account of his apparent fascination with the mysteries. So too was 'Fingers' Freddy, the infamous Italian-American conman who entertained crowds of people as his hoard of boy pickpockets descended upon the possessions of their unsuspecting victims.[83] Another suspect materialized in the form of Francis Tumblety, a man possessing considerable medical knowledge and an unsettling hobby for collecting dissected uteri. Tumblety certainly appeared to be a very likely suspect; after he was arrested for his acquisition of sexual organs on 24 November 1888, detectives could not help but notice the sudden cessation of the ghastly murders that had plagued Whitechapel for months.

Equally alluring was the possibility of James Maybrick being the Ripper. Maybrick's diary fell into the possession of the London police, revealing in remarkable detail the minutiae of the Whitechapel murders. How Maybrick had acquired this information was unclear, for most details of the cases had purposely been kept under lock-and-key to prevent the spread of misinformation amongst the public. To implicate Maybrick even further, a pocket watch bearing tiny inscriptions was found in his lodgings following his death in 1889. On closer examination, it appeared that the inscriptions 'PN', 'AC', 'ES', 'CE' and 'MK' were the initials of the canonical five victims.[84]

The mystery of Jack the Ripper will most likely never be solved, with vital evidence lost to and obscured by history. Nevertheless, the Whitechapel murders of 1888 carved out a new era of crime and punishment in the nineteenth century, where a newfound emphasis was placed on the importance of obsessively recording every shred of detail through inquest reports, eyewitness scrutinization and the popular new trend of mortuary photography. The bone-chilling legacy left on Victorian London by Jack the Ripper, as well as the other infamous criminals of his day, changed the way the police responded to reports of murder, rape and other serious criminal offences. An emphasis on penalizing criminals, the insistence of fair trials and an increase in funding for the judicial system led to a reform of penal institutions, law courts and the police force as a whole. Crime in Victorian Britain had truly changed forever.

Chapter 9

Death, Dying and the Afterlife in Victorian Britain

'The bare corpse lies there amid the living, beside them in their sleep; before them at their meals.'
Dr John Simon, *City of London Medical Reports* (1852)

Death, a deeply unpleasant but necessary evil, is inescapable, and the Victorians knew this better than most. In a world where dirt, danger and disease lurked around every corner, premature death was an accepted way of life in the nineteenth century. Children would die before they were old enough to leave their cradles; men would succumb to injuries and wounds that would otherwise be treatable had they received the correct medical assistance. Death in giving birth was still a very real threat for pregnant Victorian women, and elderly slum dwellers celebrated each year that they passed having evaded their fate. Death was forever hovering over the slums of Victorian Britain, extending its long, bony finger and claiming its next victim without discrimination.

In the nineteenth century, it was estimated that at least one death occurred per day in London alone. Whether through illness, accident or tragic events like suicide or murder, death was a natural part of the daily routine of the dark and dingy underworld of the Victorian slums. Children could expect to grow up without siblings, and parents knew that it was a reality to lose at least one, if not more, of their children before they reached adulthood. The life expectancy of the Victorian slums was set at just around 40, drastically brought down from the expectancies of their wealthier peers due to greater risks to health that their hovels and slums posed. It is especially important to note that the life expectancy statistics of the nineteenth-century slums were affected by the high rates of infant mortality, which particularly struck the poorest members of society.

However, just because their children faced high odds of dying before their first birthdays or the eve of puberty did not mean that Victorian parents loved them any less.[1] It is a common misconception, even within modern historiography, that parents in the past struggled to bond with their children in case they succumbed to childhood disease.[2] In reality, parents cared for their sick and ailing children with tenderness and affection, even when it became clear that their lives would be cut short. This affection toward children extended to distant kin, family friends and even neighbours within the community, who mourned their deaths as though the children had belonged to themselves.[3] In one heart-rending example from the late 1800s, a tight-knit community came together to mourn the death of a beloved orphaned child. 'Little Mitey', an 8-year-old girl, had been raised by her neighbours following the death of her mother and her abandonment by her father. Languishing from an illness, Mitey 'would lie with half-shut eyes softly repeating to herself, "Gentle Jesus", or singing, as well as her weakened voice would permit; "I'd like to be an angel"'.[4] Despite the efforts of Mitey's dedicated and loving neighbours, she would later succumb to the illness that plagued her. At her funeral, members of the community offered their pittances to afford the burial costs, and paid their respect at the side of her open coffin; a 'score or more of granny's, neighbours who with bowed heads and reverent air, stood round the open grave'.[5]

Members of the community also gathered to pay their respects at the funeral of an unnamed 17-year-old girl in August 1842.[6] The girl, an apparent orphan, had been drawn to commit suicide by throwing herself from the 202ft-high Monument in North London. The Monument, which served as a memorial to the Great Fire of London in 1666, was an apparent preferred location for suicidal people, and no less than five other unfortunate souls were known to have jumped from its top since 1750.[7] Another location which frequently found itself favoured by the suicidal was the Duke of York's Column in St James's Park, near to Buckingham Palace. The column, which was 124ft high, was available to thrill-seeking Victorians, who could climb to the very top up 168 rickety and dimly lit steps.[8] Once at the apex, tourists could precariously perch along a narrow platform to witness a bird's-eye view of London. On 14 May 1850, however, authorities were forced to install a solid gate around the platform, after one man, French musician Henri Joseph Stephan, had intentionally thrown himself from the top of the column to the ground below, to the horror of onlookers.[9]

In cases of suicide, or if an unfortunate soul had passed away while living exposed on the street, the body would be transported to whatever funerary home, mortuary laboratory or morgue was available nearby. If a person had died while at home, however, the body would typically remain there until it was ready for burial. Keeping the body of a deceased family member within the same room as the living was commonplace in the nineteenth and even twentieth centuries, and was not considered to be particularly unsafe or unsanitary. In his investigative report on the slums of Spitalfields, George Sims entered the homes of at least four hovels containing the corpses of the recently deceased. Though this was a sight Sims would have undoubtedly been accustomed to, given the traditions of the day, he was nonetheless horrified to find that, unlike in the cases of the wealthy – who could afford to bury their dead within days of their passing – the poor had to wait until they had raised sufficient funds before their loved ones could be removed from the homes of the living. It was no surprise, then, when Sims found himself face-to-face with the rapidly decomposing corpses of slum dwellers.

The first corpse he encountered was found at 17 Hope Street.[10] There, the body of a child who had died from scarlet fever was placed flat upon a table – the only item of furniture – in the centre of the room. The corpse, which was tinged with green and the signs of early decomposition, was watched over by its mournful parents and elder teenage sister. When Sims enquired why the child had not yet been buried, they replied that their funds were completely non-existent. It took the intervention of Sims, who called on the assistance of a council relief worker, to have the body removed and buried the next day.

Another family who were forced to live alongside a decomposing relative resided at 28 Church Street.[11] There, the body of another child who had succumbed to scarlet fever had been left entirely naked and exposed on the dining table. Immediately Sims entered the room, he noted a 'dreadful' smell as the body began to release its gases and bodily fluids. The single-room dwelling had been the home of the child, its 3-year-old sibling, its parents and its elderly grandparents, who mourned that they could not afford to bury him. It would take another ten days following Sims's visit before the child was buried.

Leaving the decaying corpses of loved ones exposed within the home would have been highly distressing and traumatic for those who were forced to live alongside it. At 26 King Street, Sims entered the home of a young couple where the corpse of their child was left exposed for nine days.[12] The father of the child admitted that the sight of the deceased infant had been so distressing, and the smell so offensive, that he was later forced to move it to an outdoor shared shed.

Finally, Sims entered the home of a young woman whose mother had died on Christmas Day.[13] A whole fifteen days had elapsed since her death, yet her decomposing body was still unburied. The woman had confessed to Sims that she could not afford to bury her mother, and that she would instead have to relinquish the corpse to the council for burial in a mass, unmarked grave. This horror was unfortunately a reality for many of the poor people who lived in the dark and dingy underworld of Victorian Britain, and who, without the assistance and charity of kind-hearted people like Sims, had to face the fact that their loved ones would receive little dignity in death.

Caring for the Dead

Once the final breath had been expelled from the dying body, the long process of mortuary care could begin.

Unlike today, where the majority of cadavers are taken to dedicated funerary homes to commence their final journeys, it was common in the nineteenth century for morticians to operate from the homes of the deceased. Here, in the 'chamber of death' (a rather macabre term that was simply used to describe the room in which someone had died), windows had to be immediately opened (if possible) and procedures conducted entirely in silence.[1] The responsibilities of the undertaker were vast, far more than just the overseeing of funerals and burials of the deceased. Their roles (sometimes referred to as 'black jobs') were hugely significant; to be entrusted with performing the final rights of the dead was truly an honour. 'After science has been baffled and death claims his victim,' wrote Auguste Renouard in 1878, 'the undertaker is the one to whom we look to perform the last sad duties.'[2]

Yet such a vital role had only just begun to emerge as its own dedicated profession by the turn of the nineteenth century. Before then, the task of preparing the dead for their burials had fallen typically to whomever had been considered the most medically qualified in the locale. In the Middle Ages, for example, this job often fell into the domain of surgeons, doctors, apothecarists or any other person possessing some degree of anatomical knowledge. However, if these figures could not be found to perform the funeral rites, as in the case of smaller, more rural societies, other people rose to the challenge. Among these were butchers, whose intricate knowledge of animalistic anatomy could be employed at a somewhat suitable standard. Midwives would also be employed, although they were often considered less capable at intellectual pursuits than men on account of their female sex. They would be avoided entirely if a man, no matter the level of his education or qualification, could instead be found.

Clergymen could also be employed. Although usually more accustomed to performing the spiritual elements of funerary rites than handling any physical remains, they were often favoured by mourners due to the belief that God would guide them to do well in their work. By the nineteenth century, this practice had mostly ceased, except in the most isolated of rural communities where the pool of medical practitioners was understandably a lot smaller. The roles of mortician, gravedigger, undertaker, pallbearer and coroner had by now all been carved out as their own distinguishable roles in society, and under the Victorians the death industry flourished.

The routines of a Victorian mortician did not discriminate by race, sex or even class. From the uppermost levels of the social strata to the very lowest, the bodies of the deceased were treated with reverence and care. 'Every person entering the store [funeral parlour], whether pauper or president, infant or adult, white or coloured, must be treated with courtesy and kindness,' stated a Victorian treatise on death.[3] Immediately after death, or as soon as was possible, the body of the deceased would be placed upon a cooling board, a long table traditionally made from wood and designed to hold slabs of ice beneath it. This would keep the body cold, allowing enough time for the coroner's inquest and post-mortem to be performed, funeral prepared and mourners to gather. The table performed the important function of keeping the corpse cool enough to stave off decay and decomposition for as long as possible – for this reason, they were particularly employed during the warmer summer months.

Once the body had been placed upon the cooling board (which would be taken to the house of the deceased by the undertaker), the limbs and joints could be positioned before rigor mortis set in (approximately around two hours after death had occurred). In doing this, the job of the mortician was made much easier for they could begin their work as soon as they were ready, and did not have to wait for the corpse's muscles to relax again, which could take at least twenty-four hours.[4] Rigor mortis renders the body entirely immovable, unless force is used to snap any wayward limbs into a manageable position. This makes the examination of the corpse difficult, particularly in cases where the person has died in an awkward position (such as sitting up). The most common technique at this stage, aside from the straightening of the limbs entirely flat, was the closing of the jaw with a ligature. Ligatures were traditionally made from a cloth bandage, and were tied around the head of the deceased and beneath their chin to firmly ensure the closure of the mouth. They were used by every undertaker, from those who served the poor to the richest of society, even being employed on the corpses of Queen Victoria and Prince Albert.[5]

After the jaw had been fastened securely with the ligature, the face would be thoroughly washed and the eyes shut. Pennies would be used to ensure that the lids of the eyes remained closed. There appears to be no particular medical or scientific reason for closing the eyes of the deceased; rather, it was a practice utilized by morticians who simply preferred their subjects not to look as though they were still alive during procedures. Upon death, the eyes traditionally glaze over and turn hues of misty blue, regardless of the eye colour of the deceased in life. It was no wonder, then, that morticians preferred not to feel as though they were being scrutinized by the very cadavers they were working on.

As well as closing the eyes, the face would be groomed and made-up as closely as possible to how it had been in life. Hair would be brushed, lips and cheeks rouged, and wounds or scars hidden to the best of the mortician's abilities. Aside from being a mark of respect for the deceased, morticians also had a duty of care to the living; as we will discover, most bodies of the deceased would be viewed before burial by family members and other mourners, so it would only further their distress if their loved ones looked repugnant in their coffins. The maintaining of faux life in the corpse was entirely psychological. Everyone knew that the cadaver was dead; that it had expired through illness, injury or old age. Yet viewing a beautiful, radiant corpse was a lot more comforting than viewing an emaciated one, and as such morticians did what they could to make the dead look alive.

With the upper half of the body pruned and primed for viewing, the gruesome work of the mortician could truly begin. With a scalpel or sharp knife, a long, deep cut was made all the way from the collarbone to the groin. As the abdominal cavity was delicately and skilfully opened – and muscle, cartilage and bone moved aside – internal organs such as the stomach, bowel and intestines would be punctured with an instrument called a 'trocar' to avoid the buildup of gases during decomposition.[6]Trocars are long, spear-like poles that have serrated tips and edges which aid in the perforating of organs.

It was not uncommon for the mortician to lightly apply pressure upon the stomach to further expel any gas; sometimes this escaped through the orifices of the body and made a rude noise as it did so. In his instructional manual for undertakers, Auguste Renouard advised to mop up any frothy, bloody discharge and other fluids that would be expelled along with the bodily gases.[7] He also instructed morticians to 'scoop out' any viscera within the body cavity before sewing shut or cauterizing the serrations.[8] Any biomaterial lifted from the body would be collected in metal pails and disposed of by the undertaker. Most often, this hazardous concoction of blood and tissue would be tipped directly into sewers through drainage systems, much as it still is today.[9]

It was no wonder, then, that morticians relied on deodorizers to keep the 'death chamber' smelling as fresh as was possible. Life in the Victorian slums, as we have seen, was cramped and overcrowded, and many of the poorest urban dwellers resided in single-room occupancies. Although unlikely that the family of the deceased would have remained in the same room where the post-mortem was being carried out, they nonetheless had to return to it once the procedure had been completed. In one example, the post-mortem of the corpse of a 2-year-old child took place within its family's dining room. Unlike in most cases, where the family would leave the room while the inspection was taking place, both of the child's parents and its three siblings decided to stay. Two journalists also attended while the undertaker performed the task, but had to abruptly leave when the overwhelming smell made them vomit.[10] Because a large number of morticians worked upon their decedents in less than ideal places, they had to make do with what sanitizing equipment they had available. In the vast majority of slum tenements, however, this was understandably very minimal.

A mortician might have carried in his bag a set of vials containing potent chemicals to assist in the staving-off of disease and miasma that erupted from the body. Carbolic soap, for instance, was used to wash down surfaces once the mortician's work had been complete; so too was carbolic powder, which would be sprinkled on the floor to act not only as a deodorizer, but also to soak up any spillages that may have occurred.[11] Cloths soaked in sweet-smelling liquids, such as lavender or other floral essential oils, would be hung around the room to further negate the smell of death and decay.[12] As one can imagine, sometimes this would have the opposite effect to that which had been intended, instead filling tiny rooms with a cloying mixture of flora, chemicals and decomposition. In more extreme cases, rags soaked in extremely dangerous chemicals such as mercury could be utilized, though to do so was inherently risky for the safety of the undertaker.

Once the body had been sewn back up, the next of kin would be alerted regarding the next step of the funerary process. This was often the family of the deceased, though in many recorded cases it could be friends, landlords or even the owners of hotels in whose establishment the dead had breathed their final breath.[13] After this, the body would be removed from the cooling board and placed within a casket of some form; often this was just temporary, and would be changed for something sturdier before burial. The body would usually be dressed by the next of kin, and always by someone of the same sex. Once this had been completed, the corpse in its coffin would be removed from the room, or simply moved to its centre if no other rooms were available, allowing for furniture to be pushed back to its usual place. This gave the family time to gather around their loved one, to adorn the body with flowers or other goods they wished to be buried alongside them. As mentioned, the coffin would most usually be left open, allowing for kin to gaze one last time upon the face of those who had left them. In cases where the deceased had died through illness or disease, however, families were warned not to go too close to the body for fear of transmission. It meant that some, particularly parents, were cruelly stolen of their final chance to kiss their dearly departed goodbye.[14]

Typically, a carriage would arrive the next day at the place where the deceased lay. This cortege would then be loaded with the coffin by pallbearers, who sought to move the corpse with haste so as to lessen the extent of decomposition and other unpleasantness lingering within the room. From there, the cortege would follow the wishes of the next of kin, usually transporting the corpse to the local church or chapel to receive the final religious rites. In other cases, however, it was led directly to the place of burial, which had not always been agreed upon by the loved ones of the deceased. Unless a will had been written, outlining the wishes of the decedent's care following their death, or unless they had hailed from a class in which they could afford the luxury of a dedicated burial plot in a well-manicured cemetery, the majority of bodies in the Victorian slums were laid to rest in simple public graves. This was not seen as a slur; rather, burial in your own grave was a luxury many of the poor could only dream of. To have your own individual burial plot was something many slum-dwellers aspired to. It was certainly the preferred alternative to a plot where you could be buried in amongst the coffins of strangers, piled high above you, or, even worse, thrown into a pauper's grave without a coffin, to be mangled for eternity with the bones of other members of the local destitute.

In the nineteenth century, a phenomenon took the Victorian death industry by storm. Never before practiced to such an extent in England, but popular in Europe and especially in America, it changed forever the way death would be viewed. Scientists and surgeons claimed to have finally found a way to put a stopper on death, promising to abolish decay and allowing the body to remain physically perfect forever. It was called embalming, and it is still incredibly popular today.

Victorian society quickly caught on to the allure of bodily incorruptness even once life itself had expired. No longer did people worry about the state of their remains after death, as conjured images of dusty bones and festering corpses were duly shooed away by the promise of eternal beauty. It was a trend that even the poor could get behind, provided they could afford to pay the £1 fee.[15] This was not as impossible as it may seem for slum dwellers, for many purposely kept aside whatever pennies they could spare to provide for a decent funeral for their loved ones. Indeed, due to such a high infant mortality rate at the time, many parents even began saving up for the funerals of their children as soon as they had been born. Many working-class families, for example, took out a so-called 'penny policy', making a small weekly payment of whatever they could afford to ensure that the funeral would be provided for should she any of their children die.[16] However, some families would later discover that documentation of the 'penny policy' insurance had been lost by the place in which it had been held, meaning that all of the pennies that parents had so scrupulously saved had been wasted, to the distress of bereaved families deep in their mourning.[17]

If you were lucky enough to be able to afford embalming, however, it may have provided a degree of comfort to those left behind. Embalming, still a favoured option by many people today, is a process which halts decomposition of the body by replacing bodily fluids and internal organs with chemicals. By being embalmed, most corpses can remain 'fresh' for much longer than if they had been left to decay naturally. The procedure, though invasive, allowed for additional time before the corpse needed to be buried, and therefore gave families a longer duration to gather for funerals, something which was greatly appreciated by those scattered across the country. As well as for aesthetic purposes, sometimes embalming would also be carried out to allow coroners more time to conduct post-mortems, and it was therefore a procedure utilized more often in cases of murder, poison or other suspicious deaths, paid for at the jurisdiction of the law.

In most cases, when a Victorian family chose to embalm their loved ones, their corpses would be taken from the place of death to mortuary parlours, much as they are today. The removal of decaying bodies to properly equipped funeral homes further attracted the living into taking the embalming route for their relatives. It no longer meant that cadavers had to remain in the centre of stuffy rooms, filling the air with the scent of death and unsettling those who had to reside alongside it. Funeral parlours thus began to grow in popularity, becoming the desired place for the dead to remain until they were buried. Before this, parlours were typically reserved only for corpses which had suffered suspicious deaths, resembling rooms akin to laboratories for the authorities to examine them to unravel the details of crimes. A room dedicated to housing the dead was also used by surgeons, doctors and medical students to allow them to perform autopsies and anatomical study. Until the popularization of embalming, funeral homes had been out of the reach of the vast majority of Victorians in Britain.

Upon death, a body would be collected from the home by an undertaker and taken to one of these parlours, where it would be washed and prepared for examination. Unlike in homes, funeral parlours allowed morticians greater space and freedom to carry out procedures with the safety of sanitizing chemicals nearby. Additionally, funeral parlours permitted greater emphasis on administrating and processing the death of the citizens they served, for they were often built with adjoining offices that filed inquest reports and registered death certificates. Unfortunately for the poor, however, this paperwork cost an additional £1 on top of every other expense they had to pay for the care of their deceased love one. For that reason, many did not bother to purchase death certificates for their own keeping.[18]

Victorian funeral parlours typically also included a private mourning room, a laboratory to conduct investigations into blood, viscera and other biological matter, and a morgue, which allowed funeral directors to house numerous bodies at once. This latter improvement alone allowed morticians more time to work on their patients without having to rush or cut corners. It did not seem to be a significant reform at the time, yet it arguably led to a greater understanding and appreciation of caring for the dead.

Funeral parlours, regardless of their size or location (whether in more affluent areas or the dingiest of slums), were expected to always be kept clean and well maintained. Although deep cleaning of morgues would typically only be carried out once per week, the hygiene standards of morticians in funeral homes were much better than they had been while conducting business from the homes of the public.[19] Here in the mortician's own personal workspace, cooling tables became permanent fixtures. No longer needing to be carried around and erected at the homes of the dead, the porous wooden tables had been replaced by alternatives made from heavy marble or even metal. These materials provided a more sturdy surface on which to work, forgoing the risk of collapse beneath the weight of a cadaver; additionally, these tables could be kept cool without the need for ice, promising to 'preserve bodies, say for five or six days'.[20] They even had their own divots and trestles carved within them, which helped drain away bodily fluids during the embalming process. Funeral parlours also usually contained chemical cupboards, washing stations (complete with a range of sponges, each used for different tasks) and a closet containing the mortician's tools, knives, handsaws, scalpels, scissors, catheters and surgeon's silk (which was used to sew up the cadaver once embalmed).[21] Auguste Renouard also encouraged funeral directors to install 'chains and hooks' within their morgues, which could be used to 'raise arteries' and keep the corpse upright while its blood was draining.[22]

The first step of the embalming process was the severing of the major arteries of the body. Once the blood had been fully drained from the corpse, antiseptic liquid would be pumped through the veins to flush out any remaining residue. This pungent acidulated liquid by all accounts disguised the smell of the corpse. Jean-Vincent Bully, a Paris perfumier and specialist dealer of scents, recommended using vinegar.[23] The body's orifices would then be stuffed with cotton or cloth, which – as explicitly expressed by Renouard – had to include the rectum.[24]

To preserve the body and stave off decay, Victorian morticians used tannic dust, which absorbed excess moisture within the abdominal cavity and tightened the skin. Cavities now desiccated; the mortician turned his attention to pumping the veins with embalming fluid, which plasticized, plumped and stiffened the body, restoring its life-like appearance. Morticians now use embalming fluids tinted with hues of peach, pink or red, so that it gives the impression of blood beneath the skin. It appears that Victorian morticians did the same, which can be gleaned from accounts of relatives viewing the scarily 'alive' corpses of their loved ones within their own coffins.

The efficiency of embalming fluid was tested by chemist William Ramsey, whose dedication to observing the properties of chemicals in the nineteenth century eventually earned him a knighthood from King Edward VII in 1902. Ramsey had concocted a solution he described only as a 'crude pyroligneous acid', into which he dipped a fresh fish and a shank of beef. When returning to his experiment eight months later, Ramsey was delighted to discover that both the fish and the beef appeared as fresh as the day he had bought them, albeit smelling disconcertedly of strong chemicals. Yet Ramsey was still not fully pleased with the results; he then took a bite of both the fish and the beef and declared them 'very agreeable to the taste'.[25] Clearly, Ramsey's experiment had worked; he had achieved the impossible.

Auguste Renouard warned morticians, however, not to be lax in their application of embalming fluids. Alumina sulphate, he cautioned, only preserved bodies for thirty days in summer and three months in winter.[26] If morticians wished to keep a corpse preserved for longer than this, they would have to adapt their embalming recipe or simply use more of it. The bodies of the fat in particular were believed to 'putrefy quicker than lean ones', as were those of children, so it was of the utmost importance that to correctly preserve them, larger quantities of fluid needed to be used.[27] Renouard proposed that embalming a body with your hands covered in oil or lard could assist in prolonging the process, allowing almost a year to go by without any outward sign of decomposition.[28] He chose to omit telling people – probably for good reason – that the bodies of their loved ones would begin to shrink, tighten and mummify after this period.

Another alternative could be chosen. As well as chemical embalming, which promised to keep the corpse aesthetically pleasing only for a number of months before it succumbed to the nature of time and eventually disintegrated, Victorian morticians also offered a process of embalming using plaster. As previously mentioned, the Victorians had a particular penchant for death, and based much of their culture around it. Art depicting the process of death, the afterlife or even bodily remains were popular amongst the nobler of classes, where it was not uncommon to hang what we might consider as macabre portraiture in one's hallway or dining room. Walks and leisurely strolls through cemeteries and graveyards was a popular pastime, and even fashion was dominated by a trend in mourning wear. When Queen Victoria commissioned a plaster cast of her beloved Albert's hand upon his death, it was little wonder that the masses sought to do the same.

Plaster casts, models or busts commemorating loved ones were not wholly unusual in the nineteenth century, and were even considered to be fashionable. Not only did it reflect the deep love and affection a family may have had for the deceased, but it also proved to be a good conversation piece. Displayed in homes from the very richest to the very poorest, casts of the body parts of the dead were integrated within the home as a strange, but subtle way of memorializing the dead. This home décor trend, popularized by Queen Victoria, who also had the hands of her nine children immortalized in plaster (although taken while they were still alive), quickly caught on.[29] Funeral directors began offering families the opportunity to take casts of hands, fingers or even faces of their loved ones. Some went even further, and radically proposed forming plaster casts of the entire body.

Upon death, a body was washed, sanitised and emptied of its viscera, before a mixture of plaster of Paris was poured in. Morticians ensured they got into every crevice, positioning limbs so that no part of the corpse would be left without. After the plaster had settled, linen dipped in embalming fluid would be tightly wrapped around the body in a style reminiscent of Egyptian mummification; the face would especially be puffed out with wads of cloth, giving the appearance of plump, lifelike cheeks.[30] A pungent mixture of balsam and turpentine would then be brushed over the body, which, although giving a yellow tinge to the body once it was unwrapped, was considered the 'best way' to embalm, lasting 'an indefinite time'.[31] The vast majority of poor Victorians were probably unable to afford this method of preserving their loved ones, but it proved to be a suitable solution for families needing to ship corpses overseas or long distances. It also led to some families visiting the coffins of their dearly departed weeks, months and sometimes even years after their death. Those fortunate and wealthy enough to do so would places bodies in catacombs and crypts so that they could be easily accessed via a monument that stood above-ground.[32]

Being a mortician in the nineteenth century could be dangerous business. Aside from all the incredibly sharp tools and implements purposefully designed to cut through tough sinews, muscles and bones, exposure to and misuse of caustic chemicals proved to be a constant danger. One chemical, chromatic acid, was regularly used in the disinfecting of the body. However, it was so corrosive that when left for twenty minutes it could completely dissolve bodily tissues and even small animals.[33] Camphor, a strong-smelling chemical made from turpentine oil, would be used to get rid of 'fetid odors [*sic*] from bodies [and] removing foul smells from the chamber of death'.[34] But in large quantities, or when used in tight spaces, exposure to camphor could cause swellings of the throat, dangerous seizures and even death.

Occasionally, morticians would injure themselves on their tools. In today's society, embalmers tend to use gloves made from chainmail or another tough material to protect slicing through their own skin.[35] Modern-day forensic and medical teams also conduct their work clad in layers of personal protective equipment, from sterile gloves to goggles and eyewear, and even respirators. Victorian morticians, however, were not so well-equipped. Some may have worn gloves, though how often these were changed will never properly be known. If gloves were worn, the materials from which they were made were probably unlikely to protect the mortician from dangers. Additionally, although the more prudent of men may have worn eye protection while dissecting cadavers in the nineteenth century, plentiful photographs taken from within laboratories, funeral parlours and lecture halls exist that show individuals diligently at work with their faces just centimetres from exposed vital organs and bodies in a state of decay.

If morticians did injure themselves upon their instruments, or accidentally get chemicals or bodily fluids upon their skin, they would douse themselves in muriatic acid.[36] Now most commonly used to disinfect swimming pools and remove cement from masonry work, this dangerously potent acid was diligent in ensuring no harmful bacteria would be left behind (but it also chemically burnt the skin immediately upon contact).

A further danger to the Victorian undertaker was handling the bodies of those who died from diseases or fell victim to poison. When preparing a corpse known to have expired from disease, special care was taken to protect against anything contagious. The lungs of tuberculosis sufferers, for example, would be incinerated to prevent the spreading of disease, while measles and typhoid patients would receive an additional wash before dissection. Sometimes, cadavers would even be covered with shrouds, which were believed to quell the spread of noxious fumes and fluids. Ulcers and glands would be carefully lanced to avoid the eruption of pus or blood upon the mortician, and in the case of patients known to have suffered from sexually transmitted disease, undertakers took considerable caution while navigating the groin and its surrounding areas.[37]

If poisoning was suspected, undertakers would work with police investigators or coroners to determine what solution had caused death. Specially trained to spot the signs of a variety of poisons within the human body, morticians and coroners carefully investigated the movement of limbs, the congealment of blood and the visual appearance of organs. Opium, for example, which was favoured in many of the dens across Victorian London, would cause the brain and lungs to dramatically swell.[38] Another favoured drug of the Victorians, laudanum, would cause extremities such as the fingers, toes and nose to turn blue.[39] Poisoning by sulphuric acid would present in blackened arteries that would droop when touched, as well as blood so thick that it resembled syrup.[40] If someone had been killed with arsenic, as had the victims of Mary Ann Cotton, their stomach and intestines would fill with a viscous liquid that resembled 'rice-water'.[41]

Knowing the signs of poisoning was a particularly important skill for morticians and coroners to have in the crime capitals of Victorian Britain such as London, Manchester and Birmingham. It was not uncommon for these cities in particular to have dedicated coroner's offices complete with wheeled gurneys that would transport the victim's body from the morgue and into tiered viewing rooms, where a handful of inspectors would gather, their pencils poised above their notebooks. Occasionally, however, some coroners were indifferent about the fates of their poor patients. 'What use or import was it to know [how someone had died]?', questioned the starkly honest Charles Manby Smith in 1857.[42] In cases like these, it was not uncommon for unethical coroners to write on the death certificates of suspected poison victims that they had died from 'natural causes', saving morticians the time and effort of dissection and close forensic examination.

Funerals

Once the mortician had finished his work, the corpse had been sewn back together and the body placed within its coffin, the funeral could finally take place. Guests would arrive at the funeral parlour or meet the cortege at the place of burial, where they could gaze one final time upon the face of their loved ones if they so wished. Attendees would dress all in black – the traditional colour of mourning – and would wear items of clothing such as gloves, veils and velvet top-hats that would be made specifically for use at funerals. Even babies and small children would be expected to wear outfits of all black when attending funerals.[1]

Indeed, mentions of children both known and unknown to the deceased are regularly found in nineteenth-century funerary records. According to Henry Mayhew, beggar children would follow along after funeral corteges and hang around by gravesides in the hope of gaining refreshments and even money for their unconvincing displays of 'mourning'.[2] On the other hand, 'funeral contractors' could be hired by families who wished to bolster the number of mourners at the funerals of their deceased loved ones. These 'contractors' would be hired to 'grieve'; for £2 10*s*, they would simply attend to make up numbers; for £5, they would 'audibly sigh'; for £7 10*s*, they would sob and cry; and for £10, they would be openly hysterical.[3] Following the funeral, refreshments would occasionally be made available at public houses or the dwellings of the mourning family. Here, the funeral contractors could fill their bellies with free food and drink, making it one form of arguably lucrative employment in Victorian Britain.

The funerals of the particularly popular poor called for greater and grander displays of grief. If a person had been especially well-loved in their community, shops and other establishments would close (either briefly or for the entire day) in order to pay respect to the deceased.[4] Additionally, curtains of houses lining the routes from funeral parlours, burial grounds and the homes of the deceased would be closed so that mourners who walked behind the cortege or followed in a carriage could appreciate the sentiments of the wider community.[5] Onlookers could also toss real or paper flowers into the path of the horses which took the coffin to its final destination.

The coffins of the poor in the nineteenth century tended to be modest and plain. Typically made from rough, unsanded wood and lacking in handles and name plates, pauper's coffins were identical to others around them. The only identifier many poor and destitute Victorians could afford for their coffin was the etching of their names or date of death upon it. In the most desperate of cases, sometimes only the initials of the deceased and the year of their death would be etched.[6] In other cases, deceased paupers of London would be laid out in empty boxes made from thin wood or even cardboard. These 'coffins' were intended to be temporary solutions only, and would be borrowed from funeral parlours which would later reclaim them once the body had been buried in the ground.[7] During the time of the Jack the Ripper murders in 1888, there was an especially high influx of paupers buried in London in this way, their 'bodies drawn out […] to be put in boxes'.[8] One contemporary, Thomas Wright, even wrote that he had heard of the corpse of an infant being buried in the curtains from the home of a neighbour, because their family could not afford to pay for a tiny casket.[9]

If, however, a person did not wish to be buried in Victorian Britain, then another option could be chosen instead: cremation. Though made legal in 1885, cremation was widely considered to be repugnant and unfashionable by Victorians, who were put off the method because it decomposes and breaks down the body faster than natural decay. As discussed previously, the Victorians who chose to embalm the bodies of their loved ones did so because the intactness of bodies was of utmost importance in their belief that the individual's soul would otherwise not rise to Heaven after death.[10] To cremate the body was to desecrate it, according to particularly pious Victorians, who questioned how they would be allowed into the afterlife without a solid body to guide them. Cremation also had other implications which dissuaded Victorians from choosing the option, including the fact that furnaces and fumes from crematoria were found to be incredibly dangerous to public health.[11] In an age before the regulation of crematoria, many would emit unsafe blankets of thick, black smoke which threatened the lives of those who were forced to live in close proximity. The Victorians also disliked the fact that without a burial, their descendants would have no permanent record of their lives in the form of gravestones and burial plots. Urns were simply not enough to be remembered, the vast majority of nineteenth-century society believed.

The belief that without a solid, physical body you could not enter into the afterlife dated back as far as the Middle Ages.[12] Just like their medieval predecessors, the Victorians believed that the souls of the dead would be trapped forever on Earth if they could not pass into the next life. The existence of wandering, morose souls has puzzled thinkers since the very dawn of man, and was a belief which the Victorians especially subscribed to. Ghosts, ghouls and other non-physical entities made up many a thrilling tale in the nineteenth century, and were a favourite amongst men, women and children alike who eagerly sought out apparitions to prove correct their theories of the existence of spirits. Indeed, Ouija boards and séances were often partaken by Victorians curious about the existence of the eerie and the supernatural. It was believed that sitting in a circle and evoking the help of a Ouija board would open portals to the afterlife, where the living could communicate with the dead and pass on messages from loved ones. Many of these sessions with supposed ghosts were entirely fabricated, with séance leaders commonly tricking their guests into closing their eyes as real, living and breathing actors made unnerving sounds around them, or played tricks with the light and with sophisticated string-operated pulleys which created the appearance of doors closing by themselves or items of furniture falling to the ground. In photographs of the time supposedly depicting these supernatural activities, many cunning Victorians used props or exposure tricks in an attempt to prove the existence of entities. One particular favourite method was tweaking the exposure time of a camera so that a real, living person could pose in one position, then move before the camera shuttered again, giving the impression of disembodied limbs and floating heads. Another favourite was the inclusion of 'ectoplasm' down the faces and chests of portrait sitters, which would later be identified as simply netting or unravelled balls of wool!

Despite this, there were many Victorians who genuinely believed in the existence of ghosts, and whose stories of unexplained ghoulish activity has trickled down to us to ponder over today. One of the most enduring ghost stories of the Victorian era came in the form of Charles Dickens's *A Christmas Carol*, in which the main character, the austere Ebenezer Scrooge, is visited by a number of ghoulish apparitions. In the tale, Scrooge is meets the ghosts of Christmases Past, Present and Future, as well as the spectral figure of his late friend and fellow miser, Jacob Marley. Through *A Christmas Carol*, Charles Dickens helped popularize tales of the paranormal which have gripped the imaginations of successive generations.

One of the most infamous of ghostly figures in the nineteenth century was believed to be that of 'Bloody Mary', a heartbroken widow whose children had all tragically perished. In some renditions of the story, Bloody Mary takes the form of the Tudor Queen Mary I, who earned the moniker for her harsh treatment of Protestants and apparent fondness for their execution in the mid-sixteenth century. The Victorians believed that by chanting her name repeatedly into a darkened mirror, Bloody Mary would appear and stare back. However, whereas the more modern belief has been that invoking Bloody Mary can bring curses and even death upon those who dare communicate with her, the Victorians believed the ghost to instead be a sage-like and guiding figure. 'On Hallowee'n look in the glass, / Your future husband's face will pass,' encouraged one guidebook for young Victorian females.[13] It was believed that Bloody Mary, so unlucky herself in love and motherhood, would offer to show the living the faces of their future sweethearts, as well as inform them of how many children they would go on to have.

Another benevolent ghost made popular in the nineteenth century was that of Queen Anne Boleyn, who was said to haunt numerous locations which had been associated with her in life. The Tower of London, Hampton Court Palace, Hever Castle in Kent and even her childhood home of Blickling Hall in Norfolk were all apparently sites in which the ghostly apparition of the ill-fated beheaded queen could be found. In 1864, a yeoman at the Tower of London said he found himself face-to-face with a tall female dressed in peculiar old-fashioned garb. When he demanded that she explain her presence, the woman ignored him and stared at him as though he was not there at all. Still, he pressed again, but the woman remained silent, now walking toward him. The yeoman guard tried to halt the silent woman with his bayonet, but she appeared to take no notice of it and continued to approach. The man closed his eyes to brace himself for impact, but nothing came. Instead, feeling as though he had just been plunged into ice, the guard was horrified to find that the woman had walked straight through him.

Anne Boleyn was not the only ghost said to haunt the Tower of London. Other spectral entities in the form of Roman soldiers, old Beefeater guards and even a grisly brown bear (from when the Tower of London had served as a menagerie) were reportedly sighted in the nineteenth century.[14] Indeed, the Tower of London was supposedly one of the most supernaturally occupied locations in the entire British Isles, and was heartily believed by even the most sceptical of Victorians to be infested with the souls of those long gone. Another of the most haunted locations in Britain was Borley Rectory in Essex, an ancient monastery which had been the site of many a murder and unexplained death in the Middle Ages. The first mention of a supposed apparition came in 1863, when visitors to Borley Rectory heard unexplainable footsteps overhead. There was no other party visiting the location at the time, and the identity of the footsteps remained unsolved. Just a few years later, four young women were wandering about the grounds of the rectory when they were stopped by the figure of a woman cloaked all in grey. The woman was wearing a nun's habit, and had a particularly solemn look upon her face. When the women approached to offer her their assistance, she disappeared into thin air.

Ghostly apparitions of women in particular seemed to be the most popular form of paranormal activity in the nineteenth century, and none was more famous than the Brown Lady of Raynham Hall in Norfolk. First sighted in 1835 at Christmas by Charles Townshead, the Brown Lady was believed to be the trapped spirit of a woman who had once inhabited the house as her own. On the fateful evening, Townshead invited his guests to the hall for an evening dance, where he was shocked to find them complain of a rude, mute woman dressed in brown who sat in their bedchambers and refused to leave when pressed. Townshead took matters into his own hands and swore to bring justice to his slighted guests by berating this mysterious indignant woman. When he finally found her hunched over in an armchair in one of the rooms, Townshead blanched at the sight. The woman was wearing clothes fashionable in decades long gone by, and, most terrifyingly of all, had empty sockets where her eyes should have been. The Christmas party was quickly disbanded, and many staff left their posts at Raynham Hall once they had heard the tale of the Brown Lady.

Despite this, a further sighting of the Brown Lady apparently occurred in 1836 by a Captain Frederick Marryat, who wished to settle the claim of her existence once and for all.[15] Marryat, who had been a good friend of Dickens, held a particular interest in the supernatural, and as such did not fear the thought of spending a night with a spectre. That evening, as he retired for bed, Marryat spied a lantern at the end of the passageway. He believed the lantern to belong to a young lady who had been checking on the nursery, so he continued onward to bed. However, as the woman slowly approached; Marryat found himself frozen in place. She moved by him, silent, but tilted her face to his in passing; a face that was sunken, skeletal and entirely otherworldly. Decades later, in 1936, an infamous photograph taken of the supposed Brown Lady was captured by Captain Hubert Provand, and remains to this day one of the most enduring pieces of pictorial evidence of a ghost of all time.

Burial

In the nineteenth century, by far the most popular way to lay a body to its eternal rest was through burials in graves dug deep into the ground. The average cost of a burial in Victorian Britain ranged between ten and thirty shillings, depending on the location of the burial plot, the depth of the grave and whether or not it would hold the coffins of other deceased persons.[1] It was true that 'wealth in London helps a man after death', for money could allow for such luxuries as quiet, private graves in beautiful spots where mourners could visit and reflect in the calming serenity of the green space around them.[2] Although the majority of Victorians, even those hailing from working-class backgrounds, could afford to purchase such plots for themselves upon death, the very poorest of society had to make do with less than ideal burial arrangements. The death industry in the nineteenth century was then, as it is now, a lucrative business. Not only would the cost of the burial of a deceased loved one be required from the living, but so too would other items deemed necessary for a proper funeral. Coffins would have to be purchased, complete with handles for the pall-bearers to carry, as well as name plates, the inscription upon it and even the nails which would bind the lid to the casket. Mourners would have to pay for the workmanship of the carpenter who made the coffin, as well as provide for the shroud, the sheet and the clothing the corpse would be dressed in. Fees were required too for such things as the cushion inserted into the coffin to keep the decedent's head slightly elevated, as well as the wages of at least four pall-bearers (if hired and not consisting of family members or friends). Other items to consider included the church fees and the price of grave digging, bell ringing and transporting the body from place of death to morgue to grave. Mourning coaches or carriages, horses, coachmen, hearses and even the pall cloth also had to be provided for by the living.

The list continued. Mourning outfits of deepest, darkest black were required to maintain a decent image within the community (no one dared turn up to a funeral in faded, tattered mourning reeds). Also required was the headstone and its inscription, the refreshments and wages owed to paid mourners, guests and workmen, and even the printing of obituaries and death notices in local newspapers or letters sent to distant friends and family. The Victorians even had to pay for the death certificates of their loved ones. All in all, it was estimated that a typical funeral in the nineteenth century would come to around £30, an extortionate fee that the working class simply could not afford to pay. As such, poorer families cut corners wherever they could, purchasing off-cuts or tester stones for the gravestones of their deceased (particularly children, which tended to naturally be smaller), as well as dying already owned clothes with black ink to prevent the need to buy new.[3] Imagine a typical nineteenth-century working-class family who would have expected at least one death if not more. That each funeral could cost £30 or upwards meant that many families desperate to provide only the best goodbyes for their loved ones found themselves in mounting debts which did little to alleviate their distress. Indeed, as mentioned previously, there are references to many poorer families in Victorian London saving up for any potential funerals immediately upon the birth of their children. Such a distressing fact was criticized in the *Morning Chronicle*, which shamed London councils for forcing families to fund funerals entirely by themselves; 'in London little attention is paid to the internment of the poor', the author wrote.

It was estimated that between forty and seventy corpses were buried per day in London cemeteries in the Victorian era, particularly in times of pandemic and disease.[5] It was little wonder that in already dangerously crowded urban areas such as London, conditions for the dead were just as claustrophobic as for the living. Indeed, W.O. Daniel wrote in his 1859 book *Ins and Outs of London* that 'it is more difficult to find room for the dead [in London] than it is for the living', given the lack of space for new burials as cemeteries threatened to overfill with corpses.[6] –'It was no uncommon site [*sic*] to see a string of such vehicles, filled with dead bodies, waiting at the gate of an unconsecrated burial ground, until they could be admitted,' wrote one source from the time.[7] Such a terrifying picture was the reality of many a Londoner in the nineteenth century. Furthermore, many more knew that without sufficient funds, they too would end up slumped upon carts with no coffins to separate them from others.

The solution of the local jurisdiction of the time was to enforce mass burials of the deceased poor. If they could not afford a decent burial, the authorities reasoned, then why should they be given the right to a dignified internment at the government's expense? Burial plots intended to hold more than one coffin or corpse would thus be left open for days until they could be sufficiently filled, and 'never covered up till the whole complement of corpses has been interred'.[8] According to the *Morning Chronicle*, 'the graves, or pits, for the reception of the lower sort of people, are made sufficiently wide to contain four, five or six wooden coffins abreast', though they commonly held more.[9] One source dating from 1838 and published in London stated that the graves of paupers would be left open until they could be filled with upwards of ten corpses, the record being eighteen buried amongst strangers without coffins to separate them.[10] Not even a thin dusting of dirt lay between the often-naked corpses, which were pressed into each other and left to putrefy without dignity. Only in the case of infectious diseases would gravediggers scatter burnt straw into the deep holes in the ground to prevent the spread of contagion and mask the horrendous smell.[11]

It will come as no surprise that the vastly overfilled cemeteries of Victorian London emitted smells of the foulest kind. Described by contemporary surgeon George Alfred Walker as 'laboratories of malaria [and] centres of infection', Victorian graveyards were said to smell like a mix of boiled cabbage leaves, rotten stinking fish, wet straw, slaughter-houses and cesspits.[12] The smell was so overpowering that 'ministers and others, upon funeral duty, stand at a considerable distance [away from graves], to avoid the horrid stench arising from them'.[13] The smell was exacerbated by the fact that even in cases where paupers had been buried in coffins, they were beginning to buckle and crack under the weight of dozens more around and above them. As more and more cheaply made and flimsy coffins were placed on top of each other, liquids produced in the body during decomposition would seep out and into those of other burials, causing an effluence of bad miasmas. It was no wonder that 'these wholesale receptacles of the dead become so offensive'.[14]

One of the most offensive-smelling burial grounds in Victorian London was at Enon Chapel on the Strand. Worshippers at the chapel began noticing foul smells and tastes within the air in the early 1840s whenever they attended Sunday services, but were assured by the vicar that nothing was amiss and that the smells were simply wafting from a nearby open sewer. This did little to assure the congregation, who returned home with 'bugs' upon their clothes and in their hair. When they demanded that the vicar properly investigate the origin of this effluvia, little could prepare them for what would be found. Underneath the floor of the chapel, and beneath the very surfaces where they had prayed, the coffins and corpses of more than a thousand people (the figure was later estimated to be 12,000) were found crammed into a cellar just 60ft by 29ft wide.[15] Policemen who were called to the scene to intervene had to plug their noses and hold their breath as they were forced to drag each and every corpse (which were all in advanced stages of decomposition, mummified or entirely skeletal) out of the cellar and into the nearest sewer entrance.[16]

That would not be the last time Enon Chapel would receive attention for its unsafe and unsanitary care of the dead. In 1852, a committee at the House of Commons gathered to discuss the origin of sixty cartloads full of human remains that had been found on the banks of the Thames.[17] When the bodies were traced back to the vicar of Enon Chapel, he swore to never again commit such heinous crimes. Instead, he vowed he would pour quicklime over the bodies so that they would dissolve and melt away, leaving room for more burials to take place.[18]

Unethical burial practices like those carried out at Enon Chapel were relatively common across cemeteries in Victorian London. Churchwardens and gravediggers would be paid for every funeral that they conducted and every body that they buried. To turn corpses away would result in a loss of profit, and that simply would not do.[19] Though not always as drastic as the methods performed at Enon Chapel in disposing of corpses, other truly awful procedures could be carried out. The bodies of babies and young children, for example, were reportedly placed into the coffins of older people who had died to save on burial space. As reported in *The Times* in 1875, some infants had even been used as the pillows of adult corpses.[20] Furthermore, some children would be buried stuffed in tight corners or small areas of a churchyard which would otherwise go to waste.[21] An even more disturbing method to ensure that gravediggers could fit as many bodies as possible within their churchyards was the mutilation of remains. 'When there was no room for a newcomer,' wrote George M. Reynolds upon a visit to the grave of his father, 'some recently-buried tenant of a grave was exhumed to afford the required space.'[22] Reynolds described the distressing scene which awaited him: 'I saw them chopping the head of his coffin away. I knew it was my father's head, and I told them to stop, and they laughed.'[23]

Unfortunately, such cases were not uncommon in London graveyards of the time. According to D.W. Bartlett in *London by Day and Night*, published in 1852, the 'ground was so full of bodies that he could not make a new grave without coming into other graves', and gravediggers had to employ pickaxes and hammers to break apart coffins and their inhabitants. One Member of Parliament, William McKinnon, even wrote in 1842 that he had 'seen them [the gravediggers] play at what is called skittles; [they] put up bones and take skulls and knock them down'.[24]

Indeed, collections of dismembered bones were surprisingly common in Victorian graveyards, with purpose-built ossuaries constructed to contain them. Ossuaries are commonly used by many cultures across the world, particularly in areas of Europe and South America, to lay their dead to rest, and are not considered particularly unethical within these contexts. For the Victorians, however, who were more accustomed to coffins and repulsed even at the thought of cremation, an ossuary was certainly out of the question.

Bunhill Fields Cemetery near Moorgate in north-west London had perhaps the largest ossuary in the whole of the city in the nineteenth century. Bunhill, literally meaning 'bone hill', had been developed upon the site of an ancient medieval mass burial ground that had been used particularly during periods of plague and natural disaster. In the eighteenth and nineteenth centuries, it had been turned into a graveyard for religious dissenters and political non-conformists, who were buried amongst the uneven ground that had been formed from literal hills of medieval bones. Bunhill Fields would later become a hotspot for tourists seeking out the graves of such people as authors John Bunyan and Daniel Defoe, and poet Isaac Watts, as well serving as a recreation ground for drunkards and drug addicts. In 1856, a Mr Jones, the proprietor of Bunhill, had been caught stealing and selling tombstones, bones and other ephemera from the graveyard, which was said to be swarming with 'slimy matter, alive with maggots'.[25] The sale of these tombstones could bring tens, if not hundreds, of pounds, providing they were well made and sturdy, and could therefore be reused to mark the grave of another deceased person. Even now, some of the gravestones moved during the time of Jones can be found slumped against other tombs and headstones in the graveyard, or lining the modern walkway through the cemetery.

Not every tombstone was valuable, however. The headstones of paupers, for example, which were often made from already-recycled stones or even just planks of wood, would not be expected to make any money if resold. Neither would the tiny headstones of babies and children, which were often accompanied by grave-goods left by grief-stricken parents and siblings in the shape of pebbles and seashells.[26] Leaving offerings such as these could provide families with an additional way to grieve, particularly considering that, due to the overcrowding of cemeteries, the grave of their loved one may not have been under their grave-marker. Indeed, it was not uncommon for headstones in Victorian London to mark the graves of the wrong people entirely, their true owner having been buried some feet away or beneath numerous other coffins. It was a sad end to the tale of many Victorian paupers, who had been forgotten about in death just as they had in life.

In an attempt to finally alleviate the mass overcrowding of cemeteries in Victorian London, local authorities would come to prohibit the burial of corpses within urban areas. Instead, parishes had to build graveyards large enough to accommodate thousands of the city's dead, and far enough away from areas of inhabitation to avoid the spread of disease and foul smell. In his 1839 pamphlet *Gatherings from Graveyards*, surgeon George Alfred Walker encouraged gravediggers to reconsider how they buried the dead, urging a gentler management of coffins to reduce the risk of coffin collapse.[27] It was hoped that by following Walker's advice, mourners paying their respects at gravesides would less frequently experience such things as headaches, heart palpitations, nausea, vomiting and other symptoms of so-called 'death by cadaverous vapours'.[28]

To further reduce the harmful effects of corpse overcrowding, Edwin Chadwick, the social reformer who campaigned tirelessly for improved sanitation, called for the passing of the Metropolitan Internments Act in 1850. This Act prescribed that should a body be buried in an urban area, it would cost the sum of 27*s*. If it was instead buried in a more remote area, as authorities encouraged, it would cost only 16*s*. In response to the Act, a total of thirty-six of the forty-three public burial sites in London's East End alone closed to further burials in 1850, bodies thereafter being interred in larger and more peaceful cemeteries.

With the closure of urban burial grounds set within the heart of busy city centres, the question of what to do with the otherwise unused land was posed to Parliament, which suggested that such land be turned into parks and green spaces to benefit the living. During the 1880s and 1890s, the Metropolitan Public Gardens Association began its lengthy cleaning up of these now-abandoned cemeteries on behalf of the government, restoring them to the green spaces they had once been. Indeed, seven of London's biggest and most overcrowded cemeteries were particularly targeted by the association, which, through dedication and unwavering hard work, turned them into botanical gardens complete with public pathways. These graveyards (called the 'Magnificent Seven') – now beautified, practical and pleasant – were visited by tens of thousands of Victorians each year, and by countless others in subsequent decades.

Nevertheless, not every visitor who set foot within the graveyards of Victorian London had such good intentions. Indeed, there were some who haunted cemeteries for their own benefit and gain, and who slunk between gravestones under the cloak of darkness to achieve their nefarious ends. These men had just one intention: they were known as the body-snatchers.

Body-Snatching

In 1844, *The Mysteries of London*, a so-called 'penny blood', spooked its readers by telling a grisly tale. Penny bloods, a favourite of Victorians, were short, often satirical horror stories that intended to scare and delight. Most often, they would be written based upon or inspired by true-life events, but were heavily embellished and injected with entirely fictional vignettes to further their terrifying impact. They were cheap and accessible to all social strata, and proved popular with men, women and children alike.

Volume One of *The Mysteries of London* series sets its story against the backdrop of a cold, foggy graveyard in Chatham, London. There, a trio of suspicious characters slink between tombstones, mausoleums and 'Bone-Houses' under the cover of darkness, laden with heavy tools such as shovels, axes and metal rods.[1] The men are described as 'Resurrectionists', and their business is a particularly morbid one.

As dawn begins to break 'in fitful gleams' through the inky sky, the men stab their iron rods into the ground, seemingly at random.[2] Deeper still they pierce the ground, until the rods thud against something solid beneath. Putting their whole weight onto the exposed ends of their rods, the men heave until the earth between them begins to crack and fall apart. They push upon the rods until they are lying almost horizontal, the ground by now resembling an erupted mound. Hastily, they pull out their shovels and toss lengths of rope to each other as they begin to dig in the mound. Within an instant, their treasure is revealed; a coffin so 'soft with decay that the iron rod had penetrated through it without much difficulty'.[3]

Victorian readers were in equal parts thrilled and horrified to read of the desecration of sacred burial grounds. Vivid descriptions of the 'sickly, fetid odours' were enough to turn delicate stomachs, but still the story grew more revolting.[4] As the Resurrectionists creak open the lid of the coffin, they are met by the unmoving face of a woman; long-dead, the corpse is 'damp and clogged with clay', and its skin has begun to recede upon its bones.[5] One of the men reaches for the skull, the eyes hollow and dark, and pulls it from the grave by the 'long hair which perhaps had once been a valued ornament'.[6] With one heave, 'the corpse is snatched from the tranquil slumber of the tomb' and tossed upon an open fire, choked with coke to disguise the smell.[7]

Resurrectionists, better known as 'Body-Snatchers', were a serious threat to Victorians, particularly the poor. Prowling local cemeteries and poring over death notices printed in newspapers, Resurrectionists would prey upon the dead to generate their income. Bodies were a lucrative trade in the nineteenth century, potentially bringing in hundreds of pounds. The bodies of the poorest members of society were particularly targeted, for their graves were often more exposed than those of the wealthy, who could afford the luxury of protection in the form of tombs and heavy lead-lined coffins. Paupers were also more likely to be buried in public graves that resembled little more than pits. In these public graves, corpses would often be buried in simple linen shrouds, their coffins recycled and reused for the next funeral of a poor decedent. Coffins for the paupers of Victorian society were not intended to be permanent; rather, they were simply receptacles to carry the corpse to its final resting place. Also not intended as items of permanence were the grave-markers of the poor, whose only recognition of their existence were small indicators made by diligent family members or friends, such as crosses made from shaped willow, stones and pebbles, or even candles. This impermanence was particularly distressing for mourners, who had no physical indicator that their loved one was buried below. Without a proper marker, the identities of the urban poor were forgotten. It was no wonder that they became such targets of the Resurrectionists.

The public graves of the desperately poor would often be dug wide enough to accommodate more than one corpse. Indeed, references of bodies buried four, five or more abreast have been found in cemetery records.[8] For body-snatchers to stumble upon crowded graves would have brought them serious profits; the poor were unfortunately such easy prey.

The fact that the corpses were extracted from their cold, earthy graves did not apparently bother the body-snatchers, nor did it matter that the poor souls now hauled into wheelbarrows or over shoulders had once been living and breathing. Neither did it matter that the corpse had come from the most destitute of society; the body-snatchers had no interest in grave goods, jewels or expensive clothing that the cadaver may have worn. Although the desecration of a burial place and the theft of a human body was technically not illegal in the 1830s, it *was* a felony for any item buried alongside the corpse to be taken and sold for profit.[9] As such, many body-snatchers are believed to have left the rest of the grave undisturbed, with its goods remaining just as they had been upon burial. But just how far Victorian body-snatchers abided by the law will probably never truly be known, and it is wholly plausible that many did not respect the rulings concerning the pilfering of grave goods. After all, they were trading in human remains, and morals did not seem to be high on their list of priorities.

Ultimately, the true value of the coffin lay within the corpse itself – and the fresher the better. In 1832, the Anatomy Act was passed, which aimed to give doctors, surgeons and physicians greater access to human bodies to conduct anatomical study. There was just one hitch; from *where* would they acquire these bodies? Although the Act had made it legal for dying patients to donate their bodies to science, the uptake was understandably very low. Many Victorians were aghast at the suggestion that their bodies be dissected, prodded and paraded in front of the wide eyes of eager medical students. Unless the deceased had been an exceptionally passionate advocate for the development of anatomy and biology – as had been the political radical Jeremy Bentham – then it was unlikely that they would sacrifice spiritual salvation in the name of medicine. Bentham, who died in 1832, had requested in his will that his body be preserved and displayed for educational purposes. His wishes were carried out by surgeon and social reformer Thomas Southwood Smith, who donated the embalmed body of his friend to University College London eighteen years later. Despite the time that had passed since his death, Bentham's body remained remarkably well preserved; even now, his clothed corpse welcomes patrons and students from behind a glass case in the hallway of the college's Student Centre.[10]

Without a constant supply of fresh corpses, anatomy schools could not carry out their work. As such, an unspoken agreement passed under the breaths of ethically unsound surgeons and their students, who argued that the theft of corpses was entirely permitted, so long as the corpse had belonged to the poorest of classes.[11] They reasoned that the corpses of paupers would be little grieved for and that their disturbed graves would go unnoticed. Due to the vast overcrowding of Victorian urban cemeteries, argued the surgeons, it was also beneficial for the ground to be less-saturated with corpses than to leave them to rot and emit their miasmas. Many physicians thus relied upon the criminal activities of the Resurrectionists, offering their powerful legal protection in return for absolute silence. Some medical schools, however, were so insistent on keeping their secrets within the institution that they sent out their own surgeons and scholars in the hunt for bodies. As early as 1788, journalists reported that,

> 'young gentlemen in this city who call themselves students of the physic [...] under cover of the night [...] dig up bodies of deceased friends and relatives [...] carrying them away without respect for age or sex.'[12]

For those who were less-inclined to dirty their hands with the crime of body-snatching, hired hands would do the duty for a fee. Doctors would keep a watchful eye on their sickly patients and warn the Resurrectionists to prepare for any imminent deaths. Once their patient had passed away and their death certificates had been signed, coffins could be taken from hospital morgues and buried. Often, however, this coffin would simply be a ruse, their occupants already dissected upon the mortuary boards of the medical school. If a coffin containing a genuine corpse did have to be exhumed, body-snatchers were encouraged to wear dark, inconspicuous clothing, and to work after nightfall. They would be provided with lengths of rope to loop around the neck, waist or limbs of the corpse, as well as wooden shovels and axes to prevent the sound of metal from alerting unwanted attention. The cadaver would then be hoisted into a covered wagon before the coffin was reburied and the gravesite covered over with soil. Targeting recent burials was beneficial not only for the freshness of the corpse, but also the fact that the soil did not give away signs of being disturbed, and could simply be brushed back to resemble a freshly dug mound without raising suspicion.

Despite attempts to keep the movements of body-snatchers hidden, mourners would occasionally raise the alarm to authorities if they felt that something was amiss. In 1875, one father grew suspicious when the doctor attending his newly born baby gave no update on the infant's health; six hours later, the baby had died and was being prepared for burial. However, as was reported in *The Times*, 'the child was not buried in [their] grave [but instead] the body had been disposed of for anatomical purposes'.[13] While the corpses of adults were appealing to Victorian surgeons, the bodies of children were even more so. However, grieving parents were reluctant to sign over the bodies of their deceased children to medical schools for anatomical research, and many Resurrectionists drew the line at exhuming the bodies of children. The acquisition of child cadavers was therefore even more difficult, and more valuable, in the eyes of anatomists.

Burke and Hare

Perhaps the best-known body-snatchers of the nineteenth century were the Edinburgh duo Burke and Hare, who, while predating the Victorian era, were well known during the Queen's reign for their dastardly deeds. Unlike other Resurrectionists of the time, Burke and Hare did not care for muddying their hands in the cemeteries of the city, and forwent the exhumation of cadavers. Instead, they cut out the middle man, targeting vulnerable paupers while they were still alive and passing off their bodies to surgeons who were none-the-wiser to the terrible crimes of the so-called 'anatomy murderers'.

William Burke and William Hare operated within the deepest warrens of Edinburgh's most decrepit of slums. Both had worked odd jobs as casual labourers, and both had known well the unease of insufficient income and job instability. The pair had been lodging at the same tenement building with their drunkard wives when word of the lucrative trade of corpses reached their ears.[1] It was an open secret that the art of body-snatching was being perfected in graveyards across the border in England, and Scottish reprobates were anxious to get a share of the easy pickings. As Resurrectionists began descending upon Scotland's dead, members of the public had reason to worry for the fate of the corpses of their loved ones. Solutions known as 'mortsafes' quickly became popular across Scotland, large structures that entombed the body in sheets of lead or sealed it in a metal coffin to prevent the theft of the corpse within. In some cases, large metal structures resembling cages would be erected around a burial plot, acting as a further deterrent to the Resurrectionists. Numerous examples of mortsafes still exist across Scotland, particularly in the cemetery and kirkyard of Greyfriars in Edinburgh. Although English examples are extant in locations such as Bunhill Fields Burial Ground in Islington and at the Science Museum in Kensington, far more have survived north of the border. Perhaps this lack of English examples is due in part to the natural degradation of materials over time. However, it is more likely that the number of mortsafes to have survived in Scotland is due to the greater evidence of body-snatching and cadaver trade that flourished there, no doubt influenced by the legacies of Burke and Hare.

In the nineteenth century, Scotland had paved the way for anatomical study and was a leading centre of medical development and advancement across the globe.

However, just as their southern neighbours had done, Scottish surgeons began to experience a lack of fresh corpses upon which to practice, their supply irrevocably cut off by the Judgement of Death Act passed in 1823. This Act significantly limited the number of executions of Victorian criminals that took place in Britain. Moralists argued that this reform was a step in the right direction, and that the total abolition of the death penalty would act as a precedent for an upheaval of the criminal justice system as a whole. On the other hand, the reduction in the number of criminal corpses that had previously streamed steadily into the lecture halls and onto the dissecting tables of hospitals and medical schools proved exceptionally problematic. Up until this time, the law had permitted surgeons the free use of the bodies of criminals to conduct medical and scientific study. Without them, anatomical study ground to a halt.

As desperation grew for fresh bodies to fill the morgues of medical schools, surgeons, doctors and students turned a blind eye to the origin of their 'patients'. Consequently, when William Hare offered Professor Robert Knox the body of a recently deceased army pensioner in order to pay off his tenancy debts, he and Burke were surprised and delighted by the lucrative future that seemed to unfurl before them. Knox had offered the men an enormous sum of £7 10*s* for the body, which they hastily pocketed. Encouraged by the relative ease with which the body had been sold for profit, the men came to a quiet understanding that they would continue their trade together with their wives.

By 1827, Burke and his mistress, Helen McDougal, had moved into a lodging house owned by Hare and his common-law wife, Margaret Laird, on Tanner's Close, Edinburgh.[2] The house was frequented by the poor and the destitute, and had such a constant stream of lodgers wandering across the threshold that neighbours had no reason to grow suspicious of the activities occurring within. However, gossip soon became aroused when locals noticed that an increasing number of lodgers appeared to disappear during the night, having been seen going about their business one day, then gone the next. Such a transitory lifestyle was not uncommon in the nineteenth century, yet nosy neighbours still grew concerned when activity in the otherwise boisterous house appeared to dramatically cease.

The first known victim of Burke and Hare is widely believed to have been a miller named Joseph, who had lodged at the house in the early months of 1828.[3] Joseph had fallen ill with influenza and a raging fever, which sparked the interest of Burke and Hare, who kept a watchful eye on the man's condition. When Joseph appeared to neither improve nor worsen, their patience grew painfully thin. Under the pretence of caring for their poor lodger, the men plied Joseph with ounces of whisky, quietly assuring him that it was medicinal and that it would soothe his symptoms. As Joseph fell into a deep slumber, Burke reached for a pillow and smothered his victim as his partner restrained his limbs and body.[4] This method of murder would eventually become favoured by the duo, who preferred the process since it left no physical mark or any sign of poison, injury or foul play. It was so preferred by the men that the method of murder even became known as 'Burking'. When the pair approached Knox with another new corpse, they were relieved that he did not question where they had found it. That the men had conveniently come across two corpses in such a small window of time did not concern Knox, who preferred not to be implicated with the pair's disreputable activities. With the need for corpses at such a high, from where they were derived was of no consequence to him.

It seemed that Burke and Hare had cracked the system, though as quickly as their fortunes had turned, they met with difficulties that blocked their path. The pair were disgruntled when a string of healthy and robust lodgers milled through the lodging house, without so much as a cough or complaint. With no unwell patrons in the boarding house, the men were forced to look elsewhere for their next victims.

In 1828, two young female prostitutes lodged at the house, at Burke's unrelenting insistence.[5] Following an evening of drinking and flirting, one of the women, Janet Brown, excused herself and left the building to resume her nightly duties of searching out lusty customers. By the time she returned later in the evening, Brown found the previously jovial kitchen now cold, quiet and empty. Upon asking the whereabouts of her friend, Mary Paterson, Brown was reassured that she had 'stepped out' with William Burke (a euphemism for engaging in sexual intercourse), and that she would soon return. After a short while, with Brown growing increasingly impatient, she decided to leave the building without Paterson. This decision undoubtedly saved Brown's life, for lying in the room next door was the corpse of her friend.[6]

When, later that day, the still-warm body of Mary Paterson was taken to the medical school stuffed in a tea-chest; the suspicions of the students were aroused.[7] Many of them recognized the deceased woman, some having even been partial to her services. Upon being asked the origin of the body and the cause of her death, Burke and Hare casually replied that they had purchased the corpse from an elderly woman.[8] Though his students were unconvinced by this evasive answer, Professor Knox did not press matters. Impressed that the corpse was so fresh, Knox pickled it in a barrel of whisky for three months, inviting artists to sketch and paint it before using it for dissection demonstrations.[9]

The hesitation of the medical students to accept the corpse of Mary Paterson did not dissuade Burke and Hare from continuing their work. Within months, the pair had murdered at least sixteen people and sold each and every one of the corpses to Knox and his team of surgeons. Amongst them were Mary and Peggy Haldane, a mother and daughter who had both been 'Burked' – smothered to death – mere months apart. In June 1828, Burke and Hare murdered an elderly woman and her intellectually disabled grandson in the same night. Having smothered the woman in her bed, the men carried the young boy up to the scene of the crime and did the same to him, but not before Burke had placed the boy over his knee and broken his spine.[10] Burke would later recount that this murder had been the one that had disturbed him the most, for the 'recollection of the piteous expression of the wistful eyes' of the boy had haunted his memories.[11]

Preying on the vulnerable, poor or helpless was the *modus operandi* of Burke and Hare. The men believed that characters such as prostitutes, the elderly, orphans or the disabled were less likely to arouse suspicion should they go missing. It was a sentiment adopted by other notable criminals of nineteenth-century Britain, including Mary Ann Cotton and Jack the Ripper, though ultimately their plan was not as watertight as it might have seemed. In late September 1828, Burke and Hare found their latest target. Known locally as 'Daft Jamie', 18-year-old James Wilson had been born with intellectual disabilities and deformed feet. A familiar face on the streets of Edinburgh, Jamie had made his living through begging, depending upon the kindness of strangers who kept a watchful eye on him from afar.

On the evening of his death, Jamie was lured into Hare's lodging house with promises of warm food and flowing whisky. When led to a bedroom (which was dutifully locked behind them by Margaret Laird), Jamie managed to fight off his attackers for a while, having not been as intoxicated as the men had hoped. Finally relenting, Jamie was battered by the duo, who stripped the corpse of its rags and hastily stuffed it in the tea-chest which had been used to transport their other victims. Upon delivery to the medical school, the suspicious students again questioned where the body had come from. They recognized Jamie, who had been such a familiar face in the area surrounding the school. Yet when the students threatened to dismiss Burke and Hare as their suppliers, fearing their illegal attainment of corpses, Knox nevertheless began to dissect Jamie's body, even though the morgue was replete with other cadavers due for inspection. By sawing off the feet of Jamie's corpse, Knox saved Burke and Hare from having their illicit actions catch up with them, ridding the body of any incriminating identifiers.[12]

Yet the final nail in the coffin for the murderous pair would come just a month later, when suspicions over Burke and Hare's activities reached fever pitch amongst Knox's students and other residents of Tanner's Close. On All Hallow's Eve 1828, Margaret Docherty entered Hare's lodging house. Docherty, who hailed from Ireland, had been enthralled by Burke's story that his mother came from the same area. Reminiscing about her hometown, Docherty fell deeper into a state of inebriation, having been plied with copious amounts of whisky by the men. Unsuspecting of anything untoward, Docherty danced with the men and their wives before she was killed at some point during the evening.[13] Too drunk to ensure that the murder had been completed to their exacting standards, Burke and Hare moved Docherty's body to the foot of a bed and covered it sparsely with straw. Had they placed the corpse in the tea-chest as usual, perhaps their exploits would never have come to light. Yet on that fateful night, one mistake was all it took for the body-snatching empire of Burke and Hare to come tumbling down.

In the morning after the drunken soiree at Tanner's Close, the body of Margaret Docherty was found by Ann Gray, a lodger searching for her stockings. Gray immediately went to the police, alerting them to the horrific sight that confronted her at the boarding house. By the time Gray and a team of policemen arrived at Tanner's Court, however, Burke and Hare had already taken the cadaver to Knox's mortuary. Gossip of body-snatching, murder and mutilated corpses soon spread around the slums of Edinburgh. Burke and Hare were arrested and put on trial, where they each gave differing testimonies of their experiences in trading illicitly with Professor Knox and his students. Upon implicating Knox, the future of anatomical study in Edinburgh seemed to have come to an end. Miraculously, however, and perhaps by virtue of his social standing as a surgeon, Knox faced no charges. Although investigators and lawyers deemed the professor 'deficient in principle and heart', his actions had not been considered untoward; rather, it was unanimously agreed that Knox had simply been doing what his profession dictated.[14]

The activities of William Burke and William Hare, however, were not taken so lightly. Under police duress, Hare confessed to everything, even aiding in the forensic examination of their victims. He maintained that throughout the serial murders, he had acted solely as Burke's right-hand man, admitting to thievery and assisting in supplying Knox with the corpses. When details of Hare's confession came to the knowledge of the public, chants of a macabre poem permeated every avenue of Edinburgh's slums:

> 'Up the close and down the stair,
> In the house with Burke and Hare.
> Burke's the butcher,
> Hare's the thief,
> Knox the man who buys the beef.
> Burke and Hare they were a pair,
> Killed a wife and didnae care.'[15]

Under the Scottish law of the time, which permitted the sale of corpses for medical study, Hare had effectively signed his release papers. It is probable that William Hare was aware of this legal loophole, and had exploited it in order to secure his freedom, aware of his fate had he been found guilty of murder. In exchange for Hare's (somewhat untruthful) confession and assistance in the investigation, he received a full pardon for his crimes. Hare's fate thereafter is unknown; some believe that he moved to London under a pseudonym, adopting an entirely new way of life and dying as an aged blind man. Another theory was that he willingly boarded a ship bound for the penal colony of Australia, where he raised a large family. Most plausible, however, was that he returned to his native Ireland and settled into a quiet life with his relatives there. Indeed, evidence indicates that Hare hitched a ride upon a mail coach (that delivered the post across Edinburgh) toward Dumfries, where he likely travelled onward to Ireland.[16]

His partner in crime did not share his fate. In exchange for his freedom, Hare had slandered the name of William Burke and placed all the blame for their crimes upon him. Burke, feeling undoubtedly slighted by his co-conspirator's betrayal, received the harshest of punishments, being sentenced to death, which was duly carried out on 28 January 1829. On the scaffold, Burke must have felt incredibly wronged by the man he had once considered his friend, whom he cursed under his breath. The legacy of William Burke did not end there, however. Never passing up the opportunity of a fresh corpse, a rival of Professor Knox, Professor Alexander Monro III, seized the chance to dissect the man whose efforts had changed the way anatomy and human biology was understood in Scottish medical schools. In front of his students – among them a young Charles Darwin – Monro carefully removed the skin from Burke's corpse and used it to bind a book that was later gifted to the

Medical College at Edinburgh University. Monro left a final ironic and gruesome tribute to Burke by dipping his quill into the still-liquid blood of the cadaver and writing:

> 'This is written with the blood of Wm Burke, who was hanged at Edinburgh. This blood was taken from his head.'[17]

Patrons of the Anatomy School at Edinburgh University can still come literally face-to-face with the corpse of William Burke. Death masks of Burke were taken following his execution, showing how he had looked in life, whilst his fully articulated skeleton gazes hollowly from a glass cabinet in the Old Medical School Building.

Though the murderous spree of William Burke and William Hare had lasted a mere two years, their legacy would influence the way that anatomical study and forensic investigation would forever be perceived. The unethical actions of Burke and Hare directly contributed to the 1832 Anatomy Act, which carefully regulated the acquiring of cadavers used for medical seminars and made it possible for the dying to leave their bodies to scientific study. The case of Burke and Hare in Edinburgh illuminated the substantial underground illicit trade in corpses across Britain, and greater effort was thereafter maintained in the prosecution of criminals found to have engaged in the act of body-snatching and exhumation. Though their intentions had never been ethical; we could perhaps credit the Scottish serial-killing duo for enlightening the hazy laws surrounding anatomical acquisitions and bringing about a new-found interest in reputable mortuary and funerary care and the rights of the dead in nineteenth-century British society.

Chapter 10

Changing Times: From Victoria to Edward

> 'The first Iron Age had been a turning point in civilisation; and one can say the same for the second.'
>
> K. Clark, *Civilisation* (1969)

'I don't mind praying to the Eternal Father,' muttered Albert Edward, the Prince of Wales, as he paced in his sitting room, 'but I must be the only man in the country afflicted with an eternal mother.'

Albert Edward (or 'Bertie', as he was known to family and friends) had good reason to grumble. For fifty-nine years, he had been styled as the Prince of Wales, the heir apparent to the British throne. He had surpassed the record of his distant uncle, King George IV, who had begrudgingly served as Prince of Wales for fifty-eight years and had acted as Regent when his incapacitated father, King George III, had been too unwell to rule. The record would not be broken for another 120 years, when Albert Edward's great-great-grandson, King Charles III, finally ascended to the throne after seventy years of principality duty. Bertie's had truly been the most enduring of occupations.

As the Prince of Wales, Albert Edward had earned a reputation as a hedonist, fond of lavishing in excess and engaging in extra-marital affairs, to the chagrin of his mother, Queen Victoria. He had been married to the fashionable and dignified Alexandra of Denmark in 1863, whose humility and gentle kindness had endeared her to the poor, the rights of whom she had ardently championed. Upon Victoria's death, Albert Edward and Alexandra ushered in a new age, a 'Belle Epoque' of prosperity and progress, sparked by their joint coronation on 9 August 1902. Though he was on the throne only for ten years, the reign of the King Edward VII marked a distinct shift from the rather straight-laced rule of his mother. The very moment the jewel-encrusted Imperial State Crown was placed upon the balding head of the aged king at Westminster Abbey, it signified change. No longer was Britain Victorian; the new Edwardian era had begun.

Edwardian Britain is best memorialized for its architectural styles, modernized fashion, penchant for decorum and permeable social classes. Under Edward VII, the cultural landscape of Britain reached new peaks. The invention of phonographs and gramophones made music more accessible to Britons, who could now listen to emerging genres like jazz and swing from the comfort of their own homes. These homes were larger, and certainly warmer, than their antecedent Victorian and Georgian houses had been. With the increase in wages and disposable income that had come from the Victorian 'Consumer Revolution', people could now afford to save, with the hope of someday buying their own new-builds and forgoing the reliance on public social housing. Indeed, Edwardian houses began popping up across the country with such speed that the period has since become known as the 'most prolific house-building period in British history'.[1]

Despite their elegant red brick exteriors and sophisticated large bay windows, Edwardian houses were affordable and therefore more accessible to the emerging middle and working classes across the country. Even the poor, who had resided in dank hovels and dilapidated buildings, could now afford to live in solidly built houses that for the first time awarded families their own privacy away from roving lodgers and transitory tenants. Though still small and occasionally cramped, Edwardian houses were brighter, cleaner and more inhabitable than their Victorian predecessors had been. Houses now came with distinct separate rooms, running water and even central heating. Under Edward, both the Liberal and Conservative governments poured money into expenditure aimed to improve construction materials and building regulations, as well as investing in more sophisticated sewage systems that vastly transformed the standards of sanitation in dense urban areas. For the first time, the dark and dingy Victorian slum hovels were replaced by comfortable and affordable Edwardian brick-and-mortar homes.

As well as stressing the importance of improvements to social housing and vagrancy, the Liberal government of the early twentieth century emphasized vital state involvement which aimed to tackle any residual poverty still lingering from Victoria's reign. Prompted to action by the publication of Seebohm Rowntree's *Poverty: A Study of Town Life* in 1901, the Edwardian government was forced to accept that much deprivation and limitation still remained across the country, particularly in pockets of London and in the North of England.[2] Though their efforts were somewhat fruitful and the country witnessed 'booming trade [...] great prosperity and wealth', there still existed a sense that more needed to be achieved for the benefit of the people.[3] This was nowhere more evident than in the case of the underrepresented, whose desperate plight and prolonged perseverance came to define Edwardian Britain.

The Struggle for Suffrage

Founded in 1889, the Woman's Franchise League campaigned for married women to gain greater independence away from their husbands, and focused their efforts particularly on gaining the right for female participation in local elections. Until this point, women had very little political enfranchisement, and could not legally vote in elections at either local or national levels. It was a desperate plight close to the heart of the group's founder, Emmeline Goulden, whose marriage to outspoken radical Richard Pankhurst had helped lead the way for the passing of two Married Women's Property Acts in 1870 and 1882 respectively.[1] These Acts were significant as they awarded married women the right to protect any wages that they had earned independent of their husbands, thus allowing wives to control their own money and financial accounts. It was the first time that women could legally lay claim to their 'own property', and was a step in the right direction in the reforming of the rights of women in Victorian Britain.

But it was not enough. Still dissatisfied with the extent of women's legal rights in Britain, Emmeline Pankhurst established a new organization, the Women's Social and Political Union (WSPU), in 1903, which quickly gained traction across the country, with married and unmarried women alike desperate for personal autonomy and political suffrage. It mirrored the efforts of another suffragist group, the National Union of Women's Suffrage Societies (NUWSS), established in 1897 by activist Milicent Fawcett, who, like Pankhurst, was deeply unsettled by the restrictive shackles placed on women in Victorian and Edwardian Britain. Of these restrictions, the most limiting of all was a statute of the 1832 Reform Act, which excluded women from the right to a vote.

The reaction to the 1832 Reform Act had been more passionate than the Government had expected, with the extent of dissent surprising Parliamentarians who watched in awe as the so-called 'gentler' of sexes grew increasingly outraged and outspoken. The NUWSS had a membership totalling around 50,000 by the turn of the century, its numbers principally comprising reform-minded women and progressive-leaning men.[2] Contrary to popular belief, the suffragist movement did not entirely consist of females, with many husbands, fathers and brothers soon finding themselves involved in the political predicament of the women they held dear.

Despite the outraged response to the Reform Act, the NUWSS campaigned for change peacefully, advocating for non-violent protests and the cordial lobbying of male Members of Parliament. By protesting peacefully, the NUWSS knew that they could not be legally reprimanded, for their campaigning efforts were entirely within the boundaries of legal dissent. This emphasis on non-violent and amicable opposition gained the NUWSS the respect of some Parliamentarians, who became increasingly aware of the pressures they were now facing. No less than 17,000 petitions were presented on behalf of the NUWSS to the Houses of Parliament throughout the nineteenth and twentieth centuries, with the most influential being submitted in 1896, having gathered the support of around 260,000 signiatures.[3] Though they strove to obtain their goals through peace and calm, clearly these suffragists were not to be dissuaded.

However, when Parliamentary action moved at a pace slower than desired, Emmeline Pankhurst and her WSPU campaigners took matters into their own hands. The peaceful protests of the NUWSS were simply not good enough; Pankhurst had much left to achieve, and no amount of gentle persuasion would convince Parliament to change its stance on female suffrage. With her daughters Sylvia and Christabel, Emmeline Pankhurst drew up a plan: they would strive to achieve their goal of women's enfranchisement by whatever means possible. Abandoning the respect for amicable relations with Members of Parliament, the Pankhursts encouraged radical suffragists to instead use other means. By committing arson, smashing windows and chaining themselves to public fences, the militant campaigners earned a new moniker which would come to define their very movement; they were no longer simply 'suffragists', now they were the 'Suffragettes'.

Due to the Suffragettes' advocation of force and haste, many, including the dominant figures of the movement, found themselves arrested for their crimes. Emmeline Pankhurst herself was arrested on three occasions, and endured painful force-feeding in response to her indignant hunger strikes.[4] Her daughter, Sylvia, vividly described suffering the practice, painting a horrific picture in her *Votes for Women*, published in 1913:

> 'Six women had got me on the bed, holding me by the ankles, knees and shoulders [...] somebody caught me by the head from behind and tied a sheet under my chin. I set my teeth like a vice and my breath came so quickly that I thought I should suffocate. I felt a man's hand trying to force my mouth open. I felt a steel instrument being forced against my gums [...] they started to force the tube down my throat. I tightened the muscles and struggled with all my might [...] it was quite a long time before I could get my breath. They left me on the bed exhausted and shaking with sobs. The same thing happened in the evening, but I was too tired to fight.'[5]

The hunger-striking militant Suffragettes had become such a problem for Parliament that it was forced to pass the Cat and Mouse Act in 1913, allowing for weakened prisoners to be temporarily discharged from prison to recover their health. In practice, the Act appeared to proactively consider the needs of the incapacitated women; in reality, however, the cycle continued when the women, now restored to full strength, would find themselves back in prison, where they resumed their obstinate hunger strikes.

The NUWSS decried the violent efforts of the Suffragettes. Helena Auerbach, the president of the Reigate, Redhill and District Society for Women's Suffrage, wrote in a 1908 letter to the press that 'aggressive political coercion is as little suited to our sex as the exercise of physical force', in an attempt to distance the NUWSS from the WSPU.[6] Yet despite this infighting within the movement, Emmeline Pankhurst would not be deterred. 'We are here, not because we are law-breakers,' she insisted in response, 'we are here in our efforts to become law-makers.'[7] By 1913, however, the activities of the Suffragettes reached new extremist heights that even Pankhurst found difficult to approve of. On 4 June 1913, radical Suffragette Emily Davison elbowed her way to the front of the crowd that had gathered to watch the King's horse, Anmer, run in the Epsom Derby. Draped in the purple, white and green flag of the Suffragette movement, Davison waited for her opportunity; as the crowd swelled and excitement reached fever pitch, Davison knew it was time to strike. 'One big tragedy may save many others,' she had stated confidently in an article for *The Suffragette* magazine.[8] It was clear what her intention would be.

As the leading horses whipped past the spectators, Davison readied herself. Upon sighting the King's horse, she ducked beneath the safety barrier and launched herself at horse and jockey. Newsreel cameras captured the moment that Davison pounced, and the subsequent seconds in which she fell to the ground, trampled by the horses. Onlookers stood, stunned, at the event that had unfolded in front of them. They did not know it then, but they had just witnessed a turning point in the Suffragette movement.

Emily Davison was transported to hospital as a flurry of negative press and hate mail flooded the desks of Emmeline Pankhurst and her Suffragettes. Even Queen Alexandra branded Davison a 'brutal lunatic', condemning the actions of the activist.[9] Davison died four days later, never regaining consciousness. Though her actions had certainly brought attention to the cause of the Suffragettes, as she had intended, it was of a negative kind. The Suffragettes were aware in the wake of the Emily Davison affair that their efforts still had far to go.

Despite the dedication and unwavering perseverance of both the NUWSS and the WSPU, women would not be granted the right to vote until 1918, and even then it was only awarded to property-owning wealthy women aged over 30. It was but a drop in the ocean; only around 8.4 million British women had been enfranchised by the Representation of the People Act.[10] This was a fraction of the around 18.9 million females of voting age in Britain at the time.[14] It would take another decade for the franchise to be further widened, but finally, in 1928 (just weeks after the death of Emmeline Pankhurst), all women and men over the age of 21 finally achieved the right to vote through the Equal Franchise Act.

The Suffragettes had succeeded.

It was not just the right to vote that Victorian and Edwardian women had so desired. Another significant change to the lives of nineteenth and twentieth-century women came in the form of a thin, pocket-sized rubber contraption: the condom.

Throughout the Victorian period, backyard abortions had been frequently sought by desperate women who had found themselves with child. Contraception as we now know it did not come into circulation until 1961, when the contraceptive pill was introduced to Britain. Victorian women had to rely on flimsy paper condoms to prevent pregnancy, many of which were reused or tore during use. It was little wonder that this method of preventing pregnancy failed more often than it worked. Single women, amorous young men and burdened parents were growing desperate.

It is thus possible to consider the condom to be one of man's greatest inventions. Not only did the vulcanized rubber material of condoms work as a barrier to contain sperm and prevent pregnancy, but the latex condom (later developed by Ernest Hopkins and Charlie Goodyear, of the tyre empire) also allowed couples to explore and engage in safe sexual intercourse.[11] The condom drastically reduced the rates of maternal deaths in childbirth and through unsafe practices such as abortion, and allowed Edwardian couples to regulate the size of their families without the risk of difficult and dangerous pregnancies and labours. Though social commentators such as Sigmund Freud had complained about the unnatural feel of the condom, it was an invention from which society as a whole had benefitted.[12] It was estimated that more than 60 per cent of Edwardian couples relied on latex condoms within the first years of their courtship and marriage, and that they would continue to rely on them even after establishing their families in order to keep practicing safe sex without the risk of falling pregnant.[13]

With this revolutionary new product, Edwardian women found themselves in positions of freedom never previously known. For the first time in history, women could choose when to stop growing their families, or even to prevent childbearing at all. It was a turning point in the history of feminism; no longer did women have to endure successive years of gruelling pregnancy, dangerous childbirth and exhausting childrearing like their mothers and grandmothers had. With such a drastic drop in birth rates, Edwardian mothers could dedicate their new-found precious time to pursuits other than the care of children. With the emphasis on education for all classes and sexes emerging toward the end of the Victorian era, more girls had grown into fully literate women. This meant that with less parental responsibility and greater academic opportunities, Edwardian women could now pursue jobs of their own. Indeed, such inventions as the sewing machine, the telephone and the typewriter truly revolutionized the world of the woman; now, their horizons were expanding.

It was not just women whose prospects greatly improved with the heralding of the Edwardian era. Like girls, young boys were also encouraged to pursue education in the early twentieth century, so much so that the legal school leaving age rose to 14 in 1900, while Balfour's Education Act of 1902 provided education for all at a secondary level. This meant that for the first time, advanced education was not reserved for the richest of communities. If a child showed great potential, or had a particular penchant for academic pursuits, colleges and even universities now accepted gifted members of even the poorest backgrounds. Many Edwardian grammar schools that chose to adopt this public schooling even invested in scholarships and funding for their exceptional prospective students, easing the burden for poor parents to provide the schooling fees for their children. As well as the establishment of dedicated secondary education, Day Trade Schools were established, particularly in urban areas such as London, Manchester and Liverpool, which thrived with the thrum of young apprentices taking up tactile skills like carpentry and mason-work. If a child had not been particularly interested in academia, many could now hope to further their careers by these other means. Indeed, students who learnt their trades at these Day Schools went on to form the backbone of Edwardian society.

As well as attractive education and employment prospects, men were targeted with new leisurely pursuits, notably in engineering and mechanics. These fields were quickly gaining in traction, so much so that a child born at the end of Victoria's reign could grow up under Edward VII in a world vastly modernized and almost entirely alien to their predecessors. In 1900, for example, young boys were astounded to hear the first transmission of human voice as it echoed across radio waves in Britain. Just three years later, mouths hung agape as the Wright brothers successfully took their first flight in a petrol-powered aeroplane. Land and sea had already been conquered; now the sky had been vanquished too.

The Edwardian era ushered in an age of rapid scientific progress, so fast that many Britons struggled to keep up. When, in 1903, business magnate Henry T. Ford introduced his first automobile, the Edwardian government was pressured into investing in motorized ambulances to respond to the motor accidents that were occurring at alarming frequency all across the country. When experiments into the effects of radium took place in the early 1900s, Edwardian scientists raced to contain it at the behest of Madame Marie Curie, who discovered that the dangerous metal threatened radioactive poisoning in all those who handled it. And when working-class men, who had been born and raised in the dark and dingy slums of Victorian Britain, were employed in engineering work for the White Star Line, little did they expect that their impressive endeavours would result in tragedy with the fateful sinking of the *Titanic* in 1912, resulting in the deaths of 1,500 people.

It was clear that Edwardian Britons had achieved so much by building upon the successes and discoveries of their Victorian predecessors. Yet they still had very much further to go.

Science, trade and engineering were not the only employment prospects available to men in the twentieth century. On the morning of 28 June 1914, events across the Continent would change the world forever. What unfurled on that bright morning would ricochet throughout Europe, launching a string of toppling political empires and collapsing economies. Hardly any nation across the entirety of the globe remained unaffected by this momentous event. It was the eve of the Great War.

A Changing World

The carriage of Archduke Franz Ferdinand rattled through the cobblestone streets of Sarajevo. Ferdinand, the heir-presumptive to the Austro-Hungarian throne, and his beloved wife, Sophie, had been on a visit to the Bosnian capital, bringing to a conclusion their Eastern European tour.[1] Generally well-liked, though chastised for his scalding opinions of Serbians, Franz had been warmly welcomed by parading crowds as his convoy made its way through the capital. Visiting schools and orphanages, army camps and city halls, Ferdinand's trip had been an apparent success.

The Archduke and his motorcade continued its journey past the Miljacka River, where huge crowds had gathered. Ferdinand felt hopeful, his confidence in establishing strong, amicable ties with Bosnia-Herzegovina growing by the hour. Such a welcoming turnout had pleased the Archduke, who, despite earlier omens of burning car axles and whispers of bomb threats, had not been persuaded to cancel his trip.[2] In their open-top carriage, Franz and Sophie reclined in the warm sun as they waved to the expectant crowd.

But just moments later, the peace was disturbed and chaos ensued. A young man by the name of Cabrinovic threw a heavy object at the Archduke and his wife, which narrowly missed the couple and bounced off the carriage's folded roof. Moments later, an explosion erupted in the crowds, injuring bystanders and army officers who had lined the route for security. Ferdinand, unfazed, insisted on completing his journey, and pressed his motorcade to press on to the city hall. Despite this earlier threat, Ferdinand's trip had otherwise run smoothly, and he was applauded for his still calmness in the face of mortality.

It appeared that Ferdinand's image was only improving with every obstacle he overcame that day. Deciding to further his positive relations with the Bosnians, Ferdinand planned to make an impromptu stop at the hospital treating the victims of Cabrinovic's failed assassination attempt. However, as the convoy bounded along the uneven roads of the city, it soon became apparent that the driver had taken a wrong turn. Stopping in a back street alley to correct their mistake, Ferdinand's carriage came to a halt just as a young man named Gavrilo Princip seized his opportunity. With just two shots from his pistol, Princip mortally wounded both the Archduke and his wife. As Franz Ferdinand sunk to his knees, the bloodied bullet lodged in the centre of his throat, he reached over to Sophie and cradled his dying wife. 'It is nothing,' he soothed, gesturing to the wound in her abdomen. 'Sophie, you must live for the sake of our children.'[3]

The assassination of Archduke Franz Ferdinand and his wife was the catalyst that sparked conflict all across the world. In response to the murder of their heir-presumptive, the Austro-Hungarians declared war on Serbia exactly one month to the day after Ferdinand's death, supported by their powerful ally, Germany. Europe was plunged into a state of war that only furthered when the other world powers of Russia, France, Great Britain and later the United States of America became drawn into the conflict.

More than 16 million people are believed to have died in the Great War, languishing in hellish trenches and on bloody battlefields. It is estimated that 6 per cent of the entire male population of Britain lost their lives during the conflict, which stretched from 1914 to its culmination in 1918.[4] Many of those men had been born in the slums of Victorian England; some had known depravity and want, had witnessed poverty and deprivation. Those young children of the Victorian slums, whose futures were just beginning to brighten, grew up to face horrors on a scale never before seen.

Life in Britain would never be the same again.

Postscript

As weary workers made their way to the public houses dotted along the seafront of Portsmouth Harbour, there was a mix of dread and nervous excitement in the air. It was 22 January 1901, and evening had begun to fall. The freezing sea mist rolling off the lapping waves cut through the wool, canvas and sack uniforms of sailors, labourers and fishermen. Chilled to the bone, the usually rowdy atmosphere of the Pompey alehouses grew hushed as eyes were turned downcast. All talk was of one thing: the health of the Queen.

Across the Solent, every bed on the Isle of Wight had been accounted for by journalists and dignitaries, clergymen and foreign ambassadors. Like the alehouses a few miles across the sea on the mainland, all conversation circled the same subject. Reporters sat poised by their telegram machines, readying themselves for the moment that they would begin typing their messages, as candlestick telephones were taken off their hooks in preparation. It would not be much longer before their vital bulletins hurtled along electrical currents and reached the principal news bureaus in London.

For at Osbourne House, the private holiday residence of the Royal Family, Queen Victoria lay dying.

The Queen, almost completely blind, tottering on weak ankles and bent double from osteoporosis of the spine, was 81. She had reigned for an incredible sixty four years, the female figurehead in a world otherwise dismissive of womanly independence. Victoria had loved and lost both people and places, from grand foreign empires to her beloved dearest Albert. She had championed social change and technological and scientific advancement, and oversaw the establishment of dedicated institutions such as hospitals, schools and places of cultural enhancement. Victoria's reign had taken Britain from the stuffy Georgian period – where the poor had been especially marginalized, life expectancy had been particularly short and epidemics had been borne and spread through inadequate sanitary conditions. By the time Queen Victoria took her last breath at 6.30 pm that night, the stinking slums of impoverished cities had largely been cleared, improved or entirely demolished. The poor emerged blinking in the light of new opportunities. Their infants had been inoculated, their jobs were now better paid, their children educated and literate, and their homes better built for inhabitation.

Surrounded by at least fourteen members of her family, as well as numerous doctors and nurses, the 'Grandmother of Europe' fixed her cloudy eyes upon a painting of Christ that hung facing the bed, uttered a final request to see her dog, Turi, and sank into her flower-adorned pillows on a small wheeled divan created specifically for her passing.[1] Her eldest son, Bertie, the Prince of Wales, had the honour of closing his mother's eyes.[2] As he turned to face his siblings, children and extended family, a grave sense of duty settled in his stomach.

As the new monarch, Bertie, now King Edward VII, continued in earnest the work that his mother, her politicians and the sanguine social reformists had started. Though compared to hers, his reign would be considerably shorter, Edwardian Britain left a lasting legacy in the form of education, sanitation and public health reforms, improved standards of housing, living and employment, and the indubitable achievement that had been the extension of the electoral franchise to women. It was an era of change, where even the prospects of the poor were beginning to reach new heights.

Though workhouses and orphanages were still in operation, labourers were still being exploited and exposed to dangerous working conditions, and the rights of the underrepresented still required much overhaul, life in Britain had incontrovertibly changed. Under Edward VII, great advances were made in sanitation, educational provision, living standards, public health, law and order, scientific progress and cultural pursuits. The dark and dingy underworld of Britain had evolved under Queen Victoria to emerge much brighter than it ever had been; under Edward and his successors, that light would only shine even brighter.

The dark and dingy underworld of the Victorian slums were now places of change, where the people who once had nothing could now grasp on to their salvation: progress.

Notes

Money Conversion

1. L. Jackson, 'Victorian Money – How much did things cost?', *The Dictionary of Victorian London* (2023). Available online.
2. The National Archives, *Currency Converter: 1270–2017* (2023). Available online.
3. *Ibid.*

Preface

1. *The Pall Mall Gazette*, Friday, 31 August 1888.
2. *The Penny Illustrated Paper*, Saturday, 1 September 1888, p.131.
3. *Ibid.*
4. *The Pall Mall Gazette*, Friday, 31 August 1888, p.10.
5. *Ibid.*, pp.15–16.
6. *Ibid.*, p.12.
7. *Ibid.*, p.12.
8. *Ibid.*, p.12.
9. A. Vale and A. Rattle, *The Woman Who Murdered Babies for Money: The Story of Amelia Dyer* (London: Andre Deutsch Ltd, 2011), and D. Arif, 'The Murder of Elizabeth Jackson', in *Casebook: Jack the Ripper* (2008).
10. *The Pall Mall Gazette*, Saturday, 1 September 1888, p.6.

Chapter 1: The Dark Underbelly of Victorian Britain

1. Demographia, 'Greater London, Inner London & Outer London Population & Density History' (2001). Available online.
2. I. Lee, 'Ragged Schools', British Library (2014). Available online.
3. Isabella Bird, *Notes on Old Edinburgh* (Edinburgh: Edmonston and Douglas, 1869), p.7.
4. Nellie Bly, *Ten Days in a Mad-House* (New York: Norman L. Munro, 1887), Chapter 11.

5. *The Hand-Book of the Toilette*, 2nd edn (London: Bradbury and Evans, 1841), p.72.
6. Richard Rowe, *Life in the London Streets* (1881).
7. *Ibid.*
8. Henry Mayhew, *London Labour and the London Poor, Volume One* (London: 1851), p.9.
9. Donald Shaw, *London in the Sixties* (1908).
10. *Ibid.*

Building Conditions

1. Isabella Bird, *Old Edinburgh*, p.8.
2. *Ibid.*
3. *Ibid.*
4. Henry Mayhew, 'Letter VI', in H. Mayhew, *The Unknown Mayhew: Selections from the Morning Chronicle, 1849–1850*, ed. E.P. Thompson and E. Yeo (London: Merlin Press, 1971), Note 9, p.103.
5. E. Cuming, '"Home is home be it never so homely": Reading Mid-Victorian Slum Interiors', *Journal of Victorian Culture*, Vol. 18 (3) (2013), p.377.
6. Isabella Bird, *Old Edinburgh*, p.8, and, Richard Rowe, *Life in the London Streets*.
7. Isabella Bird, *Old Edinburgh*, p.10.
8. *Ibid.*, p.10.
9. *Ibid.*, p.10.
10. *Ibid.*, p.12.
11. Alfred R. Bennett, *Victorian London* (1924).
12. Richard Rowe, *Life in the London Streets*.
13. *Ibid.*
14. Henry Mayhew, *London Labour and the London Poor, Volume One*, p.6.
15. Max Schlesinger, *Saunterings in and about London* (1853).
16. UK Parliament, 'Reforming Society in the 19th Century' (2023). Available online.
17. *Ibid.*
18. K. Clark, *Civilisation* (London: The BBC, 1969), p.232.
19. London School of Economics, 'Charles Booth's London: Poverty maps and police notebooks' (2016). Available online.
20. M. Denham, 'Victorian philanthropists, philosophers and activists', *British Geriatrics Society* (27 May 2017). Available online.
21. *Ibid.*
22. *Ibid.*
23. K. Clark, *Civilisation*, p.329.
24. Thomas Wright, 'The Army of London Poor, by the River-Side Visitor' (1882).
25. RA VIC/MAIN/QVJ (W) Friday 30 November 1866. (Princess Beatrice's copies), *Queen Victoria's Journals* (2013). Available online.

26. Isabella Beeton, *Mrs Beeton's Book of Household Management* (London: S.O. Beeton, 1861), p.6.
27. Isabella Bird, *Old Edinburgh*, p.7.
28. Henry Mayhew, *London Labour and the London Poor, Volume One*, p.iii.
29. *The Evening Standard*, 1 September 1888.
30. Dr Guthrie, in Isabella Bird, *Old Edinburgh*, p.14.
31. K. Clark, *Civilisation*, p.326.
32. Isabella Bird, *Old Edinburgh*, p.23.
33. William Blake, in, K. Clark, *Civilisation*, p.323.
34. Isabella Bird, *Old Edinburgh*, p.28.
35. Nellie Bly, *Ten Days in a Mad-House* (New York: Norman L. Munro, 1887), Chapter Three.

Chapter 2: City Dwellers and Street Urchins: Living in the Slums

1. Richard Rowe, *Life in the London Streets*.
2. *Ibid.*
3. E. Cuming, '"Home is home be it never so homely": Reading Mid-Victorian Slum Interiors', *Journal of Victorian Culture*, p.375.
4. Isabella Bird, *Old Edinburgh*, p.22.
5. Isabella Bird, *Old Edinburgh*, p. 8, and The *Cornhill Magazine* (1901).
6. Isabella Bird, *Old Edinburgh*, p.11.
7. S.P. Ryder, *et al.*, 'Annie Chapman', *Casebook: Jack the Ripper* (2023). Available online.
8. S.P. Ryder, *et al.*, 'Mary Ann Nichols', *Casebook: Jack the Ripper*.
9. Nellie Bly, *Ten Days in a Mad-House*, Chapter Three.
10. Karl Marx, in E. Cuming, 'Reading Mid-Victorian Slum Interiors' (2013), p.371.
11. Isabella Bird, *Old Edinburgh*, p.11.
12. *Ibid.*, p.18.
13. *Ibid.*, p.18.
14. Nellie Bly, *Ten Days in a Mad-House*, Chapter Three.
15. Henry Mayhew, *London Labour and the London Poor, Volume One*.
16. B. Watts, 'Children in the Home: Infant Wellbeing and Parent-Child Relationships in Late Medieval England, 1250–1500' (unpublished Masters Thesis: University of Wales Trinity Saint David, 2022).
17. Isabella Bird, *Old Edinburgh*, p.24.
18. Henry Mayhew, *Letter XXXI* (1851).
19. *The Times*, 23 December 1864.
20. Arthur Sherwell, *Life in West London* (1897).
21. Henry Mayhew, *Letter XXXI* (1851).
22. Henry Mayhew, *London Labour and the London Poor, Volume One*, p.20.
23. 'Walter', *My Secret Life* (1900).

Homosexuality

1. B. Watts, *Inside the Tudor Home: Daily Life in the Sixteenth Century* (Yorkshire: Pen & Sword History, 2023).
2. *The Times*, 16 February 1863.
3. *Ibid.*
4. C. Hodgman and M. Cook, 'Gay rights in 19th-Century Britain', *BBC History Magazine*, September Issue (2018), p.84.
5. *The Penny Illustrated Paper*, 5 April 1862.
6. Arthur Munby, *Diary*, 20 February 1827.
7. *The Times*, 27 July 1854.
8. *Ibid.*
9. *The Times*, 11 April 1855.
10. *Ibid.*
11. C. Hodgman and M. Cook, 'Gay rights in 19th-Century Britain', p.84.
12. *Ibid.*, p.84.
13. *Ibid.*, p.84.
14. Lola Montez, *The Arts of Beauty: Secrets of a Lady's Toilet* (New York: Dick & Fitzgerald, 1858), Introduction.

Clothing and Fashion

1. *The Hand-Book of the Toilette*, 2nd edn, p.8.
2. Richard Rowe, *Life in the London Streets*.
3. *Ibid.*
4. George Augustus Sala, *London Up to Date* (1895).
5. S.P. Ryder, *et al.*, 'Mary Ann Nichols', *Casebook: Jack the Ripper*.
6. Baroness Staffe, *The Lady's Dressing Room* (1893).
7. Lola Montez, *The Arts of Beauty*, p.51.
8. Mary Eliza Haweis, *The Art of Beauty* (1878).
9. Lola Montez, *The Arts of Beauty*, p.51.
10. *The Hand-Book of the Toilette*, 2nd edn, pp.4–5.
11. Isabella Bird, *Old Edinburgh*, p.20.
12. *The Hand-Book of the Toilette*, 2nd edn, pp.9–10.
13. Lola Montez, *The Arts of Beauty*, p.65.
14. B. Watts, *Inside the Tudor Home: Daily Life in the Sixteenth Century*.
15. S.P. Ryder, *et al.*, 'Mary Ann Nichols', *Casebook: Jack the Ripper*.
16. Isabella Beeton, *Mrs Beeton's Book of Household Management*, p.5.
17. S.P. Ryder, *et al.*, 'Elizabeth Stride', *Casebook: Jack the Ripper*.
18. S.P. Ryder, *et al.*, 'Catherine Eddowes', *Casebook: Jack the Ripper*.
19. S.P. Ryder, *et al.*, 'Mary Jane Kelly', *Casebook: Jack the Ripper*.
20. M. Marsh, *Compacts and Cosmetics: Beauty from Victorian Times to the Present Day* (Yorkshire: Pen & Sword Books Ltd, 2009), p.45.
21. *The Hand-Book of the Toilette*, 2nd edn, p.51.

22. M. Marsh, *Compacts and Cosmetics*, p.29.
23. George Augustus Sala, *London Up to Date.*
24. Nellie Bly, *Ten Days in a Mad-House*, Chapters Three and Four.

Chapter 3: Bone Grubbers, Mudlarks and Matchstick Girls: At Work in the Slums

1. The *Cornhill Magazine* (1901).
2. *Toilers in London* (1889) and Montague Williams, *Down East and Up West* (1894).
3. Henry Mayhew, *Letter VI* (1849), in Yeo and Thompson, Note 9, p.125.
4. *Toilers in London.*
5. Charles Dickens Jr, *Dickens's Dictionary of London* (1879).
6. Isabella Beeton, *Mrs Beeton's Book of Household Management.*
7. *Ibid.*, p.8.
8. *Ibid.*, p.986.
9. *Ibid.*, p.41.
10. Nellie Bly, *Ten Days in a Mad-House*, Chapter Three.
11. Isabella Beeton, *Mrs Beeton's Book of Household Management*, p.962.
12. *Ibid.*, pp.961–62.
13. *Ibid.*, pp. 961, 977.
14. *Ibid.*, p.7.
15. *Ibid.*, pp.962–64.
16. *Ibid.*, p.964.
17. William Acton, *Prostitution considered in its Moral, Social, and Sanitary Aspects* (1870).
18. S.P. Ryder, *et al.*, 'Mary Jane Kelly', *Casebook: Jack the Ripper.*
19. Henry Mayhew, *Letter XXXI* (1850).
20. *Ibid.*
21. William Acton, *Prostitution* (1870).
22. *Ibid.*
23. *Ibid.*
24. S.P. Ryder, *et al.*, 'Mary Ann Nichols', *Casebook: Jack the Ripper.*
25. H. Rubenhold, *The Five: The Untold Lives of the Women Killed by Jack the Ripper* (London: Penguin, 2019), p.43.
26. Henry Mayhew, *London Labour and the London Poor, Volume One*, p.20.
27. E. Griffin., 'Child Labour', *British Library* (2014). Available online.
28. Nathan Gould, *Information concerning the state of children employed in cotton factories* (Manchester, 1818).
29. UK Parliament, 'Reforming Society in the 19th Century' (2023). Available online.
30. Henry Mayhew, *London Labour and the London Poor*, p.6.
31. B. Watts, *Inside the Tudor Home: Daily Life in the Sixteenth Century.*

32. UK Parliament, 'Reforming Society'.
33. *Ibid.*

The Workhouse

1. Max Schlesinger, *Saunterings in and about London.*
2. K. Clark, *Civilisation*, p.326.
3. S.P. Ryder, *et al.*, 'Annie Chapman', *Casebook: Jack the Ripper.*
4. UK Parliament, 'Reforming Society in the 19th Century'.
5. E. Griffin., 'Child Labour', *British Library.*
6. L. Goldfinch, 'Fathering Christmas', *History Revealed Magazine*, Issue 37 (2016), p.39.
7. *Ibid.*, p.39.
8. Nathan Gould, *Information concerning the state of children employed in cotton factories* (Manchester, 1818).
9. I. Lee, 'Ragged Schools'.
10. M. Denham, 'Victorian philanthropists, philosophers and activists'.
11. *Ibid.*
12. P. Higginbotham, *The Workhouse* (2023). Available online.
13. M. Denham, 'Victorian philanthropists, philosophers and activists'.
14. *Ibid.*
15. Thomas Wright, *The Great Army of London Poor, by the River-side Visitor* (1882).
16. Richard Rowe, *Life in the London Streets.*
17. Henry Mayhew, *London Labour and the London Poor, Volume One*, p.6.
18. E. Griffin, 'Child Labour'.
19. Henry Mayhew, *London Labour and the London Poor, Volume One*, p.3.
20. *Ibid.*, p.3.
21. I. Lee, 'Ragged Schools'.
22. Henry Mayhew, *London Labour and the London Poor, Volume One*, p.3.
23. *Ibid.*, p.3.
24. *Ibid.*, p.5.
25. *Ibid.*, p.5.
26. *Ibid.*, p.6.
27. The *Cornhill Magazine* (1901).
28. Max Schlesinger, *Saunterings in and about London.*
29. Charles Dickens Jr, *Dickens's Dictionary of London.*
30. Alfred R. Bennett, *Victorian London.*
31. Henry Mayhew, *London Labour and the London Poor, Volume One*, p.27.
32. B. Watts, 'Children in the Home: Infant Wellbeing and Parent-Child Relationships in Late Medieval England, 1250–1500'.
33. Henry Mayhew, *London Labour and the London Poor, Volume One*, p.34.
34. B. Watts, 'Children in the Home: Infant Wellbeing and Parent-Child Relationships in Late Medieval England, 1250–1500'.

Chapter 4: Health, Hygiene and Medicine: Keeping Clean in the Slums

1. Isabella Bird, *Old Edinburgh*, p.3.
2. Mrs Panton, *Leaves from a Life* (1908).
3. Henry Mayhew, *Letter VI*, (1849), in Yeo and Thompson, Note 9, p.125.
4. Isabella Bird, *Old Edinburgh*, p.7.
5. *The Hand-Book of the Toilette*, 2nd edn, p.4.
6. Henry Mayhew, *London Labour and the London Poor, Volume One*, p.23.
7. Isabella Beeton, *Mrs Beeton's Book of Household Management*, p.975.
8. Francis Pears, *The skin, baths, bathing, and soap* (London: Pears, 1859), p.77.
9. *Ibid.*, p.69.
10. Isabella Beeton, *Mrs Beeton's Book of Household Management*, p.2.
11. M. Marsh, *Compacts and Cosmetics*, p.33.
12. *The Hand-Book of the Toilette*, 2nd edn, p.12.
13. *Ibid.*, p.12.
14. Francis Pears, *The skin...*, pp.65–66.
15. *Ibid.*, pp.65–66.
16. Isabella Beeton, *Mrs Beeton's Book of Household Management*, p.972.
17. *The Hand-Book of the Toilette*, 2nd edn, p.7.
18. *Ibid.*, p.10.
19. R. Goodman, *How to Be a Tudor: A Dawn-to-Dusk Guide to Tudor Life* (London: Penguin, 2016).
20. Isabella Beeton, *Mrs Beeton's Book of Household Management*, pp.965–66.
21. *The Hand-Book of the Toilette*, 2nd edn, p.12.
22. Lola Montez, *The Arts of Beauty*, p.32.
23. *Ibid.*, p.32.
24. *Ibid.*, p.33.
25. *Ibid.*, p.62.
26. *The Hand-Book of the Toilette*, 2nd edn, p.108.
27. *Ibid.*, p.110.
28. *Ibid.*, p.105.
29. Lola Montez, *The Arts of Beauty*, p.62.
30. *Ibid.*, p.61.
31. S.P. Ryder, *et al.*, 'Annie Chapman' and 'Catherine Eddowes', *Casebook: Jack the Ripper*.
32. Francis Pears, *The skin...*, p.95.
33. *Ibid.*, pp.81, 90.
34. *Ibid.*, p.82.
35. *Ibid.*, p.82.
36. *Ibid.*, p.95.
37. M. Marsh, *Compacts and Cosmetics*, p.40.
38. *Ibid.*, p.40.
39. *Ibid.*, p.34.

40. *Ibid.*, p.33.
41. *Ibid.*, p.34.
42. Francis Pears, *The skin....*, p.82.
43. *Ibid.*, p.94.
44. *Ibid.*, p.94.
45. *Ibid.*, p.98.
46. *Ibid.*, p.98.
47. L. Goldfinch, 'Fathering Christmas', *History Revealed Magazine*, p. 36.
48. B. Watts, *Inside the Tudor Home: Daily Life in the Sixteenth Century.*
49. *Ibid.*
50. Isabella Bird, *Old Edinburgh*, p.14.
51. S.P. Ryder, *et al.*, 'Annie Chapman', 'Catherine Eddowes' and 'Elizabeth Stride', *Casebook: Jack the Ripper.*
52. S.P. Ryder, *et al.*, 'Elizabeth Stride', *Casebook: Jack the Ripper.*
53. S.P. Ryder, *et al.*, 'The Suspects: Albert Victor', *Casebook: Jack the Ripper.*

Death and Disease

1. C.A. Almenara, A. Aimé, and C. Maïano, 'Vinegar and weight loss in women of eighteenth-century France: a lesson from the past', *History of Psychiatry*, Vol. 31 (2) (2019).
2. *The Hand-Book of the Toilette*, 2nd edn, p.141.
3. *Ibid.*, p.141.
4. Eugene Rimmel, *Book of Perfumes* (1867).
5. Francis Pears, *The skin ...*, p.103.
6. *Ibid.*, p.103.
7. M. Marsh, *Compacts and Cosmetics*, p.27.
8. Museum of the Mind, 'Explore Bethlem', *Bethlem Royal Hospital* (2023). Available online.
9. Isabella Bird, *Old Edinburgh*, p.6.
10. *Ibid.*, p.6.
11. *Ibid.*, p.10.
12. *Ibid.*, p.10.
13. *The Hand-Book of the Toilette*, 2nd edn, p.1.
14. *Ibid.*, p.1.
15. *Ibid.*, p.2.
16. *Ibid.*, p.2.
17. *Ibid.*, p.4.
18. Francis Pears, *The skin...*, pp.72–73.
19. *Ibid.*, p.77.
20. *Ibid.*, p.77.
21. Barnardo's, 'Our History' (2023). Available online.
22. P. McGuinness, '1854: Dr John Snow Cures London of Deadly Cholera', *History Revealed Magazine*, Issue 46 (2017), pp.20–21.

23. *Ibid.*, p.20.
24. *Ibid.*, p.20.
25. *Ibid.*, p.20.
26. *The Hand-Book of the Toilette*, 2nd edn, p.x.
27. *Ibid.*, p.3.
28. Barnardo's, 'Our History'.
29. M. Denham, 'Victorian philanthropists, philosophers and activists'.
30. Max Schlesinger, *Saunterings in and about London.*
31. Black, *Black's Guide to London and Its Environs* (1882).
32. L. Goldfinch, 'Fathering Christmas', *History Revealed Magazine*, p.37.
33. Henry Mayhew, *Letter III*, Friday, 26 October 1849.
34. Isabella Bird, *Old Edinburgh*, p.20.

Mental Illness

1. Museum of the Mind, 'Explore Bethlem', *Bethlem Royal Hospital* (2023). Available online.
2. *Ibid.*
3. *Ibid.*
4. Isabella Bird, *Old Edinburgh*, p. 24.
5. Museum of the Mind, 'Patients – Ada Jane Warren', *Bethlem Royal Hospital* (2023). Available online.
6. *Ibid.*
7. Museum of the Mind, 'Patients – Hannah Levy Bensusan', *Bethlem Royal Hospital* (2023). Available online.
8. *Ibid.*
9. Museum of the Mind, 'Patients – Thomas George Callaghan', *Bethlem Royal Hospital* (2023). Available online.
10. Museum of the Mind, 'Patients – Henry Leotine Gamlen', *Bethlem Royal Hospital* (2023). Available online.
11. Richard Rowe, *Life in the London Streets*.
12. Nellie Bly, *Ten Days in a Mad-House*, Chapter Six.
13. *Ibid.*, Chapters Eleven and Three.
14. Museum of the Mind, 'Explore Bethlem'.
15. *Ibid.*
16. *Ibid.*
17. *Ibid.*
18. *Ibid.*
19. *Ibid.*
20. *Ibid.*
21. *Ibid.*
22. *Ibid.*
23. *Ibid.*
24. *Ibid.*

25. *Ibid.*
26. *Ibid.*
27. L. Jackson, *Dirty Old London: The Victorian Fight Against Filth* (London: Yale University Press, 2014).
28. Museum of the Mind, 'Explore Bethlem'.
29. *Ibid.*
30. *Ibid.*
31. *Ibid.*
32. *Ibid.*
33. A. Brereton, 'Morphinomania in the 19th century', *National Trust for Scotland* (2020). Available online.
34. National Museum of American History, 'Stomach Pump: MG.M-07432 (c. 1861–1865)', *Smithsonian Institution* (2023). Available online.
35. Nellie Bly, *Ten Days in a Mad-House*.
36. Museum of the Mind, 'Explore Bethlem'.
37. *Ibid.*
38. M. Marsh, *Compacts and Cosmetics*, p. 24.
39. Henry Mayhew, *London Labour and the London Poor, Volume One*, p. 7.
40. S.P. Ryder, *et al.*, 'Annie Chapman', *Casebook: Jack the Ripper*.
41. A. Brereton, 'Morphinomania in the 19th century'.
42. See Image 11.
43. J.R. Nash, *Look For the Woman: A Narrative Encyclopaedia of Female Poisoners, Kidnappers, Thieves, Extortionists, Terrorists, Swindlers and Spies from Elizabethan Times to the Present* (London: Evans, 1981).
44. A. Brereton, 'Morphinomania in the 19th century'.
45. *Ibid.*
46. *Ibid.*
47. Mayo Clinic, 'Opium' (2023). Available online.
48. A. Brereton, 'Morphinomania in the 19th century'.

Beauty

1. Lola Montez, *The Arts of Beauty*, p.25.
2. *Ibid.*, pp.20–22.
3. *Ibid.*, pp.20–22.
4. *Ibid.*, pp.20–22.
5. *Ibid.*, pp.20–22.
6. *The Hand-Book of the Toilette*, 2nd edn, p.92.
7. Lola Montez, *The Arts of Beauty*, p.62.
8. Isabella Beeton, *Mrs Beeton's Book of Household Management*, p.2, and Lola Montez, *The Arts of Beauty*, p.35.
9. Lola Montez, *The Arts of Beauty*, p.25.
10. *Ibid.*, p.52.
11. D. Sessions, 'Victorian Makeup Guide and Beauty Products: History', *Vintagedancer* (2023). Available online.

12. *Ibid.*
13. *The Daily News*, 5 April 1851.
14. M. Marsh, *Compacts and Cosmetics*, p. 25.
15. *Ibid.*, p.27.
16. Lola Montez, *The Arts of Beauty*, p.98.
17. *Ibid.*, p.98.
18. Francis Pears, *The skin ...*, p.23.
19. *Ibid.*, p.31.
20. *Ibid.*, p.31.
21. *Ibid.*, p.32.
22. Lola Montez, *The Arts of Beauty*, p.96.
23. Francis Pears, *The skin ...*, p.32.
24. C.A. Almenara, A. Aimé and C. Maïano, 'Vinegar and weight loss in women of eighteenth-century France'.
25. Francis Pears, *The skin ...*, p. 38.
26. *The Hand-Book of the Toilette*, 2nd edn, p.77.
27. *Ibid.*, p.77.
28. Lola Montez, *The Arts of Beauty*, p.35.
29. *Ibid.*, p.35.
30. *The Hand-Book of the Toilette*, 2nd edn, pp.76–77.
31. *Ibid.*, pp.76–77.
32. Isabella Beeton, *Mrs Beeton's Book of Household Management*, p.977.
33. *The Hand-Book of the Toilette*, 2nd edn, p.87.
34. M. Marsh, *Compacts and Cosmetics*, p.34.
35. C.Arnold, *Edward VII: The Prince of Wales and the Women He Loved* (London: St Martin's Press, 2017).
36. S.P. Ryder, *et al.*, 'Catherine Eddowes', *Casebook: Jack the Ripper*.
37. Mrs C.S. Peel, *Early Victorian England, 1830–1865*, ed. G.M. Young (Oxford University Press, 1934).
38. *Ibid.*
39. C. Arnold, *Edward VII*.
40. *The Hand-Book of the Toilette*, 2nd edn, p.99.
41. *Ibid.*, p.99.
42. *Ibid.*, p.98.
43. *Ibid.*, p.55.
44. *Ibid.*, p.55.
45. *Mothers and Daughters* (*c.* 1840s).
46. *The Hand-Book of the Toilette*, 2nd edn, p.72.
47. *The Hand-Book of the Toilette*, 2nd edn, p.58, and Lola Montez, *The Arts of Beauty*, p.59.
48. Baroness Staffe, *The Lady's Dressing Room*.
49. Francis Pears, *The skin ...*, p.103.
50. M. Marsh, *Compacts and Cosmetics*, p.34.
51. Lola Montez, *The Arts of Beauty*, p.59.
52. *The Hand-Book of the Toilette*, 2nd edn, p.73.

53. *Ibid.*, p.73.
54. *The Hand-Book of the Toilette*, 2nd edn, pp.70, 65.
55. J.J. Atwood, *Advertisement* (*c*. 1800s).

Cosmetics

1. Lola Montez, *The Arts of Beauty*, p.41.
2. *Ibid.*, p.42.
3. M. Marsh, *Compacts and Cosmetics*, p.9.
4. *The Hand-Book of the Toilette*, 2nd edn, p.85.
5. *Ibid.*, pp.48–49.
6. Lola Montez, *The Arts of Beauty*, p.55.
7. *The Hand-Book of the Toilette*, 2nd edn, p.91.
8. *Ibid.*, p.164.
9. Lola Montez, *The Arts of Beauty*, p.49.
10. M. Marsh, *Compacts and Cosmetics*, p.37.
11. Lola Montez, *The Arts of Beauty*, p.48.
12. *The Hand-Book of the Toilette*, 2nd edn, p.91.
13. *Ibid.*, p.91.
14. *Ibid.*, p.165.

Hair

1. *The Hand-Book of the Toilette*, 2nd edn, p.26.
2. *Ibid.*, p.35.
3. Isabella Beeton, *Mrs Beeton's Book of Household Management*, p.981.
4. Lola Montez, *The Arts of Beauty*, p.82.
5. *Ibid.*, p.89.
6. *The Hand-Book of the Toilette*, 2nd edn, p.27.
7. *Ibid.*, p.28.
8. *Ibid.*, p.23.
9. *Ibid.*, p.23.
10. *Ibid.*, p.25.
11. *Ibid.*, pp.25, 37.
12. Baroness Staffe, *The Lady's Dressing Room.*
13. Isabella Beeton, *Mrs Beetons Book of Household Management*, p.982.
14. *The Hand-Book of the Toilette*, 2nd edn, p.39.
15. *Ibid.*, p.41.
16. Alfred R. Bennett, *Victorian London.*
17. M. Marsh, *Compacts and Cosmetics*, p.30.
18. Isabella Beeton, *Mrs Beeton's Book of Household Management*, p.978, and *The Hand-Book of the Toilette*, 2nd edn, p.31.
19. *The Hand-Book of the Toilette*, 2nd edn, p.29.
20. *Ibid.*, p.29.
21. Isabella Beeton, *Mrs Beeton's Book of Household Management*, p.978.

22. *The Hand-Book of the Toilette*, 2nd edn, p.100.
23. Lola Montez, *The Arts of Beauty*, p.91.
24. *Ibid.*, p.91.
25. *The Hand-Book of the Toilette*, 2nd edn, p.86.
26. *Ibid.*, p.83.
27. *Ibid.*, p.162.

Cleaning the Home

1. Isabella Beeton, *Mrs Beeton's Book of Household Management.*
2. *Ibid.*
3. *Ibid.*
4. *Ibid.*, p.986.
5. *Ibid.*, p.972.
6. *Ibid.*, p.994.
7. *Ibid.*, p.994.
8. *Ibid.*, p.983.
9. *Ibid.*, p.994.
10. *Ibid.*, p.986.
11. *Ibid.*, p.986.
12. *Ibid.*, p.994.
13. Baroness Staffe, *The Lady's Dressing Room.*
14. *Ibid.*
15. Isabella Beeton, *Mrs Beeton's Book of Household Management*, p.986.
16. *Ibid.*, p.972.
17. *Ibid.*, p.984.
18. *Ibid.*, p.984.
19. *Ibid.*, p.985.
20. *Ibid.*, p.983.
21. *Ibid.*, p.986.
22. Charles Dickens Jr., *Dickens's Dictionary of London.*
23. Max Schlesinger, *Saunterings in and about London.*
24. *Ibid.*

Chapter 5: 'Please Sir, I Want Some More': Food and Diet in the Slums

1. Isabella Beeton, *Mrs Beeton's Book of Household Management*, p.905.
2. Alexis Soyer, *A Shilling Cookery for the People* (1854).
3. S.P. Ryder, *et al.*, 'Elizabeth Stride', *Casebook: Jack the Ripper.*
4. Isabella Beeton, *Mrs Beeton's Book of Household Management*, p.31.
5. Mrs C.S. Peel, *Early Victorian England, 1830–1865.*
6. Isabella Bird, *Old Edinburgh*, p.8.
7. Richard Rowe, *Life in the London Streets.*

8. B. Watts, 'Children in the Home: Infant Wellbeing and Parent-Child Relationships in Late Medieval England, 1250–1500'.
9. Isabella Beeton, *Mrs Beeton's Book of Household Management*, p.43.
10. *Ibid.*, p.974.
11. *Ibid.*, p.974
12. *Ibid.*, p.974.
13. *Ibid.*, p.974
14. Francis Pears, *The skin ....*
15. Isabella Beeton, *Mrs Beeton's Book of Household Management*, p.965.
16. *Ibid.*, p.965.

Meals

1. Mrs C.S. Peel, *Early Victorian England, 1830–1865.*
2. *Ibid.*, and D.W. Bartlett, *London by Day and Night* (1852).
3. Isabella Beeton, *Mrs Beeton's Book of Household Management*, p.95.
4. *Ibid.*, p.95.
5. Alexis Soyer, *A Shilling Cookery for the People.*
6. Isabella Beeton, *Mrs Beeton's Book of Household Management*, p.95.
7. *Ibid.*, p.95.
8. *Ibid.*, pp.95, 565.
9. *Ibid.*, p.250.
10. *Ibid.*, p.215.
11. *Ibid.*, p.226.
12. *Ibid.*, p.37.
13. Richard Rowe, *Life in the London Streets.*
14. Isabella Beeton, *Mrs Beeton's Book of Household Management*, p.38.
15. *Ibid.*, p.38.
16. *Ibid.*, p.38.
17. *Ibid.*, p.37.
18. *Ibid.*, p.37.
19. Alexis Soyer, *A Shilling Cookery for the People.*
20. *Ibid.*
21. *Ibid.*
22. Alexis Soyer, *A Shilling Cookery for the People*, and Isabella Beeton, *Mrs Beeton's Book of Household Management*, p.341.
23. Isabella Beeton, *Mrs Beeton's Book of Household Management*, p.341.
24. *Ibid.*, p.316.
25. *Ibid.*, p.351.
26. *Ibid.*, p.127.
27. Alexis Soyer, *A Shilling Cookery for the People.*
28. Isabella Beeton, *Mrs Beeton's Book of Household Management*, p.127, and Alexis Soyer, *A Shilling Cookery for the People.*
29. Alexis Soyer, *A Shilling Cookery for the People.*
30. Isabella Beeton, *Mrs Beeton's Book of Household Management*, pp.587, 584, and Alexis Soyer, *A Shilling Cookery for the People.*

31. Isabella Beeton, *Mrs Beeton's Book of Household Management*, pp.558, 575, 570.
32. Alexis Soyer, *A Shilling Cookery for the People*.
33. Isabella Beeton, *Mrs Beeton's Book of Household Management*, p.83.
34. *Ibid.*, p.83.
35. *Ibid.*, p.61.
36. Alexis Soyer, *A Shilling Cookery for the People*.
37. *Ibid.*
38. *Ibid.*
39. Charles Dickens, *Oliver Twist* (London: 1837; Penguin Red Classic, 2007 edn).
40. Alexis Soyer, *A Shilling Cookery for the People*.
41. Isabella Beeton, *Mrs Beeton's Book of Household Management*, pp.426, 445.
42. *Ibid.*, pp.458, 71.
43. Alexis Soyer, *A Shilling Cookery for the People*.
44. Isabella Beeton, *Mrs Beeton's Book of Household Management*, p.852.
45. Mrs C.S. Peel, *Early Victorian England, 1830*–1865.
46. Isabella Beeton, *Mrs Beeton's Book of Household Management*.
47. Alexis Soyer, *A Shilling Cookery for the People*.
48. *Ibid.*
49. Douglas Jerrold, in Isabella Beeton, *Mrs Beeton's Book of Household Management*, p.907.
50. *The Dover Telegraph and Cinque Ports General Advertiser*, 'The Poisonings by Arsenic at Bradford', Saturday, 13 November 1858.
51. Isabella Beeton, *Mrs Beeton's Book of Household Management*, p.893.
52. *Ibid.*
53. *Ibid.*, p.894.
54. B. Watts, 'Children in the Home: Infant Wellbeing and Parent-Child Relationships in Late Medieval England, 1250–1500'.
55. Isabella Beeton, *Mrs Beeton's Book of Household Management*, p.887.
56. *Ibid.*, p.894.
57. *Ibid.*, pp.904, 903.
58. Nellie Bly, *Ten Days in a Mad-House*, Chapter 10.
59. *Ibid.*, Chapter 10.
60. *Ibid.*, Chapter 10, Chapter 11.
61. S.P. Ryder, *et al.*, 'Mary Jane Kelly', *Casebook: Jack the Ripper*.
62. E. Brand, 'Did the original Coca-Cola drink really contain cocaine?', *History Revealed Magazine*, Issue 46 (2017), p.78.
63. S.P. Ryder, *et al.*, 'Annie Chapman', *Casebook: Jack the Ripper*.
64. Isabella Beeton, *Mrs Beeton's Book of Household Management*, p.974.
65. *Ibid.*

Beverages

1. Auguste Renouard, *The Undertakers' Manual* (New York: A.H. Nirdlinger & Co., 1878), p.137.
2. Isabella Bird, *Old Edinburgh*, p.5.

3. *Ibid.*, p.4.
4. *Ibid.*, p.4.
5. Auguste Renouard, *The Undertakers' Manual*, p.137.
6. E. Brand, 'Did the original Coca-Cola drink really contain cocaine?', p.78.
7. *Ibid.*
8. *Ibid.*
9. *Ibid.*
10. *Ibid.*
11. *Ibid.*
12. Cassell, *Cassell's Household Guide: Being a Complete Encyclopaedia of Domestic and Social Economy and Forming a Guide to Every Department of Practical Life* (London: Cassell, Petter and Galpin, 1869).
13. *Ibid.*
14. *Ibid.*
15. The *Cornhill Magazine* (1901).
16. Isabella Beeton, *Mrs Beeton's Book of Household Management*, p.879.
17. Cassell, *Cassell's Household Guide.*
18. *Ibid.*
19. *Ibid.*
20. *Ibid.*
21. Mrs C.S. Peel, *Early Victorian England, 1830–1865.*
22. Cassell, *Cassell's Household Guide.*
23. *Ibid.*
24. S.P. Ryder, *et al.*, 'Catherine Eddowes', *Casebook: Jack the Ripper*.
25. *The Leisure Hour* (1852).
26. M. White, 'Juvenile crime in the 19th century', *British Library* (2014). Available online.
27. 'Walter', *My Secret Life* (1900).
28. Isabella Bird, *Old Edinburgh*, p.6.
29. *Ibid.*, p.6.

Diet

1. Lola Montez, *The Arts of Beauty*, p. 26.
2. *Ibid.*, pp.29–30.
3. C.A. Almenara, A. Aimé and C. Maïano, 'Vinegar and weight loss in women of eighteenth-century France'.
4. Pierre Virard, *Essai sur la santé des filles nubiles* (1779), p.5.
5. Peter Cunningham, *Handbook of London* (1850), p.42.
6. Francis Pears, *The skin …*, p.35.
7. J. Gregory, 'Veggie Victorians', *BBC History Magazine*, September Issue (2018), p.43.
8. *Ibid.*, p.44.
9. *Ibid.*, p.44.
10. *Ibid.*, p.45.

11. Auguste Renouard, *The Undertakers' Manual*, p.136.
12. J. Gregory, 'Veggie Victorians', p.44.
13. *Ibid.*, p.44.
14. *Ibid.*, p.44.
15. Isabella Beeton, *Mrs Beeton's Book of Household Management.*
16. J. Gregory, 'Veggie Victorians', p.44.
17. *Ibid.*, p.44.

Purchasing Food

1. Arthur Sherwell, *Life in West London* (1897).
2. The *Cornhill Magazine* (1901).
3. *Ibid.*
4. *Ibid.*
5. *Ibid.*
6. *Ibid.*
7. Arthur Sherwell, *Life in West London.*
8. Gauldie, *Cruel Habitations*, p.153, in E. Cuming, '"Home is home be it never so homely": Reading Mid-Victorian Slum Interiors', *Journal of Victorian Culture*, Vol. 18 (3) (2013), p.375.
9. Richard Rowe, *Life in the London Streets.*
10. Henry Mayhew, *London Labour and the London Poor, Volume One*, p.3.
11. *Ibid.*, p.3.
12. *Ibid.*, p.3.
13. *Ibid.*, p.5.
14. *Ibid.*, p.3.
15. The *Cornhill Magazine* (1901).
16. Henry Mayhew, *London Labour and the London Poor, Volume One*, p.6.
17. *Ibid.*, p.3.
18. *Ibid.*, p.3.
19. H. Mayhew, *The Adventures of Mr and Mrs Sandboys, and Family, who came up to London to 'enjoy themselves' and to see the Great Exhibition* (1851).
20. *The Leisure Hour* (1856).
21. Cruchley, *Cruchley's London in 1865: A Handbook for Strangers* (1865).
22. George Augustus Sala, *London Up to Date.*
23. *Ibid.*

Chapter 6: Fun and Games: Entertainment in the Slums

1. Bishop Hall, in Isabella Beeton, *Mrs Beeton's Book of Household Management*, p.9.
2. Henry Mayhew, *London Labour and the London Poor, Volume One*, p.11.
3. *Ibid.*, p.15.
4. *The Times*, Advertisement, 1870.

5. B. Watts, 'Children in the Home: Infant Wellbeing and Parent-Child Relationships in Late Medieval England, 1250–1500'.
6. *The Times*, Advertisement, 1870.
7. *Ibid.*
8. *Ibid.*
9. Henry Mayhew, *London Labour and the London Poor, Volume One*, p.15.
10. *Ibid.*, p.15.
11. B. Watts, 'Children in the Home: Infant Wellbeing and Parent-Child Relationships in Late Medieval England, 1250–1500'.
12. *Ibid.*
13. *Ibid.*
14. Henry Mayhew, *London Labour and the London Poor, Volume One*, p.15.
15. T. Tate, 'A Game of One's Own: Women's Football in Victorian Britain', *History Workshop* (2018).
16. *Ibid.*
17. *The Queen's London: a Pictorial and Descriptive Record of the Streets, Buildings, Parks, and Scenery of the Great Metropolis* (1896).
18. 'Walter', *My Secret Life* (1900).
19. B. Watts, *Inside the Tudor Home: Daily Life in the Sixteenth Century*.
20. The National Archives, 'Currency Converter: 1270–2017' (2023). Available online.

Excursions

1. H. Rubenhold, *The Five: The Untold Lives of the Women Killed by Jack the Ripper*.
2. Isabella Bird, *Old Edinburgh*, p. 26.
3. *Ibid.*, p.26.
4. Charles Dickens Jr, *Dickens's Dictionary of London*.
5. *Ibid.*
6. Peter Cunningham, *Handbook of London*, and Friedrich von Raumer, *England in 1835* (1835).
7. *The Queen's London* (1896).
8. Cruchley, *Cruchley's London in 1865: A Handbook of Strangers*.
9. Charles Dickens Jr, *Dickens's Dictionary of London*.
10. *Ibid.*
11. *Punch Magazine* (1850).
12. Uncle Jonathan, *Walks In and Around London*, 3rd edn (1895).
13. Cruchley, *Cruchley's London in 1865: A Handbook of Strangers*.
14. *Ibid.*
15. Charles Ricketts, *Self Portrait* (1866).
16. Black, *Black's Guide to London and Its Environs*, 8th edn (1882).
17. *Ibid.*
18. Grant Richards, *Memories of a Misspent Youth* (1932).
19. *Ibid.*

20. *Ibid.*
21. George Augustus Sala, *London Up to Date.*
22. *Punch Magazine* (1851).
23. H. Mayhew, *The Adventures of Mr and Mrs Sandboys, and Family.*
24. *Ibid.*
25. *The Queen's London* (1896).
26. *Ibid.*
27. Henry Mayhew, *London Labour and the London Poor, Volume One*, p.18.
28. *Ibid.*, p.15.
29. C. Timms, *Newington Causeway Advertisement* (1857).

Special Occasions

1. N. Orme, *Medieval Children* (Yale: Yale University Press, 2003), and B. Watts, 'Children in the Home: Infant Wellbeing and Parent-Child Relationships in Late Medieval England, 1250–1500'.
2. B. Watts, 'Children in the Home: Infant Wellbeing and Parent-Child Relationships in Late Medieval England, 1250–1500'.
3. *Ibid.*
4. *Ibid.*
5. Isabella Beeton, *Mrs Beeton's Book of Household Management*, p.907.
6. *Ibid.*, p.752.
7. *Ibid.*, p.854, and B. Watts, 'Children in the Home: Infant Wellbeing and Parent-Child Relationships in Late Medieval England, 1250–1500'.
8. L. Goldfinch, 'Fathering Christmas', *History Revealed Magazine*, p.37.
9. B. Watts, 'Children in the Home: Infant Wellbeing and Parent-Child Relationships in Late Medieval England, 1250–1500'.
10. *The Los Angeles Herald*,1 April 1906.
11. *The San Francisco Call*, Vol. 95 (118), 27 March 1904.
12. Henry Mayhew, *London Labour and the London Poor, Volume One*, p.20.
13. *Ibid.*, p.20.
14. D.W. Bartlett, *London By Day and Night.*
15. L. Goldfinch, 'Fathering Christmas', *History Revealed Magazine*, p.40.
16. *Ibid.*, p.41.
17. *Ibid.*, p.41.
18. Alexis Soyer, *A Shilling Cookery for the People.*
19. *Ibid.*
20. D.W. Bartlett, *London By Day and Night.*
21. L. Goldfinch, 'Fathering Christmas', *History Revealed Magazine*, p.41.
22. Isabella Beeton, *Mrs Beeton's Book of Household Management*, p.891.
23. D.W. Bartlett, *London By Day and Night.*
24. *Ibid.*
25. Henry Mayhew, *London Labour and the London Poor, Volume One*, p.25.
26. *Ibid.*, p.25.
27. *Ibid.*, p.22.

28. Cassell, *Cassell's Household Guide.*
29. *Ibid.*
30. Mrs C.S. Peel, *Early Victorian England, 1830–1865.*

Chapter 7: Growing Up in Victorian Britain: The Children of the Slums

1. M. Denham, 'Victorian philanthropists, philosophers and activists'.
2. Henry Mayhew, *London Labour and the London Poor, Volume One*, p.20.
3. *The Times*, 6 and 7 July 1853.
4. V. Walsh, 'The History of Condoms', *Condoms.uk* (2022). Available online.
5. Augustus K. Gardner, *The Conjugal Relationships as regards Personal Health and Hereditary Wellbeing* (1894).
6. *Ibid.*
7. *Ibid.*
8. *Ibid.*
9. *The Times*, 6 and 7 July 1853.
10. *Ibid.*
11. *Ibid.*
12. Augustus K. Gardner, *The Conjugal Relationships*.
13. Charles Dickens, *Oliver Twist.*
14. Isabella Bird, *Old Edinburgh*, p.13.
15. Author's notes taken from an exhibit at The Foundling Museum, Bloomsbury (2023).
16. Barnardo's, 'Our History'.
17. *Ibid.*
18. P. McGuinness, '1854: Dr John Snow Cures London of Deadly Cholera', p. 20.
19. Isabella Bird, *Old Edinburgh*, p.22.
20. Henry Mayhew, *London Labour and the London Poor, Volume One*, p.10.
21. B. Watts, 'Children in the Home: Infant Wellbeing and Parent-Child Relationships in Late Medieval England, 1250–1500'.

Infancy and Childhood

1. Richard Rowe, *Life in the London Streets.*
2. Isabella Bird, *Old Edinburgh*, p.20.
3. *Ibid.*, p.19.
4. *Ibid.*, p.13.
5. *Ibid.*, p.12.
6. See sources such as Henry Mayhew's *London Labour and London Poor*, George Augustus Sala's *London Up to Date* (1895) and Alfred R. Bennett's *Victorian London* (1924).
7. Isabella Bird, *Old Edinburgh*, p.4.

8. *Ibid.*, p.4.
9. *Ibid.*, p.9.
10. B. Watts, 'Children in the Home: Infant Wellbeing and Parent-Child Relationships in Late Medieval England, 1250–1500'.
11. *Ibid.*
12. Henry Mayhew, *London Labour and the London Poor, Volume One*, p.20.
13. *Ibid.*, p.39.
14. *Ibid.*, p.38.
15. *Ibid.*, p.37.
16. *Ibid.*, p.36.
17. *Ibid.*, p.37.
18. Henry Mayhew, *Letter XXXI* (1851).
19. I. Lee, 'Ragged Schools'.
20. L. Goldfinch, 'Fathering Christmas', *History Revealed Magazine*, p.36.
21. Isabella Bird, *Old Edinburgh*, p.10.
22. *Ibid.*, p.13.
23. Henry Mayhew, *London Labour and the London Poor, Volume One*, p.36.
24. London School of Economics, *Charles Booth's London: Poverty maps and police notebooks* (2016). Available online.
25. I. Lee, 'Ragged Schools'.
26. Charles Dickens, *The Daily News* (1846).
27. *Ibid.*
28. I. Lee, 'Ragged Schools'.
29. RA VIC/MAIN/QVJ (W) Wednesday 22nd June 1887. (Princess Beatrice's copies). *Queen Victoria's Journals* (2013), pp.280–81. Available online.
30. Henry Mayhew, *London Labour and the London Poor, Volume One*, p.20.

Chapter 8: Crime, Punishment and the Victorian Justice System

1. Henry Mayhew, *London Labour and the London Poor, Volume One*, p.3.
2. A. Davies and J. Rowbotham, 'How mean are the streets of modern Britain?', *BBC History Magazine*, September Issue (2018), p.16.
3. *Ibid.*, p.16.
4. Ibid., p.16.
5. Henry Mayhew, *London Labour and the London Poor, Volume One*, p.23.
6. *Ibid.*
7. M. White, 'Juvenile crime in the 19th century'.
8. *Ibid.*
9. Alfred R. Bennett, *Victorian London.*
10. *Ibid.*
11. A. Davies and J. Rowbotham, 'How mean are the streets of modern Britain?', p. 17.
12. *Ibid.*, p.17.

13. National Museum of American History, 'Stomach Pump: MG.M-07432 (c. 1861–1865)', *Smithsonian Institution* (2023). Available online.
14. Arthur Sherwell, *Life in West London* (1897).
15. K. Clark, *Civilisation*, p.330.
16. Henry Mayhew, *Letter XXXI* (1851).
17. *Ibid.*
18. M. White, 'Juvenile crime'.
19. *Ibid.*
20. *Ibid.*
21. S.P. Ryder, *et al.*, 'Fingers Freddy', *Casebook: Jack the Ripper* (2023). Available online.
22. M. White, 'Juvenile crime'.
23. *Ibid.*
24. *Ibid.*
25. *Ibid.*

Cold-Blooded Killers

1. D. Wilson, *Mary Ann Cotton: Britain's First Female Serial Killer* (Hampshire: Waterside Press, 2013), and J.R. Nash, *Look For the Woman.*
2. D. Wilson, *Mary Ann Cotton* (2013).
3. *Ibid.*
4. J.R. Nash, *Look For the Woman.*
5. *The Examiner*, 13 June 1846.
6. G. Spicer, 'The Thames Torso Murders of 1887–1889', *Casebook: Jack the Ripper*. Available online.
7. *Ibid.*

Jack the Ripper

1. S.P. Ryder, *et al.*, 'Emma Elizabeth Smith', *Casebook: Jack the Ripper* (2023). Available online.
2. *Ibid.*
3. *Ibid.*
4. S.P. Ryder, *et al.*, 'Martha Tabram', *Casebook: Jack the Ripper* (2023). Available online.
5. R. Jones, 'Martha Tabram, Murdered August 7th 1888', *Jack the Ripper 1888* (2023). Available online.
6. *Ibid.*
7. *Ibid.*
8. Walter Dew, *I Caught Crippen: Memoirs of Ex-Chief Inspector Walter Dew, C.I.D. of Scotland Yard* (London: Blackie, 1938).
9. *The Daily News*, 'The East-End Murders', Tuesday, 9 September 1888.
10. *The Daily News*, 'The Whitehall Mystery: Inquest: Medical Evidence', Tuesday, 9 September 1888.

11. D. Arif, 'The Murder of Elizabeth Jackson', *Casebook: Jack the Ripper* (2008). Available online.
12. *Ibid.*
13. S.P. Ryder, *et al.*, 'Mary Pearcey', *Casebook: Jack the Ripper* (2023). Available online.
14. *Ibid.*
15. *Ibid.*
16. S.P. Ryder, *et al.*, 'Jill the Ripper', *Casebook: Jack the Ripper* (2023). Available online.
17. *The East London Observer*, 'Another Horrible Tragedy in Whitechapel: A Woman Murdered in Buck's Row', Saturday, 1 September 1888.
18. S.P. Ryder, *et al.*, 'Mary Ann Nichols', *Casebook: Jack the Ripper*.
19. *Ibid.*
20. *The East London Observer*, 'Another Horrible Tragedy in Whitechapel…',. Saturday, 1 September 1888.
21. *The Times*, London, 'Another Murder in Whitechapel', Saturday, 1 September 1888.
22. *Ibid.*
23. *Ibid.*
24. *The Evening Standard*, London, 'Murder in Whitechapel', Saturday, 1 September 1888.
25. *The East London Advertiser*, 'Another Whitechapel Mystery: Horrible Murder in Buck's Row, Whitechapel', Saturday, 1 September 1888.
26. *The East London Observer*, 'Another Horrible Tragedy in Whitechapel…', Saturday, 1 September 1888, and *The Evening Standard*, London, 'Murder in Whitechapel', Saturday, 1 September 1888.
27. S.P. Ryder, *et al.*, 'Mary Ann Nichols', *Casebook: Jack the Ripper*.
28. *Ibid.*
29. H. Rubenhold, *The Five: The Untold Lives of the Women Killed by Jack the Ripper*, p.43.
30. S.P. Ryder, *et al.*, 'Mary Ann Nichols', *Casebook: Jack the Ripper*.
31. *Ibid.*
32. *The Evening Standard*, London, 'Murder in Whitechapel', Saturday, 1 September 1888.
33. *The Daily Telegraph*, 'Inquest: Annie Chapman', Tuesday, 11 September 1888.
34. *Ibid.*
35. *Ibid.*
36. S.P. Ryder, *et al.*, 'Annie Chapman', *Casebook: Jack the Ripper*.
37. R. Jones, 'The Murder of Annie Chapman – 8th September 1888', *Jack the Ripper 1888* (2023). Available online.
38. *Ibid.*
39. *The Illustrated Police News*, 'The Terrible Tragedy of Annie Chapman's Life', September 1888.
40. R. Jones, 'The Murder of Annie Chapman', *Jack the Ripper 1888*.
41. *Ibid.*

42. S.P. Ryder, *et al.*, 'Annie Chapman', *Casebook: Jack the Ripper* (2023).
43. *Ibid.*
44. *The Daily Telegraph*, 'Inquest: Annie Chapman', Tuesday, 11 September 1888.
45. *Ibid.*
46. *Ibid.*
47. H. Rubenhold, *The Five: The Untold Lives of the Women Killed by Jack the Ripper*, p.122.
48. *Ibid.*, p.128.
49. S.P. Ryder, *et al.*, 'Annie Chapman', *Casebook: Jack the Ripper.*
50. *Ibid.*
51. *The Daily Telegraph*, 'Inquest…', Tuesday, 11 September 1888.
52. S.P. Ryder, *et al.*, 'Annie Chapman', *Casebook: Jack the Ripper.*
53. *The Daily Telegraph*, 'Inquest…', Tuesday, 11 September 1888.
54. *Ibid.*
55. H. Rubenhold, *The Five: The Untold Lives of the Women Killed by Jack the Ripper*, p.168.
56. *Ibid.*, p.173.
57. S.P. Ryder, *et al.*, 'Elizabeth Stride', *Casebook: Jack the Ripper* (2023).
58. H. Rubenhold, *The Five: The Untold Lives of the Women Killed by Jack the Ripper*, p.206.
59. S.P. Ryder, *et al.*, 'Elizabeth Stride', *Casebook: Jack the Ripper.*
60. *Ibid.*
61. *Ibid.*
62. J.J. Eddleston, *Jack the Ripper – An Encyclopaedia* (CreateSpace Independent Publishing Platform, 2019), p.36.
63. S.P. Ryder, *et al.*, 'Elizabeth Stride', *Casebook: Jack the Ripper.*
64. R. Whittington-Egan, *Jack the Ripper: The Definitive Casebook.* (Gloucestershire: Amberley, 2013), p.234.
65. *Ibid.*, p.239.
66. *Ibid.*, p.248
67. S.P. Ryder, *et al.*, 'Catherine Eddowes', *Casebook: Jack the Ripper.*
68. Medical Report, *Coroner's Inquests No. 135* (Corporation of London Records, 1888).
69. *Ibid.*
70. S.P. Ryder, *et al.*, 'Mary Jane Kelly', *Casebook: Jack the Ripper.*
71. S.D. Wood, 'Room 13 Millers Court', *Casebook: Jack the Ripper* (2005).
72. S.P. Ryder, *et al.*, 'Mary Jane Kelly', *Casebook: Jack the Ripper.*
73. *Ibid.*
74. *Ibid.*
75. *Ibid.*
76. *Ibid.*
77. J. Louhelanien, 'Forensic Investigation of a Shawl Linked to the "Jack the Ripper" Murders', *Journal of Forensic Sciences*, Vol. 65 (1) (2019), pp.295–303.

78. S.P. Ryder, *et al.*, 'Aaron Kosminksi', *Casebook: Jack the Ripper* (2023).
79. Melville Macnaghen, *Days of My Years* (London: 1914).
80. R. Jones, 'The DNA and the Shawl', *Jack the Ripper 1888* (2023).
81. *Ibid.*
82. S.P. Ryder, *et al.*, 'Prince Albert Victor', *Casebook: Jack the Ripper* (2023).
83. S.P. Ryder, *et al.*, 'The Suspects', *Casebook: Jack the Ripper* (2023).
84. S.P. Ryder, *et al.*, 'James Maybrick', *Casebook: Jack the Ripper* (2023).

Chapter 9: Death, Dying and the Afterlife in Victorian Britain

1. B. Watts, 'Children in the Home: Infant Wellbeing and Parent-Child Relationships in Late Medieval England, 1250–1500'.
2. *Ibid.*
3. *Ibid.*
4. Thomas Wright, *The Pinch of Poverty* (1892).
5. *Ibid.*
6. Peter Cunningham, *Handbook of London.*
7. *Ibid.*
8. John Timbs, *Curiosities of London* (1867).
9. *Ibid.*
10. George Sims, *How the Poor Live* (London: 1883).
11. *Ibid.*
12. *Ibid.*
13. *Ibid.*

Caring for the Dead

1. Auguste Renouard, *The Undertakers' Manual*, p.6.
2. *Ibid.*, p.11.
3. *Ibid.*, p.179.
4. R. Shrestha, T. Kanchan and K. Krishnan, 'Methods of Estimation of Time Since Death', *National Library of Medicine* (2023).
5. See Image 26 in this book. Beneath Prince Albert's chin and along the side of his face is the cloth ligature used to keep his jaw shut.
6. Auguste Renouard, *The Undertakers' Manual*, p.36.
7. *Ibid.*, p.36.
8. *Ibid.*, p.36.
9. R. Atkinson and S. Tavner, 'What really happens when you die?', *The Guardian*, Saturday, 16 February 2008.
10. George Sims, *How the Poor Live*.
11. Auguste Renouard, *The Undertakers' Manual*, p.155.
12. *Ibid.*, p.153.

13. *Ibid.*, p.146.
14. *Ibid.*, p.169.
15. Pember Reeves, *Round About a Pound a Week* (London: G. Bell and Sons, Ltd, 1913).
16. P. Cryer, 'Costs of dying in Victorian and Edwardian England', *1900s* (2023). Available online.
17. *Ibid.*
18. Pember Reeves, *Round About a Pound a Week.*
19. Auguste Renouard, *The Undertakers' Manual*, p.179.
20. *Ibid.*, p.18.
21. *Ibid.*, p.18.
22. *Ibid.*, p.18.
23. *Ibid.*, p.19.
24. *Ibid.*, p.18.
25. *Ibid.*, p.23.
26. *Ibid.*, p.29.
27. *Ibid.*, p.32.
28. *Ibid.*, p.49.
29. The hands of some of Victoria's children can be viewed at the Victoria and Albert Museum in London. Some are available to view in online collections.
30. Auguste Renouard, *The Undertakers' Manual*, p.86.
31. *Ibid.*, p.86.
32. *Ibid.*, p.86.
33. *Ibid.*, p.25.
34. *Ibid.*, p.21.
35. C. Valentine, *Past Mortems: Life and Death Behind Mortuary Doors* (London: Sphere, 2018).
36. Auguste Renouard, *The Undertakers' Manual*, p.19.
37. *Ibid.*, p.30.
38. *Ibid.*, p.46.
39. A. Brereton, 'Morphinomania in the 19th century'.
40. Auguste Renouard, *The Undertakers' Manual*, p.44.
41. *Ibid.*, p.45.
42. Charles Manby Smith, *The Little World of London* (London: Virtue and Co., 1857).

Funerals

1. B. Watts, 'Children in the Home: Infant Wellbeing and Parent-Child Relationships in Late Medieval England, 1250–1500'.
2. H. Mayhew, *London Labour and London Poor*, Letter III, Friday, 26 October 1849.
3. *Punch Magazine*, 17 October 1857.
4. Richard Davey, *A History of Mourning* (1889).
5. *Ibid.*

6. James Greenwood, *The Mysteries of Modern London* (1883).
7. Thomas Wright, *The Great Army of London Poor, by The River-side Visitor.*
8. *The Daily Telegraph*, 'Inquest: Annie Chapman', Tuesday, 11 September 1888.
9. Thomas Wright, *The Great Army of London Poor, by the River-side Visitor.*
10. *The Penny Illustrated Paper*, 17 July 1875.
11. *Ibid.*
12. B. Watts, 'Children in the Home: Infant Wellbeing and Parent-Child Relationships in Late Medieval England, 1250–1500'.
13. Hallowe'en Greeting Card, *c.* 1920, in B. Ellis, *Lucifer Ascending: The Occult in Folklore and Popular Culture* (2004).
14. B. Watts, *Inside the Tudor Home: Daily Life in the Sixteenth Century.*
15. F. Marryat, *There is No Death* (1917).

Burial

1. *The Times*, 1 June 1875.
2. D.W. Bartlett, *London by Day and Night.*
3. B. Watts, 'Children in the Home: Infant Wellbeing and Parent-Child Relationships in Late Medieval England, 1250–1500'.
4. *The Morning Chronicle*, 9 February 1778.
5. James Greenwood, *The Wilds of London* (1874).
6. W.O. Daniel, *Ins and Outs of London* (1859).
7. L. Jackson, *Dirty Old London: The Victorian Fight Against Filth.*
8. *The Morning Chronicle*, 9 February 1778.
9. *Ibid.*
10. *Bell's Life in London and Sporting Chronicle*, 9 September 1838.
11. *Ibid.*
12. George Alfred Walker, *City Medical Reports* (1849).
13. *The Morning Chronicle*, 9 February 1778.
14. John Simon, *City Medical Reports* (1849).
15. D.W. Bartlett, *London by Day and Night.*
16. *Ibid.*
17. *Ibid.*
18. *Ibid.*
19. L. Jackson, *Dirty Old London: The Victorian Fight Against Filth.*
20. *The Times*, 1875.
21. James Greenwood, *The Wilds of London.*
22. D.W. Bartlett, *London by Day and Night.*
23. *Ibid.*
24. L. Jackson, *Dirty Old London: The Victorian Fight Against Filth.*
25. *Ibid.*
26. James Payn, *Lights and Shadows of London Life* (1867).
27. L. Jackson, *Dirty Old London: The Victorian Fight Against Filth.*
28. *Ibid.*

Body-Snatching

1. George W.M. Reynolds, *The Mysteries of London*, Vol. 1 (London: John Dicks, 1844).
2. *Ibid.*, Chapter CVI, 'The Grave-Digger', p.323.
3. *Ibid.*, p.323.
4. *Ibid.*, p.323.
5. *Ibid.*, p.323.
6. *Ibid.*, p.323.
7. *Ibid.*, p.323.
8. B. Shillace, 'Body Snatching', *Case Western Reserve University: Dittrick Medical History Center* (2017). Available online.
9. *Ibid.*
10. University College London, 'Auto-Icon' (2023). Available online.
11. B. Shillace, 'Body Snatching'.
12. *The New York Times*, February 1788.
13. *The Times*, 1 June 1875.

Burke and Hare

1. B. Johnson, 'The Story of Burke and Hare', *Historic UK* (2017). Available online.
2. National Museums Scotland, 'Edinburgh at the time of Burke and Hare' (2023). Available online.
3. O. Dudley Edwards, *Burke and Hare* (Edinburgh: Birlinn, 2014), p.106.
4. B. Johnson, 'The Story of Burke and Hare'.
5. *Ibid.*
6. *Ibid.*
7. A. Knight, *Burke and Hare* (London: The National Archives, 2007), p.41.
8. *Ibid.*, p.41.
9. L. Rosner, *The Anatomy Murders: Being the True and Spectacular History of Edinburgh's Notorious Burke and Hare and of the Man of Science Who Abetted Them in the Commission of Their Most Heinous Crimes* (Philadelphia: University of Pennsylvania Press, 2010), pp.100–25.
10. A. Knight, *Burke and Hare*, p.45.
11. 'The Proceedings of the Trials of Burke and Hare, 24th December 1828', in, *Burke and Hare*, ed. W. Roughead (Edinburgh: William Hodge & Company, 1921), p.19.
12. L. Rosner, *The Anatomy Murders*, pp.189–90.
13. A. Knight, *Burke and Hare*, p.56.
14. 'The Proceedings of the Trials …', p.87.
15. The Anatomical Museum, 'William Burke', *The University of Edinburgh* (2019). Available online.
16. The Anatomical Museum, 'William Hare', *The University of Edinburgh* (2019). Available online.
17. The Anatomical Museum, 'William Burke'.

Chapter 10: Changing Times: From Victoria to Edward

1. H.C. Long, *The Edwardian House: The Middle-class Home in Britain* (Manchester: Manchester University Press, 1993).
2. B. Seebohm Rowntree, *Poverty: a study of town life* (London: Macmillan, 1901).
3. V. Bonham Carter, *Winston Churchill: An Intimate Portrait* (London: Smithmark Pub., 1995).

The Struggle for Suffrage

1. BBC, 'Emmeline Pankhurst', *History* (2014). Available online.
2. UK Parliament, '1897 Foundation of the National Union of Women's Suffrage Society' (2023). Available online.
3. C. Culpin, 'Parliament and the Suffrage Movement', *Women's Suffrage* (2023). Available online.
4. B. Cook, 'The Suffragette Hunger Strikes', *Museum of London* (2018). Available online.
5. Sylvia Pankhurst, *Miss Pankhurt's Terrible Experiences. Votes for Women* (1913), p.369.
6. Helena Auerbach, 'Women's Suffrage', 12 February 1908, SHC ref 3266/1.
7. Emmeline Pankhurst, 'Speech from the Dock', in *Votes for Women* (1908), p.1.
8. Emily Davison, 'A Year Ago. A Statement by Miss Emily Wilding Davison on her Release From Holloway, June 1912', *The Suffragette*, 13 June 1913, p.577.
9. Queen Alexandra, 'Telegram to Herbert Jones', 4 June 1913, University of Central Lancashire.
10. BBC, 'Emmeline Pankhurst', *History*.
11. The House of Commons, 'Population Statistics, England And Wales', Vol. 209, debated on 28 July 1927, (2023).
12. V. Walsh, 'The History of Condoms'.
13. *Ibid.*

A Changing World

1. J. Greenspan, 'The Assassination of Archduke Franz Ferdinand', *History* (2014).
2. *Ibid.*
3. *The Sarajevo Newspaper*, 'Austrians Are Furious Over Assassination of Ferdinand and Wife, 29 June 1914.
4. UK Parliament, 'The Fallen' (2023). Available online.

Postscript

1. L. Worsley, *Queen Victoria: Daughter, Wife, Widow, Mother* (London: Hodder, 2018), p.406.
2. *Ibid.*, p.409.

Bibliography

Archival Sources

RA VIC/MAIN/QVJ (W) Friday 30th November 1866. (Princess Beatrice's copies). *Queen Victoria's Journals* (2013). Available online at: queenvictoriasjournals.org.

RA VIC/MAIN/QVJ (W) Wednesday 22nd June 1887. (Princess Beatrice's copies). *Queen Victoria's Journals* (2013). Available online at: queenvictoriasjournals.org.

Primary Sources

Beeton, Isabella, *Mrs Beeton's Book of Household Management* (London: S.O. Beeton, 1861).

Bird, Isabella, *Notes on Old Edinburgh* (Edinburgh: Edmonston and Douglas, 1869).

Bly, Nellie, *Ten Days in a Mad-House* (New York: Norman L. Munro, 1887).

Campbell, Lady Colin, *The Lady's Dressing Room* (London: Cassell & Company, 1893).

Cassell, *Cassell's Household Guide: Being a Complete Encyclopaedia of Domestic and Social Economy and Forming a Guide to Every Department of Practical Life* (London: Cassell, Petter and Galpin, 1869).

Child-Villiers, Margaret, *Fifty-One Years of Victorian Life* (London: John Murray, 1922).

Combe, Andrew, *The Principles of Physiology: Applied to the Preservation of Health, and to the Improvement of Physical and Mental Education* (London: Harper & Brothers, 1841).

The Daily News, 'The East-End Murders', Tuesday, 9 September 1888.

The Daily News, 'The Whitehall Mystery: Inquest: Medical Evidence', Tuesday, 9 September 1888.

The Daily Telegraph, 'Inquest: Annie Chapman', Tuesday, 11 September 1888.

Dew, Walter, *I Caught Crippen: Memoirs of Ex-Chief Inspector Walter Dew, C.I.D. of Scotland Yard* (London: Blackie, 1938).

Dickens, Charles, 'A letter on ragged schooling', *The Daily News*, February 1846.

Dickens, Charles, *Oliver Twist* (London: 1837; Penguin Red Classic, 2007 edn).

Dickens, Mary Angela, *Dickens' Dream Children* (London: Raphael Tuck & Sons Ltd, 1926).

The Dover Telegraph and Cinque Ports General Advertiser, 'The Poisonings by Arsenic at Bradford', Saturday, 13 November 1858.

The East London Advertiser, 'Another Whitechapel Mystery: Horrible Murder in Buck's Row, Whitechapel', Saturday, 1 September 1888.

The East London Observer, 'Another Horrible Tragedy in Whitechapel: A Woman Murdered in Buck's Row', Saturday, 1 September 1888.

Engels, Friedrich, *Condition of the Working Class in England*, 2nd edn (London: 1887).

The Englishwoman's Domestic Magazine (London: 1852–1879).

The Evening Standard, London, 'Murder in Whitechapel', Saturday, 1 September 1888.

The Examiner, London, 'The Murders by Poison in Norfolk', Saturday, 13 June 1846.

Francatelli, Charles Elmé, *A Plain Cookery Book for the Working Classes* (London: Routledge, 1852).

Godwin, George, *London Shadows: A Glance at the 'Homes' of the Thousands* (London: George Routledge & Co., 1854).

Gould, Nathan, *Information concerning the state of children employed in cotton factories* (Manchester: 1818).

The Hand-Book of the Toilette, 2nd edn (London: Bradbury and Evans, 1841).

Kitchiner, William, *The Cook's Oracle; and Housekeeper's Manual.* (New York: J. & J. Harper, 1830).

London, Jack, *The People of the Abyss* (Piedmont: 1902).

Mayhew, Henry, *London Labour and the London Poor, Volume One* (London: 1851).

Mayhew, Henry, *London Labour and the London Poor, Volume Two* (London: 1861).

Mayhew, Henry, *London Labour and the London Poor, Volume Three* (London: 1861).

Mayhew, Henry, *London Labour and the London Poor, Volume Four* (London: 1865).

Montez, Lola, *The Arts of Beauty: Secrets of a Lady's Toilet* (New York: Dick & Fitzgerald, 1858).

Moritz, Karl Philipp, *Travels in England in 1782* (1795).

The Morning Chronicle, 9 February 1778.

The New York Times, 'Adelaide Bartlett', Monday, 19 April 1886.

Nightingale, Florence, 'Introductory Notes on Lying-In Institutions', *Nature*, Vol. 5 (106) (1871).

Nightingale, Florence, *Notes on Nursing for the Labouring Classes* (London: Harrison, 1861).

The Pall Mall Gazette, Friday, 31 August 1888.

The Pall Mall Gazette, Saturday, 1 September 1888.

Payn, James, *Lights and Shadows of London Life* (1867).

Pears, Francis, *The skin, baths, bathing, and soap* (London: Pears, 1859).

The Penny Illustrated Paper, Saturday, 1 September 1888.

'The Proceedings of the Trials of Burke and Hare, 24th December 1828', in *Burke and Hare*, ed. W. Roughead (Edinburgh: William Hodge & Company, 1921).

Reeves, Pember, *Round About a Pound a Week* (London: G. Bell and Sons, Ltd, 1913).

Renouard, Auguste, *The Undertakers' Manual* (New York: A.H. Nirdlinger & Co., 1878).

Riis, Jacob A., *How the Other Half Lives: Studies Among the Tenements of New York.*

Rowntree, B. Seebohm, *Poverty: a study of town life* (London: Macmillan, 1901).

Simon, John, *City of London Medical Reports: Special report on Intramural Internments* (London: 1852).

Sims, George, *How the Poor Live* (London, 1883).

Smith, Adolphe, *Street Life in London* (London, 1877).

Smith, Charles Manby, *The Little World of London* (London: Virtue and Co., 1857).

Soyer, Soyer, *A Shilling Cookery for the People* (London: Geo. Routledge & Co., 1854).

The Times, London, 'Another Murder in Whitechapel', Saturday, 1 September 1888.

Virard, Pierre, *Essai sur la santé des filles nubiles* (1779).

Wright, Thomas, *The Pinch of Poverty* (1892).

Secondary Sources

Almenara, C.A., Aimé, A., and Maïano, C., 'Vinegar and weight loss in women of eighteenth-century France: a lesson from the past', *History of Psychiatry*, Vol. 31 (2) (2019).

Arnold, C., *Edward VII: The Prince of Wales and the Women He Loved* (London: St Martin's Press, 2017).

Begg, P., and Bennett, J., *Jack the Ripper: The Forgotten Victims* (London: Yale University Press, 2014).

Bennett, J., *Mob town: a history of crime and disorder in the east end* (London: Yale University Press, 2017).

Brand, E., 'Did the original Coca-Cola drink really contain cocaine?', *History Revealed Magazine*, Issue 46 (2017), p.78.

Clark, K., *Civilisation* (London: The BBC, 1969).

Cohen, W.A., and Johnson, R., *Filth: Dirt, Disgust, and Modern Life* (Minneapolis: University of Minnesota Press, 2005).

Cox, M., *The Oxford Book of Victorian Ghost Stories* (New York: Oxford University Press, 2003).

Crystal, P., *The History of Sweets* (Yorkshire: Pen & Sword Books Ltd, 2021).

Cuming, E., '"Home is home be it never so homely": Reading Mid-Victorian Slum Interiors', *Journal of Victorian Culture*, Vol. 18 (3) (2013), pp.368–86.

Davies, A., and Rowbotham, J., 'How mean are the streets of modern Britain?', *BBC History Magazine*, September Issue (2018), pp.16–17.

Fletcher, A., *Growing Up in England: The Experience of Childhood, 1600–1914* (New Haven: Yale University Press, 2008).

Gauldie, E., *Cruel habitations; a history of working-class housing 1780–1918* (New York: Barnes & Noble, 1974).

Goldfinch, L., 'Fathering Christmas', *History Revealed Magazine*, Issue 37 (2016), pp.34–41.

Green, B.S., 'Learning from Henry Mayhew: The Role of the Impartial Spectator in Mayhew's London Labour and the London Poor', *Journal of contemporary ethnography*, Vol. 31 (2), (2002), pp.99–134.

Gregory, J., 'Veggie Victorians', *BBC History Magazine*, September Issue (2018), pp.42–45.

Hands, T., *Drinking in Victorian and Edwardian Britain: Beyond the Spectre of the Dunkard* (London: Palgrave Macmillan, 2018).

Hayward, S., '"Those who cannot work": an exploration of disabled men and masculinity in Henry Mayhew's London Labour and the London Poor', *Prose Studies*, Vol. 27 (1) (2005), p.53.

Herdman, J.M., 'Curious Conversations: Henry Mayhew and the Street-Sellers in the Media Ecology of London Labour and the London Poor', *Journal of Victorian Culture*, Vol. 26 (3) (2021), pp.384–403.

Hodgman, C., and Cook, M., 'Gay rights in 19th-Century Britain', *BBC History Magazine*, September Issue (2018), pp.82–85.

Hwang, H., *London's underground spaces: representing the Victorian city, 1840–1915* (Edinburgh: Edinburgh University Press, 2013).

Jackson, L., *Dirty Old London: The Victorian Fight Against Filth* (London: Yale University Press, 2014).

Kilday, A-M., and Nash, D., 'The Ripper of Our Nightmares', *BBC History Magazine*, September Issue (2018), pp.31–34.

Koven, S., *Slumming: sexual and social politics in Victorian London* (New Jersey: Princeton University Press, 2006).

Long, H.C., *The Edwardian House: The Middle-class Home in Britain* (Manchester: Manchester University Press, 1993).

Marsh, M., *Compacts and Cosmetics: Beauty from Victorian Times to the Present Day* (Yorkshire: Pen & Sword Books Ltd, 2009).

McGuinness, P., '1854: Dr John Snow Cures London of Deadly Cholera', *History Revealed Magazine*, Issue 46 (2017), pp.20–21.

Morgan, M., *The Battered Body Beneath the Flagstones & Other Victorian Scandals* (London: Robinson, 2018).

Nash, J.R., *Look For the Woman: A Narrative Encyclopaedia of Female Poisoners, Kidnappers, Thieves, Extortionists, Terrorists, Swindlers and Spies from Elizabethan Times to the Present* (London: Evans, 1981).

Rosenman, E.B., *Unauthorised Pleasures: Accounts of Victorian Erotic Experience* (Ithaca: Cornell University Press, 2018).

Rosner, L., *The Anatomy Murders: Being the True and Spectacular History of Edinburgh's Notorious Burke and Hare and of the Man of Science Who Abetted Them in the Commission of Their Most Heinous Crimes* (Philadelphia: University of Pennsylvania Press, 2010), pp.100–25.

Rubenhold, H., *The Five: The Untold Lives of the Women Killed by Jack the Ripper* (London: Penguin, 2019).

Wallis, J., *Investigating the Body in the Victorian Asylum: Doctors, Patients, and Practices* (London: Palgrave Macmillan, 2017).

Watts, B., *Inside the Tudor Home: Daily Life in the Sixteenth Century* (Yorkshire: Pen & Sword History, 2023).

Whittington-Egan, R., *Jack the Ripper: The Definitive Casebook* (Gloucestershire: Amberley, 2013).

Wilson, D., *Mary Ann Cotton: Britain's First Female Serial Killer* (Hampshire: Waterside Press, 2013).

Worsley, L., *Queen Victoria: Daughter, Wife, Widow, Mother* (London: Hodder, 2018).

Online Sources

Arif, D., 'The Murder of Elizabeth Jackson', *Casebook: Jack the Ripper* (2008). Available online at: casebook.org.

Bank of England, 'Inflation Calculator' (2023). Available online at: bankofengland.co.uk.

Barnardo's, 'Our History' (2023). Available online at: barnardos.org.uk.

Bloy, M., 'Victorian Legislation: a Timeline', *The Victorian Web* (2014). Available online at: victorianweb.org.

BNA, *The British Newspaper Archive* (2023). Available online at: britishnewspaperarchive.co.uk.

Brereton, A., 'Morphinomania in the 19th century', *National Trust for Scotland* (2020). Available online at: nts.org.uk.

Denham, M., 'Victorian philanthropists, philosophers and activists', *British Geriatrics Society* (27 May 2017). Available online at: bgs.org.uk.

Fleming, R.S., 'Victorian Make-up Recipes', *Kate Tattershall* (2014). Available online at: katetattersall.com.

Gale Primary Sources, *19th century British Library newspapers* (2023). Available online at: gale-com.

Griffin, E., 'Child Labour', *British Library* (2014). Available online at: bl.uk.

Hicks, G., 'An analysis of first names from the 1851 Glamorgan census', *Genuki UK & Ireland Genealogy* (2002). Available online at: genuki.org.uk.

Higginbotham, P., *The Workhouse* (2023). Available online at: workhouses.org.uk.

Jackson, L., *Dictionary of Victorian London* (2012). Available online at: victorianlondon.org.

Jackson, L., 'Victorian Money – How much did things cost?', *The Dictionary of Victorian London* (2023). Available online at: victorianlondon.org.

Jones, R., 'Martha Tabram, Murdered August 7th 1888', *Jack the Ripper 1888* (2023). Available online at: jack-the-ripper.org.

Landow, G.P., *et al.*, *The Victorian Web* (2023). Available online at: victorianweb.org.

Lee, I., 'Ragged Schools', *British Library* (2014). Available online at: bl.uk.

London School of Economics, *Charles Booth's London: Poverty maps and police notebooks* (2016). Available online at: booth.lse.ac.uk.

Museum of the Mind, 'Patients – Explore Bethlem', *Bethlem Royal Hospital* (2023). Available online at: museumofthemind.org.uk.

The National Archives, *Currency Converter: 1270–2017* (2023). Available online at: nationalarchives.gov.uk.

National Museum of American History, 'Stomach Pump: MG.M-07432 (c. 1861–1865)', *Smithsonian Institution* (2023). Available online at: americanhistory.si.edu.

ProQuest, *British Periodicals* (2023). Available online at: proquest.com.

Ryder, S.P., *et al.*, *Casebook: Jack the Ripper* (2023). Available online at: casebook.org.

Shillace, B., 'Body Snatching', *Case Western Reserve University: Dittrick Medical History Center* (2017). Available online at: artsci.case.edu.

Spicer, G., 'The Thames Torso Murders of 1887–1889', *Casebook: Jack the Ripper*. Available online at: casebook.org.

Vale, A., and Rattle, A., *The Woman Who Murdered Babies for Money: The Story of Amelia Dyer* (London: Andre Deutsch Ltd, 2011).

UK Parliament, 'Reforming Society in the 19th Century' (2023). Available online at: parliament.uk.

White, M., 'Juvenile crime in the 19th century', *British Library* (2014). Available online at: bl.uk.

Unpublished Sources

Watts, B., 'Children in the Home: Infant Wellbeing and Parent-Child Relationships in Late Medieval England, 1250–1500' (Unpublished Master's Thesis: University of Wales Trinity Saint David, 2022).

Index